Paying Respect to
The Sopranos

Paying Respect to *The Sopranos*

A Psychosocial Analysis

CHRISTOPHER J. VINCENT

McFarland & Company, Inc., Publishers
Jefferson, North Carolina, and London

LIBRARY OF CONGRESS CATALOGUING-IN-PUBLICATION DATA

Vincent, Christopher J. 1977–
    Paying respect to The Sopranos : a psychosocial analysis /
Christopher J. Vincent
        p.   cm.
    Includes bibliographical references and index.

    ISBN 978-0-7864-3608-8
    softcover : 50# alkaline paper ∞

    1. Sopranos (Television program)   I. Title.
    PN1992.77.S66V56   2008
    791.45'72 — dc22   2008020874

British Library cataloguing data are available

Cover photograph ©2008 Shutterstock

Manufactured in the United States of America

*McFarland & Company, Inc., Publishers
    Box 611, Jefferson, North Carolina 28640
    www.mcfarlandpub.com*

Acknowledgments

I'd like to thank my parents, Veronica Vincent and Robert Wertheimer, for their immeasurable support.

Thanks to Mr. Tim Prosser and Mr. Michael Duffy, for opening my eyes to meaning in literature. Thanks to Dr. Sylvester Kreilein for linguistic consultation.

For their perspectives and support, I'd like to thank all of the wonderful HBO.com message boarders, but especially Sfogliatella, MankindTGA, newsgrrl12, BabylonDon, 50Bill, mhodnov, macaroniandgravy, shablap, jenjen8788 and allieboy.

Thanks to Diego Viturro, Scott Runde and Derrick Juengst for their valuable and much appreciated feedback.

Thanks to my family, the Aratas, for their enthusiasm — especially my grandmother Dorothy Arata.

I'd like to thank the inventor of the Digital Video Recorder.

Special thanks to my "Soprano daddy," Greg Youra, for introducing me to *The Sopranos* experience and...

A very special thanks to Lisa Frey for giving me the push to write this book.

I'd also like to thank all the members of the creative team behind the scenes of *The Sopranos*, who deserve as much credit as those on screen. Of course there is David Chase (creator, executive producer, writer, director) but I'd like to acknowledge the phenomenal family that created the greatest art of the twenty-first century — Robin & Mitchell Burgess (writers, executive producers), Terence Winter (writer, executive producer, director), William B. Stitch, A.C.E. (editor), Bob Shaw (production designer),

Phil Abraham (director of photography), Gianna Maria Smart (producer), Andrew Schneider (supervising producer, writer), Matthew Weiner (writer, executive producer), Tim Van Patten (director, executive producer), Brad Grey (executive producer), Frank Renzulli (writer, producer), Henry Bronchtein (writer, director, unit production manager and co-executive producer), Martin Bruestle (producer), Georgianne Walken, C.S.A., and Sheila Jaffe, C.S.A.(casting), Ilene Landress (executive producer), Diane Frolov (writer, supervising producer), John Patterson (director), Alan Taylor (director), Allen Coulter (producer, director) Peter Bucossi (stunts), Dan Castleman (technical consultant), Juliet Polcsa (costume designer), Kathryn Dayak (music editor) and all other members of the crew.

Table of Contents

Preface

Friends, Romans, countrymen —*Howyoudoin'*? If you're like me, you miss *The Sopranos*. For eight years Tony Soprano and his New Jersey family became an extension of our own families. We shared their joys and their sorrows. We soared to unprecedented and unimagined heights of entertainment combined with meaning. *The Sopranos* transcended our concepts of the possibilities of a weekly one-hour drama. Its absence from the pinnacle of the television landscape and also our lives has been felt deeply by us all. This volume celebrates the incomparable HBO program by studying its unique creative palette, demystifying its subtle messages and meanings, and eulogizing its wonderfully complicated characters. In short, I have come both to bury Caesar *and* to praise him.

I am convinced that *The Sopranos* is the greatest American art of the twenty-first century. It goes beyond gangster genre, family drama, psychological study, sociological portrait and any other attempt at classification. It is a complex universe — a tapestry of human behavior, emotion and motivation. The tone of *The Sopranos* does not dictate morals and meanings. Rather, it simply presents pieces of a puzzle and lets the viewer do the work of putting them together. No two people have exactly the same interpretation of the show and that is a testament to its artistic power and merit. I believe that it holds, for everyone, a key to greater understanding of their lives and the world in which they live. Whether regarding family relationships, work-related stress, the climate of American society, or personal demons — it's all in there if you're willing to unpack it, and that's exactly what I undertake in the following pages.

Unlike Tony Soprano, I was fortunate enough to get in on the ground floor — as a fan of this unparalleled phenomenon in 1999. I and millions of other people were introduced to the most engaging, exhilarating, provocative and downright entertaining television show of our lives. First, the realistic portrayal of working organized criminals intrigued me. Then, its characters endeared themselves to me. The unique tempi of storytelling seduced me. And it was funny! It touched thoughts and feelings in its audience that networks had discarded as unprofitable. It had an appealing like-mindedness, acutely aware of a previously under-represented American *zeitgeist*. Season after season I became more obsessed with Tony Soprano and his two families. I watched episodes over and over again, each time picking up on a finer nuance and each time finding more appreciation for the richness of this story. The writing, the acting, the directing, the sets, the costumes, the music — all contributed to my fascination with this familiar yet entirely original world that came from the mind of its creator, David Chase. *The Sopranos* kept its audience in laughter, tears, terror and always on the edge of its seats.

My intentions in this book are twofold. First, to add an element of closure to the *Sopranos* experience but also to rekindle in you the fire for Tony Soprano and his family. I hope to show you things in *The Sopranos* that you had not seen before and to give you the tools to make your own insights and personal connections. Second, I will make a cohesive presentation of the themes and messages of the series. I will lay out a concept blueprint and proceed to illustrate how characters and key events fit into this scheme. I weave together the myriad of seemingly unrelated aspects to show you how, together, they form a monument that demarcates the American experience at the beginning of the third millennium. My intention is not to give you all the answers because such a proposition is ridiculous. Rather, the goal is to get you to ask the right questions.

Such compelling art as *The Sopranos* has inspired analytical works before mine. The insightful perspective from Maurice Yacowar in *The Sopranos on the Couch* and those essays collected and edited by David Lavery (*This Thing of Ours, Investigating* The Sopranos and *Reading* The Sopranos, *Hit TV from HBO*) are excellent examples. Other notable works include Gabbard's *The Psychology of* The Sopranos, Green and Vernezze's The Sopranos *and Philosophy — I Kill Therefore I Am*, and Schneider's *Tony Soprano on Management*. After fueling my own fire with these and other books, I felt that there were still greater depths to be plumbed. The majority of existing *Sopranos* literature is either collected short essays, episode guides or analysis within a specific scholarly field. This volume presents a breadth and coherency afforded by a single author unrestricted by the boundaries of any single discipline. Most importantly, this volume deals with the finale of the series. Tony's journey has been a long and winding one. Previous works dealt with the fascinating stops along the way. This one, though, is the only book to have the perspective of the entire run of the series, right up to the final stop where we all got off in the summer of 2007.

My research has been fanatical immersion and obsessive deconstruction of the source material, accompanied by thorough and painstaking documentation of recurring themes, artistic choices and minutiae. My zealous passion for *The Sopranos* has led me to innumerable viewings of all eighty-six episodes. Each one has been given full examination with my microscope, calibrated and highly sensitized for detail and meaning. Participation in the vibrant online community has also been a great source of inspiration and I extend my gratitude to those who were and continue to be a part of it. Eight years of obsession has led me to countless observations, interpretations, theories and opinions about *The Sopranos*. The result is this book in which I flesh out meanings and present a distillation of the latent messages of its creator, David Chase. When I'm done, the varied dots (like *The Sopranos'* "made guys") are connected. I take the hundreds of puzzle pieces and assemble them to share with you the Big Picture.

A caution: Before continuing, I would like to clarify that this book discusses all major plot points of The Sopranos. *It is intended as a digestiv to be enjoyed after the wonderful experience of witnessing the New Jersey family saga. Salud.*

1

The Big Picture

The Sopranos is a feast for an audience hungry for entertainment of substance. Its exceptional quality and popularity can be credited to the wonderful talent of the creative team that has fashioned this truly unique television show which boldly transcends the medium into a work of pure art. The writing is appealing for its engaging stories told in rhythms that are fresh and exciting. The direction is thoughtful and impeccable in its understated realism. The acting is compelling in its authentic humanity. Receptive ears and open minds at HBO allowed a warm home for this revolutionary program. Good timing and a little luck didn't hurt either. The serendipitous conjunction of all of these elements brought about the greatest television show ever, *The Sopranos*.

This show has personality! It tells the story of Tony Soprano, the boss of a New Jersey "Family" of organized criminals. Although the principal attraction is the allure of a mob story, *The Sopranos* goes far beyond all previous entries in the genre. The otherworldliness of the gangster lifestyle is combined with familiar tropes such as work, family dynamics and stress. From there it delves into psychotherapy and self-awareness. The elements of north New Jersey and Italian-American heritage create a sense of folk portraiture. Above all, the series is very much driven by its characters. Tony, brilliantly portrayed by James Gandolfini, struggles with the two halves of his life — his family and his Other Family. He loves his wife and children and to provide for them he manages an organization of thieves and murderers. Conflict in serving both families results in questioning, from without and within, of his personal worth. Tony's quest for happiness within this scenario is the core of *The Sopranos*. Gandolfini endears

Tony to his audience with a remarkable ability to express a broad spectrum of emotion, from genuine tenderness to violent rage. Tony has become a cultural icon not as a hero but an evolutionary step beyond antihero.

Surrounding Tony Soprano is a collection of unique north Jersey characters superbly brought to life by a gifted cast of actors. Edie Falco plays Carmela, Tony's worrying wife. She is at times conflicted about Tony's crimes unless distracted with a gaudy sapphire ring or mink coat. She wavers between her dependence on Tony and a nagging desire to escape, from him or herself. Their children are typical suburban kids whose greatest struggle is coming to terms with the apparent hypocrisy of their parents' lives. Their daughter Meadow (Jamie-Lynn Sigler) is cynical about her father's line of work and her mother's complicity in it. This manifests itself in deliberate acts of rebellion that challenge her parents' values. Unlike his older sister, AJ (Robert Iler) is a classic underachiever. His story is that of a young man looking for a place to fit in. As he chronically stumbles trying to find a path in life, he unwittingly runs afoul of Tony and Carmela. His difficulty in accepting responsibility for the consequences of his actions is a symptom of the ambiguous moral dynamic of the Soprano household. Regardless of any temporary personal differences, Tony, Carmela, Meadow, and AJ are bound together by the tradition of family and what it means to be a Soprano.

Tony's extended family is very much a part of his life as well. The initial premise of the show revolves around Tony's relationship with his mother, Livia, who is extraordinarily brought to life by actress Nancy Marchand. With her pretense of martyrdom, Livia is a bitter, manipulative and emotionally abusive matriarch who can make an audience cringe with horror or laugh in disbelief. Although Livia dies at the beginning of the third season, her ghost haunts the breadth of the series, looming in the minds of those she touched with her toxicity. Tony's sister Janice (Aida Turturro) has adopted her share of Livia's idiosyncrasies. She pushes people's buttons without qualms if it will get her what she wants. Janice is genuinely emotional but she frequently overplays it, fishing for sympathy. Her chameleonic nature is rooted in the survival instinct that came from growing up with Livia and Johnny Boy Soprano.[1]

The line between Tony's two families begins to blur with his uncle and his nephew, both of whom are part of Tony's crime Family. Tony's Uncle Junior (Dominic Chianese) is "old school," involved in the Family business stretching back to the 1950s. Junior is exceptionally self-involved and his concerns rarely extend beyond his own well-being. After Tony's mother dies, Junior represents the sole remaining link to the bygone era that Tony romanticizes for so much of his life. Tony's nephew, Christopher Moltisanti (Michael Imperioli), is torn between his twin desires to rise through the ranks of north Jersey criminals and his dreams of being a Hollywood mover and shaker. This is further complicated by his chronic battle with chemical dependencies. The other players in Tony's Family are equally colorful. With unimpeachable fashion sense, Silvio Dante (Steven Van Zandt) is the pompadoured manager of the Bada Bing! Club. As a trusted friend he found his calling as Tony's *consigliere*, a position in which he acts as a sounding board and adviser regarding the Family business. Paulie "Walnuts" Gualtieri (Tony Sirico), with trademark silver wings in his hair, has been in the Family almost as long as Junior. Paulie's reputation as a true tough guy, though well-earned, belies his numerous superstitions, phobias and obsession with betrayal.

Helping Tony address the stress that results from living with and trying to serve his two families is Dr. Jennifer Melfi. Dr. Melfi is guided by a dedication to her profession and her patients' mental health. Her work with Tony in the context of psychiatric therapy is the fulcrum of *The Sopranos*. Tony's feelings are explored in their sessions together and by this device Melfi helps Tony and the audience gain insight into his condition and his journey.

Series creator David Chase takes his audience through the lives of complicated characters in a manner so compelling that they are given much greater importance than those of the average television drama. The level of scrutiny and interpretation draws parallels to the act of meditation. By meditating on these characters and situations, one is able to learn lessons that apply to one's own personal experience. Chase acts as the therapist as he asks the probing questions of his viewers. The audience emulates the therapist-patient relationship with each other when they take it upon themselves to discuss and explore their feelings about *The Sopranos*. They ask themselves, "Who are we and where are we going?" While the focus is on Tony Soprano, HBO's Chris Albrecht points out that David Chase is "the intellectual, creative, spiritual, conscious and unconscious leader of the show."[2] His method of storytelling is unique and powerful, creating an irresistible addiction to this show as he slyly plants seeds of change in the American subconscious. Tony's just a piece in a game — no doubt the king on the board — but Chase is the one making the moves. Tony is a front. Chase is the wizard behind the curtain, the Godfather pulling the strings. David Chase is the real Boss of this Family, Tony Soprano's just a lightning rod put in place to take the hits.

In the form of *The Sopranos*, David Chase holds up a mirror to the American public. Despite the underpinning of Italian heritage of these characters, this is an American story. It is set in a specific place and time, that of New Jersey at the beginning of the twenty-first century. The depiction of modern America is created in the rich detail which surrounds the characters and their experiences. Popular cultural elements are ubiquitous. Television is a staple of American lives, a fact that is constantly represented in *The Sopranos*. America's fixation on television is faithfully portrayed whether it's Tony and the History Channel, Adriana watching *The A-Team*, Sunday football or the constant background appearance of infomercials. The show is peppered with pop culture references (AJ playing Nintendo, a mention of the musical *Jersey Boys*, discussion of who won *American Idol*). These simple but familiar elements help the audience to accept this as a convincing, though fictional, world. The frequency of real consumer products has been criticized by some as a compromise of the show's integrity in conciliation to product placement. Tony drives a Cadillac Escalade, gets Raid roach killer sprayed in his eyes and likes Tropicana Orange Juice With *Some* Pulp. However, rather than detracting from the experience, these examples enhance believability because they are specific and relatable. They also reflect a certain mentality of consumerism in America. These details create and strengthen the connection between the characters and the audience. The episodes are very current, with fictional setting and real broadcast dates typically falling within a few months of each other. Inclusion of news headlines such as Hurricane Katrina, Terry Schiavo or Scott Peterson enrich the contemporaneous quality of the show. Allusions to the Bush administration are littered throughout the series. Understated inclusion of September 11, mentions of the Taliban, homeland security and recent paranoia regarding Middle Easterners outline a chronology of actual events parallel to those through which the United States has lived. These subtle touches not only empower the sense of reality in the fiction but call on strong emotions stemming from a common American experience.

The concept of personal journey will be used throughout this book. Chase professes the "psychological and emotional journey" of Tony Soprano to be most important to him.[3] He and the whole creative team behind *The Sopranos* have invented a universe which acts as a path on a journey of self-awareness for the audience as well as Tony. Human behavior, emotions, relationships, ambitions and motivations are all dealt with in unique and stimulating ways. The show appeals to so many people because they struggle with these things in their own lives. Chase has created a forum for something that the public felt but could not express. He guides his audience to recognize both similarities and differences between themselves and the fictional characters of *The Sopranos*.

The Sopranos is a mirror held up to modern human experience. It is up to the audience to make the connections between fiction and reality, to look into the mirror and examine how they live their values. Then Chase asks questions that encourage them to acknowledge and understand their own personal feelings. The climate of American life is in a rare conjunction with what Chase has to say and the message has fallen on ears that are ready to hear it. The search for happiness is the impetus for embarking on the psychological and emotional journey. The *Sopranos* journey does not fit common preconceptions. It's not "bad person turns good"— Tony Soprano acknowledges the error of his ways and resolves to go straight. On the other hand, neither is it the reverse — Tony Soprano's evolution from innocent child to evil and immoral criminal adult. It's more accurately "good and bad person remains good and bad." Tony Soprano has strengths and weaknesses at the beginning of the series and the same can be said at the end. He gains understanding of some of his problems and addresses them. New problems arise, though. Some are his own doing and some are externally sourced. As in real life, the difference of eight years can be as simple as "same thing, different day." Uncle Junior counsels Tony that there aren't always answers to life's problems. His advice to Tony is to steer the ship the best way he knows how and find little pleasures in the meantime.[4] This brings about a re-evaluation of what brings pleasure and happiness and how that relates to one's individual identity. The journey of Tony Soprano and his audience is the discovery and acceptance of their identities.

In a Nutshell

In its eight-year run, *The Sopranos* featured a variety of interrelated themes. However, these themes are not always addressed in a linear fashion and so they can be obscure at times. They are presented in the context of the stories of its characters and how their individual journeys intersect. It is necessary to clarify at the outset of this book the dominant themes that are presented over the breadth of the show. As Tony would say, it's important to be aware of The Big Picture.

From the beginning to end of the series, these characters deal with their identity in a search for happiness. In the smallest, simplest of nutshells, that's what the show is about. Their distance from that goal is illustrated in their countless bouts with feelings of emptiness, disappointment, guilt, shame, fear, depression, sorrow and anger. For the most part, the causes of these emotions are internal, of the characters' own doing. Once this is established, the next part of their struggle is acceptance of personal responsibility. Character unwillingness to accept responsibility leads them to negative behaviors. They constantly lie to each other and themselves. They go about in pity for themselves by complaining and displacing blame on circumstances or others. They indulge in vices such as gambling, drugs or infidelity. They unleash their frustrations on others — verbally, emotionally and physically. These are all symptoms but they feed back into the initial feelings of emptiness, creating a negative cycle that prevents them from attaining their simple and reasonable goal of happiness. Ultimately the characters have control over the choices they make in their lives and they must accept the consequences of their actions.

At the same time the characters engage in these negative patterns of behavior, they try to escape the negative cycle. They try to improve their condition via psychotherapy, higher education, real estate licensure, etc. They strive to give their children good lives. Motivated by desires to love and be loved, they look for support from their family and peers. Unfortunately they often don't know how to support each other. In the endeavor to achieve happiness, they stumble on a journey of self-acceptance, recognizing and sometimes changing negative behaviors. They deal with questions of morality and identity. As they do, they learn about themselves. That is The Big Picture.

There is a common symptom of egocentric self-pity demonstrated in these characters' words and behaviors. Characterization often takes the form of complaining and whining. Whatever rollercoaster of emotions they experience, these characters are rarely happy or even content. Tony's nephew Christopher Moltisanti is constantly dismayed by daily tedium. AJ is always making excuses for his selfish behavior, unwilling to accept adult responsibilities. Paulie Walnuts is obsessed with betrayal. Virtually every character not only feels that life's circumstances have been unfair to them but they insist on convincing those around them of that belief. Even Tony has been known to disparage his luck despite the blessings and comforts he has. The ease with which these characters place blame on externals indicates that the level of accountability for their troubles is practically nonexistent. Most of the time they are in a state of denial. They don't see that they are displacing blame from themselves. Rather, these characters seek validation as victims and they spread the grief around as consolation.

If they didn't have anything to complain about, they wouldn't know what to do with themselves. Each, focused solely on themselves, feels that they are alone with their problems. When they've got lemons, they make sour lemonade to serve to their family, friends and associates. Meanwhile, nobody's problems are getting solved.

The discontent of these characters is largely a result of their misunderstanding about what will provide them happiness. They are lost on their journey. That confusion results from an uncertainty or misconception of who they truly are as individuals. In the sixth season, Dr. Melfi counsels Tony that the modern onset of adulthood is delayed by a bombardment of information that people must endure.[5] Though she says this in the context of AJ's maturation, it applies to all of the characters. Along with delayed adulthood, another consequence of the assault of input is that it becomes difficult for one to separate their own intrinsic qualities and convictions from those that are learned. From a very young age, people learn from others and their experiences. Their original identity is changed and molded over time. For the most part these experiences strengthen them and are part of the growth process, but some of the messages they receive are misinterpreted or corrupted, especially on *The Sopranos*.

The processing of all of this input is demanding yet necessary for a healthy and consistent way of living. It is compromised, however, by the modern American "go, go, go" mentality, where productivity has become so ingrained as the goal of their daily lives that it becomes the mode of *internal* operation as well. When it requires the most valuable commodity — time — and tangible results are unquantifiable, the processing of that information is not given sufficient attention. This approach does not accommodate reflection and healthy interpretation of the things they see and hear every day. Information is misinterpreted when it is ignored or processed in haste. This is symptomatic of the American modus operandi. The adoption of misinterpreted lessons leads to behaviors detrimental to themselves such as pursuing unhealthy relationships, idleness or in the more extreme cases criminality and violence.

There are different origins for the corrupt messages these characters accept as truth but a few common sources are presented in *The Sopranos*. Often characters values are based on those of their parents. Whether adopting or deviating from those values, their behaviors are developed from the starting point of someone else's ideology. For example, Tony emulates his father's idea of manhood and this, in turn, results in frustration in his relationship with his own son when AJ doesn't fit that definition. In a deviation from a parent's behavior, Tony eschews his mother's propagation of misery. Janice, however, learned her guile and manipulation from Livia. Christopher inherits and/or learns his parents' substance abuse. Carmela has more than a little of her father's stubbornness. For a time, Meadow defines herself by rebellion from her parents. Each characters' parentage sets a foundation for them and so no one ever truly starts with a clean slate but rather they start with the slate they were given — that of their parents' teachings. The misinterpreted lessons learned by the parents become the corrupted messages imparted to their children.

Television is one of the easy external culprits to finger because it sends so many corrupted messages regarding who or what people should be, what is worthwhile and what provides happiness. It tells them how to act and gives a distorted presentation of what normal, successful life is. This is certainly a contributing factor to Christopher's difficulty in accepting life's wearisome monotony which can't possibly live up to the non-stop excitement presented in the movies he loves and the television to which he is so frequently glued. This same condition is exhibited in others, primarily members of the younger generations such as Adriana, AJ and to a lesser extent Meadow. This idea regarding television's role in the disintegration of individuality and individual happiness coming from a television show is in harmony with the often tongue-in-cheek commentary presented by David Chase and company.

Corrupt messages also come from within these characters. Time and again they are shown to make excuses for their negative behaviors. Business and survival tenets rationalize the practice of extortion and racketeering. The concepts of honor and loyalty are used to excuse physical violence, even to the extent of whacking someone. These characters can live with their destructive behavior by advocating these concepts as higher guiding principles. This deception is so thorough that they, themselves, believe it. The price they pay is a lingering guilt which haunts them and threatens to deliver retribution upon them at any moment. Subconsciously, they sweep the issues under the rug in hopes of avoiding them. This illustrates a microcosm of the gambler mentality which pervades the *Sopranos* universe: Maybe they'll get their comeuppance or maybe they'll outrun their own reckoning. It is this question that is foremost in the minds of fans as this tension plays with their own values system. The bottom line is that all of these conflicting messages contribute to the complicated nature of their worlds and their confusion of personal identity.

Peer perception is directly related to the identity of these characters. The necessity of maintaining a certain appearance for the benefit of others is exhibited in all of the characters. To different extents they each accept compromises to gain degrees of freedom. There is a measure of deception in the safeguarding of one's image — deception of others and themselves. They establish and preserve a persona, a mask that fits with the expectations of their peers. The problem is that their peers are doing the same thing. It is artifice based on a façade built on a lie and the net result is a world of pretense with no real foundation. Each character is constantly struggling with their own sense of self in the face of every secondary character's deluded identity, further obscured by the secondary character's posturing to satisfy the deluded identity of the primary character. Just as these characters deceive others and themselves about their own identity, the situation is further complicated when they also deceive themselves about the personalities of others. When considering the behavior of others, there are lessons to be learned and there is a subconscious decision by these characters to listen to certain lessons and ignore others. It is a web of self-corrosive cognitive and behavioral habits which dilute and degrade their individuality, compounded by every lie told to each other and to themselves.

Tony's cousin, Tony Blundetto, is a good example of all of this. Tony B. comes out of prison wanting to pursue a legitimate career as a massage therapist, a great disappointment to Tony S. When Tony B. is lured by the luxury of the criminal life, he abandons that dream by returning to organized crime. Tony S. helps him but not to the degree Tony B. feels he deserves. Rather than accepting responsibility for his own delayed career in The Family, Tony B. blames Tony S., convincing himself that his cousin is fixated solely on the acquisition and maintenance of personal wealth, prioritizing it above familial allegiances.[6] In this way he is able to be the victim with a clear conscience rather than sleeping in the bed he made for himself. The lesson he should have derived, or at least *could* have derived, was that his choices have consequences and he has to be willing to live with those. Tony B. is just one example of this behavior common to most of the characters in *The Sopranos*. On one hand they truly desire to be "good." However, they tend to hear what they want to hear — that which does not complicate their lives by forcing them to accept responsibility for attitudes and behaviors which they instinctually feel are wrong. They would rather continue unencumbered by the pain required of personal growth.

The Sopranos' representation of lying, egotism, complaining, violence, vice indulgence and self-involvement is familiar to its audience. These are only symptoms, however, of a greater discontent. The characters complain from a deep sense of disenchantment. They gamble and cheat on their wives as distractions from their pain. In different ways they are each aware of an emptiness in their lives, the promise of happiness unfulfilled. Regardless of their supposed successes, status and luxuries, there is an inescapable sentiment of disappointment. Their accomplishments are hollow because they don't bring true happiness. The frustration is compounded by a sense of entitlement, the feeling that they have been cheated of that which was owed to them. With a trend towards wealth and idleness, these characters feel entitled to a satisfying, happy life. Too often they sit back and wait for the good things to happen for them without exerting the effort, without enduring the pain required to earn them. Eventually they either change or they do not. David Chase forces his audience to recognize that same crossroads before them.

The Journey

From the mire of these convoluted causes and effects, Tony Soprano strives for happiness in the face of relentless internal and external challenges. The art of *The Sopranos* is so transcendent that Tony's journey becomes that of the audience. Everyone struggles to come to terms with feelings of frustration, disappointment, rage and doubt in their own lives. The growth of Tony Soprano is effected by the central device of *The Sopranos,* that of psychiatric therapy. Tony is first seen in a waiting room as he is about to meet psychiatrist Dr. Melfi. When Tony goes into that office, the audience goes with him and when new episodes aired they would return, sitting down on the couch at the same time each week for an hourlong session with *The Sopranos.* Whether it's the first or fiftieth viewing, those sessions are not passive television watching, either. They demand close attention, active participation, thorough consideration and application to one's life. This audience is such a tightly bonded group because they have gone to therapy together for years, every Sunday night. They have been able to vicariously experience therapy for themselves and instead of a typical $200 per hour fee they only had to pay twenty bucks a month for HBO! A motivated community of mental health therapists could file a class action suit for loss of livelihood when HBO provided millions of potential patients with cheap, effective therapy.

Tony's initial reticence to engage in psychotherapy reflects a stigma toward the profession but also toward the patient. Tony has been taught that those who cannot help themselves are weak. Having that philosophy so ingrained in him would have led Tony to consider himself weak for seeking the help of a psychotherapist. The fact that it would be a cognitive weakness rather than a physical one only complicates the situation. If it were a simple physical ailment, it would be understood and accepted by Tony's associates. However, their Old World views do not allow for the invisible ailments of the mind. For Tony it is an especially difficult consideration in light of his pride in his own acuity and mental toughness. His decision to participate in psychotherapy is a rebellion from the old school of thought and indicates an evolution in Tony's thinking beyond the corrupted lessons taught to him throughout his life. He allows for the possibility that having a weakness does not invalidate him.

Dr. Melfi counsels Tony, and by extension the viewing audience, about his tumultuous feelings. She normalizes the emotional struggle and assuages feelings of isolation with the recognition that such a condition is not particular to Tony but is an epidemic, a crisis symptomatic of cultural and societal factors of twenty-first century America. This acknowledgment is representative of the voice of *The Sopranos*. It appeals to so many fans because it addresses those feelings of isolation and gets them out in the open where they can be wrestled with on a level playing field. In one way or another, fans of the show identify with this sense of crisis whether in their jobs or at home, in their relationships or within themselves. Where mainstream popular entertainment is typically satisfied with sweeping the difficult issues under the rug, Melfi provides an alternative, a treatment solution. *The Sopranos* scratches the itch in its viewers that no one else has been able or willing to touch.

What allows this device of therapy to work so uniquely is the manner and tone of presentation. The universe fashioned by David Chase's team has been rewarding to such large numbers of viewers because of the neutral voice employed in the telling of this story. The audience is never told how to feel with musical score, pointed camera moves or tidy morals.[7] To do so would be the equivalent of inviting them to cheat on a test. It would compromise the integrity of the journey. There would be no real progress. The only accomplishment would be the temporary relief from necessary growing pains, made all the more difficult by their delay. Rather than dictating a specific lesson about these characters' behavior, Chase treats his audience as adults and asks them to do the work of deriving significance from the material. Because they are challenged to find the meanings on their own, the result is that the lessons are rooted within themselves. What one learns from the show is heard in their own voice with a foundation of the values, emotions and intricacies of their own life experiences. This tailor-made aspect results in a magnification of the lessons' power and efficacy. They speak to so many people because they are drawn out of the beliefs which already existed inside them. What was intangible within is made concrete.

In taking its audience through the therapeutic process, *The Sopranos* helps its audience to know themselves. Chase acts as the über-therapist, not pushing a philosophy or opinion but asking the difficult questions and forcing his audience to probe their feelings. They are confronted with difficult situations, pressed to re-evaluate their beliefs and given insight on the motivations of both themselves and others. Therapy is a long-term enterprise with no quick or easy answers. Likewise, *The Sopranos* is a gradually unfolding story presenting pieces of the puzzle a few at a time. Therapy is undertaken for greater self-awareness and understanding leading to peace of mind through healthy behaviors, just as *The Sopranos* teaches. Even though it can be a slow, painful and frustrating process, it is important that one sees it through. One does so both for their own edification in witnessing the fate of Tony Soprano, but also to further the process of learning about themselves. In the show and in one's life, the end of the road is unknown but the journey is a reward in itself. Along that path, one becomes more in touch with who they are and what they believe. An important characteristic of good art is that it has an infinite number of meanings and interpretations. By its therapeutic virtues, *The Sopranos* meets those criteria exceptionally.

The struggle with personal identity is succinctly laid out for the audience in the popular episode in which Tony reads this quotation from Nathaniel Hawthorne: "No man can wear one face to himself and another to the multitude without finally getting bewildered as to which may be true."[8] In the context of that specific episode, it forces Tony to consider the great dichotomy he has created in his life where, in the same day, he takes his daughter to visit prospective colleges and then brutally garrotes a former business associate who disappeared into the witness protection program. It is not the morality of his actions that is a concern to Tony but rather the potential bewilderment, which he instinctively knows is linked to his happiness.

Tony Soprano's journey is the arc of *The Sopranos*. This book examines that journey and that which guides him. It begins with an accounting of Tony's early, influential life experiences. Then, in chapters 3 and 4, Tony's work life is presented. His wife and children play a critical role in Tony's journey and are discussed in chapters 5 and 6. Chapter 7 studies internal conflicts and behavioral symptoms common to the populace of Tony's world. The therapeutic device and its essential role in Tony's journey are elaborated upon in Chapter 8. Chapter 9 analyzes the roles of symbolism, food and storytelling in creating the *Sopranos* universe. The book concludes in Chapter 10 with an evaluation of each of the Sopranos' journeys.

Although this book is framed in the context of Tony's journey, it is critical to understand that there is no ultimate arrival point at which the journey ends, for Tony or the reader. Tony's positive and negative behaviors are in a yin and yang relationship, ebbing and flowing. There are successes and there are failures. Tony Soprano takes two steps forward in one episode and takes two steps back in another. It is inaccurate to box one's perception of Tony's journey into the linear trajectory of a rise and fall, typical of the gangster genre. Rather, Chase has expressed the belief that Tony is constantly experiencing his rise and his fall simultaneously.[9] This is the journey of *The Sopranos*. Chase shines a light on the dark corners of the minds of his audience, prompting scrutiny and encouraging the desire for understanding. The psychiatric method and quest for self-knowledge are inextricably linked to that overarching theme of *The Sopranos*— the deceptively simple journey for identity and happiness.

2

Family History

In order to understand Tony Soprano's journey, it is necessary to be familiar with where he came from. As evidenced in innumerable sessions with Dr. Melfi, much of Tony's unhappiness stems from his childhood. Whether regarding his mother, father, sister, friends or associates — the people and environment of his youth directed the path he would take in life and how he would experience it. Throughout the course of the series, there have been recollections, clues, hints, scraps and allusions to Tony's earlier years. Using these various pieces of Tony's puzzle, this chapter is a presentation of his life in the years up to the very first episode.

Growing Up Soprano

Tony is a third generation Italian-American. In the 1920s his grandfather on his father's side was a master stonemason named Corrado Soprano. Corrado came to the United States from the village of Avellino with his brother Frank, who was a marble worker. Avellino is a small village in the Naples region of Italy and Corrado was part of a large transmigration in which many people from Avellino made the Atlantic crossing to eventually settle in the North Ward of Newark, New Jersey. He put his skills as a stonemason to work, along with his brother, on a crew of laborers. Their most notable project was a church in which their fellow Italian immigrants could worship. This church stands to this day and carries for Tony Soprano deep significance, symbolic of family and tradition.[1]

Shortly after arriving in the United States, Corrado Soprano married.

He and his wife were blessed with three sons. The first, Corrado Soprano Jr., took his father's name. This oldest son would later be known to the *Sopranos* audience as Uncle Junior. Following Junior came Hercule, nicknamed "Eccle." Eccle was a challenge for his parents because he was developmentally disabled, although in those days they favored the term "slow." The family preferred to focus on his handsome features.[2] Their third and last child they gave the name Giovanni but he would later become known as Johnny Boy Soprano.

Tony's mother Livia was born a few years later, in 1929.[3] Livia had three sisters — Settimia, Gemma and Quintina.[4] She also had a brother, Mickey.[5] There was a close-knit quality of the North Ward that reflected the tightness of the Italian immigrant community. Johnny and Livia met, married and got a house on 6th and Orange.[6] Their first child arrived in 1958, a baby girl they named Janice.[7] Two years later, in 1960, Livia gave birth to their first boy.[8] They named him Anthony. This is the anti-hero who would one day grow up to be the boss of north Jersey's organized crime family. About five years after Tony was born came his sister Barbara.[9]

The Soprano home was a complicated household, to say the least. Tony's father, Johnny, was supposedly an early community leader and champion of Italian-Americans in the North Ward.[10] Livia was a full-time mother and homemaker. In the early to middle sixties Johnny Soprano was sentenced to a jail term. While Johnny was away in prison, the children were told that he was in Montana being a cowboy.[11] It was during this time that Uncle Junior took on certain characteristics of a father figure to the Soprano children, especially Tony. The relationship between Junior and Tony hinged on baseball. Junior taught Anthony the rules and how to play. They would play catch together, a tradition that would continue even after Johnny had finished serving his term.[12] Junior's relationship with Janice was less idyllic. He remained distrustful of her as a result of at least two incidents — one in which she allegedly stole money from his wallet and another in which he caught her with pyromaniacal intentions in his home.[13] When Johnny did return home, his manner of fatherhood was epitomized by his use of the belt as a means of discipline.[14]

As Tony's sister Janice would later put it, their mother Livia would play the children off each other to toughen them.[15] From as far back as is remembered, Livia was always a bitter person. She found next to nothing to take pleasure in — not her children, her husband, nor herself. This created a difficult environment for her husband to enjoy or her children to grow and learn good habits. Dysfunctionality was the norm in the Soprano home. Livia was unable to experience joy and Johnny was frustrated at her condition and its effects on his and the children's lives.[16]

Young Tony looked up to his sister. She was older and consequently an authority figure. She also had a fighting spirit in an environment that was not always nourishing and loving. The relationship that Tony has with his older sister, Janice, has contributed greatly to the understanding of the Soprano family. In their childhood, Anthony and his sister were good friends. They would "play house" together, steal cigarettes, and so on.[17] Janice gradually found that her position of elder gave her power and authority over Anthony, which she would begin to abuse. She began to take for granted that she could command Tony to do whatever she said. Once she fed Tony a Milk Bone under the guise of a cookie.[18] When her father took her on secret trips to the amusement park, Janice lorded the secret over Tony and rubbed his nose in exclusion. This situation led Tony to believe that Janice got whatever she wanted and that she was spoiled while his needs were dismissed as unimportant.[19]

When Tony made such an assertion to his mother, she replied in a very telling manner, exploding in a rage. Livia unloaded her bitterness and frustration on her son by threatening to stick a fork in his eye. This may have been the first time that young Anthony was confronted with the baffling concept of his own mother willing to perpetrate violence upon her son. So immediate and so graphic was the image that it seems a certainty that this would have traumatized Tony in some way, regardless of how repressed. Evidence indicates that this type of comment was not unheard of from Livia. In later years, when Tony shared this incident with Dr. Melfi, he discarded it as being without real intent and only a symptom of his mother's personality. Apparently remarks of this nature were so commonplace they were disregarded. The other possibility is that by minimizing the weight of such an awful thing, Tony was able to live with this paradoxical threat of cruel physical violence from his own mother. As if he were pretending that it never happened, Tony was able to sleep under the same roof as someone who would willfully put the fear of pain into him.[20]

In the spring of 1967 Tony became aware of an aspect of his father which he had not seen before. One morning on his way to school, he was witness to Johnny Boy, with the help of his Uncle Junior, chasing and beating a man named Rocco Alatore. This was a revelation to Tony who was impressed by Johnny's skill in administering a beating, showing that he was tough and not someone to be trifled with. Young Anthony bragged to his schoolmates about his father being a tough guy and found that it gave him some credential and respect from his peers.[21]

Newark was undergoing dramatic demographic changes in the sixties. With an unprecedented influx of African-Americans into the city of Italian-Americans, racial tensions came to the surface. Anthony Imperiale, a controversial figure know as "The White Knight," fought for the rights of the white community in the face of the arrival of other ethnic groups. From what we know about his purported work as an early community leader, it is likely that Johnny Boy Soprano associated with Imperiale.[22] The racial tension eventually exploded in the Newark Riots of July, 1967.

Concurrent with the riots, Tony's familiarity with his father's work expanded. With resentment towards the apparent favoritism his father showed Janice, Tony followed them on one of their secretive excursions. He discovered that they had developed a tradition of going to a local amusement park together. What Tony also unexpectedly witnessed was his father being arrested in a raid. In violation of his parole, Johnny Soprano was booked for association with known undesirables. This was traumatic for Janice to witness and caused Anthony to re-evaluate his father. His mother gave the defense that Johnny was innocent and he was the victim of ethnic discrimination against the Italians, an argument that Tony himself would adopt later in life. It became apparent that Johnny Boy was actually using Janice as cover for secret meetings with business associates. However, the sentiment Tony had towards Janice remained the same. He felt as if she was favored and given special treatment.

Later that year Johnny's frustration with Livia grew. An opportunity presented itself through one of Johnny's associates, Rocco Alatore, the victim of the beating that young Tony witnessed. Rocco would gamble and borrow money from Johnny. Rocco's reputation for book smarts gave him credence when he came to Johnny with a business proposal. Rocco saw the growing city of Reno full of possibilities. He sought Johnny's help as a business partner. As an investor and possible restaurant manager and host, Johnny saw a chance to be a success by getting in on the ground floor with a hot prospect. Friction resulted, though, when Livia disapproved. She refused to endorse the plan and actively disallowed it. So frustrated was Johnny that he threatened to take the children to Reno without Livia. Livia vetoed his threat by one-upping him with one of her own: She would rather smother her children than let Johnny take them away. Johnny felt that he was held back by Livia, that she was dragging him down and preventing him from attaining happiness and success. Unfortunately, young Tony overheard this argument with its threats, further enlightening him about his mother's disposition. The Sopranos never left New Jersey while Rocco Alatore moved to Reno and eventually became a millionaire.[23]

In Tony's early years there were two other peers who would have a profound impact on him the rest of his life. First there was his cousin, Tony Blundetto, the son of Livia's sister Quintina and Albert Blundetto.[24] The two Tonys would play together as children and grow up together. In the third grade, Tony met a classmate named Arthur Bucco.[25] Even at such a young age something in Artie won Tony's heart and they would be like brothers for the rest of their lives. Although quiet when around his parents, Tony was a magnetic and boisterous personality with his friends.

By the time he was nine, Tony began to exhibit the husky physique which would be his characteristic trademark later in life. Tony's knowledge of his father's affairs expanded even further in October of 1969. While accompanying his father and Uncle Junior one Saturday afternoon, Tony was directed to wait in the car while they paid a visit to Mr. Satriale, the local butcher. Satriale had been a compulsive gambler who did his betting and borrowing with Johnny Boy. Tony decided to follow his father and uncle into the pork store where he witnessed his father chop off Satriale's pinky finger with a butcher's knife. This was another pivotal moment in Anthony's youth. Despite the horror of the situation, he found it to be an exhilarating rush of adrenaline.

The aftermath of that incident was equally impactful on Tony's experience of the world. In framing his son's experience of the incident, Johnny Boy Soprano opened up to his son that gambling was his livelihood. He emphasized the point that even though his actions seemed horrible, it was Mr. Satriale's gambling, avoidance and weakness that were truly reprehensible. He stressed to young Tony the importance of individual honor, paying one's debts and the evils of gambling. At the same time he demonstrated some of the suave manipulation and management that Tony would become so good at when he followed his chastising with laudatory praise at Tony's courage in a situation in which others would have run. As these complicated and conflicting messages swirled in his head, Tony came to the dinner table. His father amorously danced with Livia as she prepared the meat his father obtained from Satriale, the meat they were all about to eat. At this moment Tony experienced his first panic attack, losing consciousness and cracking his head on the table. The family wrote it off as a fainting spell but this was to be the first demonstration of Tony's internal warning system short-circuiting in stressful situations.[26] Sadly, Mr. Satriale committed suicide not long after this incident and consequently Johnny Soprano became one of the primary proprietors of Satriale's Meat Market.[27]

Later in their youth, Janice took another opportunity to prey on

Anthony by tape recording him and younger sister Barbara having a fight. Janice then proceeded to blackmail them both with it, making them do her bidding. From Tony's demeanor in session with Dr. Melfi, it is clear that he recalls that incident as one of torture. Janice took advantage of her younger, less worldly brother for personal gain. This was likely Tony's primary first-hand experience with extortion. An experience like that alone would affect him but even more so when the persecutor was his own flesh and blood: An older sister, his mentor and protector, betrayed him. In later life Tony would characterize his childhood home as operating under the principle of "Every man for himself."[28] This "survival of the fittest" mentality would introduce him to concepts of Darwinism that would later resonate with him.

Another prominent figure in Tony's youth was Richard "Dickie" Moltisanti. Dickie was a charismatic tough guy who married Tony Blundetto's older cousin, Joanne. Tony looked up to Dickie like an older brother, with love and admiration. Dickie served in the United States Navy. When he returned, he did a stint in jail during which his cellmate was killed on orders of an associate, Jilly Ruffalo. After his jail term Dickie retaliated by taking out Ruffalo's eye. This vicious demonstration was typical of the characteristic loyalty that was respected in his circle. Dickie and Joanne had a son, Christopher, in 1968. Tony would give baby Christopher rides in the basket of the Satriale delivery bicycle.[29] From an early age Tony had a special bond with Christopher Moltisanti. The relationship became even deeper when Dickie was gunned down while carrying TV trays into his home. It was revenge contracted by Ruffalo through a cop on his payroll, Barry Haydu. Tony was devastated by Dickie's death. Out of respect for Dickie, Tony accepted the lifelong role of a father to Chris.[30]

It was around this time that Tony began to exhibit the behavior of problem child. His wayward ways likely resulted from the male role model presented him and also the friends he associated with. Artie Bucco was always a straight-and-narrow kid but Tony's other boyhood friends did not live up to that standard. First and foremost there was Salvatore Bonpensiero, who would earn the nickname "Big Pussy" due to the paradoxical nature of his large size and his pursuit of cat-burgling. Though a little older than Tony, Pussy would be his dear, lifelong friend. Tony also made the acquaintance of Giacomo "Jackie" Aprile. Jackie was a neighborhood kid who looked up to his older brother, Richie. Unfortunately, Richie was another less-than-desirable role model, a classic hoodlum. Richie relished the adoration of his kid brother and Tony, fueling it by demonstrating his toughness with symbolic acts like taking a leather jacket off a neighbor-hood tough guy, Rocco DiMeo.[31] Luckily, Jackie had more sensibility than Richie and it would serve him well. Tony and his friends' pranks started small. They exploited a neighborhood boy named Jimmy Smash for the entertainment they found in his speech impediment, a cleft palate.[32] According to Livia, she practically lived in the vice principal's office on account of the boyhood mischief that Tony would get himself into. Tony, with his friends, would steal lobsters down at the docks and then sell them on Bloomfield Avenue for a buck. At the age of ten, Tony stole a car, barely able to see over the steering wheel.[33]

In the early seventies the Soprano family was able to build a home in Verona on 55 Benedict, about ten miles north of their old residence in Newark.[34] Johnny Boy was achieving some financial success for himself and his family. The relationship between Johnny and Livia deteriorated over the years. The tension and frustration between them came to a boil and exploded on the way back from an evening out at the popular New York nightclub, The Copacabana. Johnny was a Cadillac man and, with Junior and his *goomah*, Rosemary, in the back seat, Johnny and Livia argued. In an act of absolute frustration and anger, Johnny felt the need of a dramatic statement. In response to Livia's nagging he unholstered his handgun and discharged a round of ammunition through Livia's beehive hairdo. This is a clear indication of the discontented state of affairs between the two.[35]

It is not totally surprising, given Johnny's unhappiness with Livia and her toxic personality, that he saw other women extramaritally. Most made guys had girlfriends, known as *goomahs,* and Johnny Boy was no exception. The most notable was a young lady named Fran Fellstein, a young beauty who had a reputation as a classy dame with expensive tastes and a young son from a previous relationship. She had schmoozed with the likes of no less than the president of the United States, John F. Kennedy. Junior was smitten with Fran and pined for her from afar. By the time he nearly worked up the nerve to pursue her, it was too late — Johnny had stepped in. She and Johnny began seeing each other circa 1970 and they would continue that relationship until Johnny's death. They had what Fran would describe as "crazy love." Junior claims this turn of events was the reason he never married and suffered in silence for years after. However it seems that he dealt with his grief in a manner more consistent with a stalker, such as phone calls and skulking outside Fran's apartment. Fran even suspected Junior's jealousy led him to tell Livia about the secret rela-tionship although this remains unconfirmed.[36] Eventually Junior would move on when he met a young woman named Roberta Sanfillippo, with whom he would have a romantic relationship for nineteen years.[37]

The Soprano family got a golden retriever named Tippy. However, Livia didn't much care for Tippy and finally nagged Johnny into getting rid of him. Under the cover story of Tippy having worms and going to live on a farm, Johnny gave Tippy to his *goomah*, Fran, whose son renamed him Freckles. While Tony accepted the farm story, Janice was more cynical, believing Tippy to have been gassed. This was only inaccurate in that Tippy lived another ten years before finally being put to sleep by Fran. When Tony learned the truth about Tippy he was hurt and confused, once again calling into question his relationship with his parents.[38]

Tony benefited from other family members as well. His grandfather, Corrado Sr., would let Tony drive backhoes at his construction site. It was also around this time that Tony first visited his Uncle Pat Blundetto's farm. Uncle Pat had the hiccups for nearly a year and as an accommodation he was allowed to retire to a farm in upstate New York. It would become a summer tradition for the boys in the extended family to spend their summers there. For Tony it became a bonding experience for him and his cousin, Tony Blundetto. They would go to the farm and Uncle Pat would "school" them: develop their work ethic by having them clear brush with a scythe, tend to his vegetables, and regale them with his great stories.[39]

When Tony began high school he already had a shady reputation. He made new friends such as Davey Scatino, an army brat whose father had been newly stationed in New Jersey. Davey and Artie Bucco were two of Tony's good friends but Tony was also making new friends in a different circle.[40] Tony played sports in high school. He was a lineman on the football team and played left field for the school's baseball team. He nearly made the All County team but his shortcoming there was consistent with his uncle's critical evaluation that Tony never had the makings of a varsity athlete.[41] Regardless, sports was a positive influence on Tony. He would spent countless extra hours working out and practicing.[42] His football coach noticed Tony's potential. Coach Molinaro took a special interest in Tony, discouraging him from associating with the troublemakers he had gotten in with. He advised Tony to recognize his own leadership potential and put it to its greatest use on the playing field. Tony did not heed his advice, disregarding him as a clueless old man.[43] Under unspecified circumstances Tony saw his first dead body at the age of fifteen.[44]

Even with his growing reputation and his brushes with the law, Tony also exhibited genuine tenderness and caring. When Sal Bonpensiero's sister, Nucci, was hospitalized with spinal meningitis, Tony was a source of remarkable support. Though only fifteen years old Tony demonstrated great sensitivity and concern for Pussy and his ill sister. Tony would go with Pussy to the hospital every day to sit with her and the Bonpensiero family. It was Tony who was at Nucci's bedside when she passed away. The support that Tony showed Pussy was something which separated him from the typical high school chum and it earned Pussy's love and allegiance.[45]

Considering Livia's overburdening idea of mothering, it is reasonable that Janice, as older sister, partly fulfilled a matronly role to Tony. Once that relationship is established, it is understandable for the adolescent Tony to disconnect her sexuality, just as he would have regarding Livia. In fact, acute awareness of Livia's sexuality was a contributing factor in Tony's very first panic attack. Tony's discomfort with Janice's sexuality comes further into play as Dr. Melfi hypothesizes that Janice would have been a focus for early sexual feelings on his part and that she likely had similar feelings. Though Melfi tries to explain the normalcy of such a phenomenon, Tony is unsettled by such a consideration.[46]

Despite their differences, Tony admired his sister Janice for her ability to withstand Livia's vitriol and dish out some of her own as well. Janice was strong in his eyes although Livia's abuse took its toll. From a young age Janice expressed herself very directly. She would grow up to be tough, taking no disrespect. Years later Janice would remark how she shared more in common with her father than Tony and in some ways this is true.[47] The fact that Janice is bold in her youth gives Tony reason to respect her. However, that did not mean she took up the role of defender and champion of the downtrodden Soprano siblings. It was still every man for himself. Janice's boldness also took her along a path of rebellion against her parents. She chose to explore alternative lifestyles such as new-age spirituality, free love, recreational drug use and rock 'n' roll (allegedly cavorting with roadies for touring musicians).[48]

Tony recalls that Janice used to be quite a hot item with the boys. Would-be suitors, like Richie Aprile, would try to get close to her by appealing to Tony. By treating him well, they aimed to impress Janice and win her approval. Janice was very expressive of her sexuality in her teenage years. Livia was especially disapproving and hurtful in her exchanges on the subject with Janice. Tony held his sister to the same standards as he did his mother when it came to romantic relations. He was taught by his parents that women should be chaste, or at least monogamous, and be held to the higher standard of strictly marital sex. This standard, however, does not apply to the men as they feel that it is their right to pre-marital and extra-marital sex. Tony had conflicting feelings on Janice's sexuality. In session with Melfi, Tony expresses the sentiment that no one wants their sister to be known as an "easy" girl.[49] Janice rebelled from this male chauvinistic attitude by freely expressing herself sexually throughout her life.

When Janice graduated high school in 1976 she left home to escape the controlling and dysfunctional Soprano family environment. Clinging to a hippie lifestyle, she went to California to be near the socially liberal community of Berkeley. She was attracted to Buddhism and changed her name to Parvati. She met a Cirque du Soleil performer named Eugene when she lived in Santa Monica in 1978. They conceived a child and Janice gave birth to a baby boy whom she named Harpo, after the Phoebe Snow song, "Harpo's Blues."[50]

Meanwhile, back in New Jersey, Tony was left to deal with his home situation without Janice's help. Despite the relationship between Johnny and Livia continuing to sour, they conceived another child. It was an unplanned pregnancy, what was commonly termed a "change-of-life baby." But Livia miscarried. When she was hospitalized, her sisters were unable to find Johnny. When he finally got word that there were complications in her pregnancy he was at Fran's. Despite the seriousness of the situation he chose to stay with his *goomah*, waiting until the next day to go to Livia in the hospital. When confronted with his absence, Johnny lied. What's more is that he made Tony an accomplice, claiming that they were together at a Yankee game and stayed with a relative in the city. Tony went along with the story, either out of a sense of allegiance and obedience to his father or simply in uncomfortable confusion. Livia, though, knew Johnny too well and saw through the lie. Unfortunately, Tony was guilty by association and this added to the distance between Tony and his mother. She very likely saw his deceit as choosing sides, or favorites between his parents. As they continued through the years, Livia would take her toll on Johnny. According to Tony, his once strong and proud father was worn down by Livia's negativity to the point that his spirit was crushed. Johnny found solace in the company of Fran and it seems that, at times, he practically lived with her.[51]

Tony proved his merit to his peers in the old-fashioned tradition of schoolyard fights. One specific instance was his face-off against another tough guy named Dominic Tedesco. In a showdown in the parking lot at Pizza World, Tony proved his dominance in front of a crowd of onlookers. In that crowd he caught the eye of a young lady by the name of Carmela DeAngelis. Though they had never met, they both felt an immediate chemistry between them.[52] Soon, they began dating. Tony made it clear that he was different from other boys when, on their second date, he brought Carmela and her mother each a dozen roses and to her father he gave a power drill. While Carmela tacitly understood that Tony had associations on the wrong side of the law, her parents were somewhat in denial. Carmela found it to be an attractive, alluring quality and she was excited by the danger and illicit nature of it all.[53] Tony and Carmela dated through much of high school. During one summer, though, the two of them stopped seeing each other for a while. In that time Tony briefly but romantically saw a friend of Carmela's named Charmaine. It did not last long, though, as Charmaine soon realized that Tony's morally questionable lifestyle was not what she was looking for. Rather, she eventually met Artie Bucco. The two of them were later to marry.[54] When Carmela and Tony were going steady they would frequently double date with Artie and Charmaine. The four of them spent a lot of time together, frequently going down to the shore to relax and enjoy their youth. Charmaine had a habit of being worse for wear when tangling with the Atlantic — she twice nearly drowned. The first incident was due to a head injury from a large wave and another due to calzone cramp.[55]

When Tony and Carmela graduated they both attended college. Tony went to Seton Hall while Carmela went to Montclair State to study business administration. During this time they maintained a close relationship.[56] While trying to go to school, Tony also maintained associations with his criminally minded friends such as Jackie Aprile. Also in the mix were Silvio Dante and Ralph Cifaretto. The four of them cohered into a "crew." They would buy and sell marijuana and fence stolen goods. Even though their operation was insignificant compared to the major crime operations in New Jersey, they had a high opinion of themselves.[57]

Tony's college career was short-lived, however: Getting into some unspecified trouble, he dropped out at Seton Hall.[58] He decided to forget about further education and he made the criminal life his full-time pursuit. He and his crew made their move into the big time with one especially bold heist. The inspiration came from a card game (run by Tony's Uncle Junior) called the Executive Game, so named for its higher caliber players gambling for higher stakes. Tony and Silvio used to spy on the operation, dreaming of one day being a part of it. With the glamour of the Executive Game and aspirations in their heads of moving up the Family ladder, Jackie struck upon the plan of robbing another high-profile card game, that of Feech LaManna. Feech, an associate of Johnny and Junior's, had close connections to the homeland. When it came time to execute the plan, Ralph was unable to go, supposedly due to a venereal disease he claims to have contracted from a hippie girlfriend. Tony, Jackie and Silvio went ahead with the job, robbing the game, much to everyone's astonishment. In order to make things right with Feech and the other made guys, they paid restitution. However, the broader effect was that these three young upstarts demonstrated themselves to be industrious and bold. They were the type of individual who could become earners, finding ways to create revenue for the Family, and from then on they would be treated with respect.[59]

Tony was on the fast track in the Family organization. His reputation became that of a big earner with an acute business mind, a sense of the big picture, and a way with people. In 1981 Tony and Carmela DeAngelis were married. This meant, though, that she would not be finishing her business administration studies. In the culture of a crime family it is expected that the men earn the money and the women fulfill the responsibilities of mothers and homemakers. With this understanding she left school to marry Tony.[60] Livia was less than encouraging. On Tony and Carmela's wedding day she told Carmela that Tony would tire of her and would pursue other women. The behavior of Livia was so offensive that Carmela's parents refused to associate with Livia, essentially estranged from their own daughter.[61] Tony and Carmela quickly got to work on starting a family and Carmela bore a daughter the following year, Meadow Mariangela.

Just as Tony's new life was taking form, the Soprano family received devastating news: Johnny Soprano, Tony's father, was diagnosed with emphysema. Due to its irreversible nature, this was a death sentence to the patriarch. Smoking his entire life finally caught up with him. In his final months, even Livia quit to ease the burden on her husband and the family. Johnny's condition continued to deteriorate. They had an oxygen tent installed in the house. Even with his ailing health, Johnny continued to see Fran but she declined to quit smoking around Johnny. In 1986 Johnny passed away. This premature end to a once indomitable man would leave the entire Soprano clan grief-stricken. Any sorrow that Livia had, she dealt with in her own way. She hardly ever visited Johnny's grave, if at all.[62] The grief was countered with a joyous event later that same year: the birth of Tony and Carmela's son, Anthony Junior, who would be commonly referred to as AJ. Tony was overjoyed at having a son and his hopes were high for the boy.

Janice returned for her father's funeral but she spent the majority of the eighties traveling the world. She had been estranged from her son who had gone to live with his father. With nothing to tie her down, Janice decided to indulge her fervor for Buddhism and make a pilgrimage to Tibet. She continued her journey in Europe, spending time in France and other countries.[63] When she returned to the United States she lived and waitressed in Detroit for a time. Her biggest memory of that time was serving Barry Sanders.[64] By this time Janice felt that she knew enough about jobs to know that she never wanted to have another one. In Seattle she practiced her art of freeloading from government aid programs by making exaggerated claims of carpal-tunnel syndrome and Epstien Barr. She remained in Seattle until Livia had a stroke in 1999. With her prospects dwindling, she chose to swallow her pride and return to New Jersey. In hopes of scavenging money from Tony, Janice returned under the guise of the desire to help the family and her mother in need.[65]

It is clear that despite rebellion and physical distancing, Janice has appropriated many of Livia's mannerisms. She has a flair for drama, especially when it will focus attention on her. She can produce crocodile tears and piercing, hurtful remarks. She shares the Soprano skill for assessing situations and people's motivations, fears and weaknesses and then manipulating them for her own purposes. She has only her own well-being in mind and rarely shows any signs of thinking of anyone else. Barbara (Tony and Janice's younger sister) is married and has two children. She is willing to help in family matters but generally stays out of Family concerns.

This is the story of Tony Soprano and his family up to the period in which he is first introduced in Dr. Jennifer Melfi's waiting room, as he embarked on a new leg of his journey. His formative years saw him through a colorful family and personal history, with notable dysfunctionality and moral ambiguity. His upbringing would be a rich source of material for the years of therapy he would undertake. Despite the unusual familial challenges he endured as a child, as an adult Tony created his own family, a source of great pride for him. At the same time he also established himself as someone to be respected in the Family business and it is this aspect of Tony Soprano's journey that shall be examined next.

3

Tony's Other Family

Now that the history of Tony's blood family had been established, the next important consideration is his business Family. How Tony came to be at the head teaches us about his skills and informs us about his environment. As Tony proceeds on his journey, the dichotomy between his two families creates conflict for him. To better understand the conflict, one must understand both families.

A Different Corporate Culture

Organized crime has changed with the times but it typically involves itself with fraud, extortion, racketeering, the servicing of vices, influence-peddling and murder. Tony Soprano and his associates have roots in Italy where organized crime goes by the name *La Cosa Nostra,* roughly translated: "This Thing of Ours." The name communicates the secret and familial nature of these organized groups of criminals under the leadership of a single boss at the head of their Family. To be part of a Family, one was often required to prove his worth with murder, known as "making their bones." Once accepted, he is required to take a vow of secrecy and allegiance called *omertà.* Once taking this vow, he is a "made guy" and receives the protection of the boss. Typical Family structure consists of a single Boss as the supreme leader directing a group of captains, or *capos.* Each *capo* is in charge of a crew of "soldiers" who do the street-level business with "associates" outside the Family. It's a pyramid system in which the large base of soldiers and associates pay percentages up to their capos who in turn pay the boss at the top. Serving at the side of a Family boss are an Underboss in charge of large-scale operational aspects and a *consigliere,* a close and trusted adviser.

In America, organized crime families became known as the mafia, or the mob, and were especially prevalent around New York City. The mafia experienced its heyday beginning with Prohibition in the 1920s and continued into the 1950s and '60s when new, successful law enforcement was put in place. Legislators developed and signed into law the Organized Crime Control Act of 1970. Though primarily aimed at illegal gambling, this act also included the subsidiary measure of the Racketeer Influenced and Corrupt Organizations Act, RICO for short. The RICO statutes provided for significantly greater penalties for those convicted of participating in organized crime. It also gave the federal government new powers in surveillance and evidence-gathering in order to assemble cases which could carry severe penalties for the heads of these organizations.

Among the new tools of law enforcement came the Witness Protection Program which provides for the personal safety of individuals willing to provide testimony in service of a conviction of organized criminals. The seeds of self-destruction took root. In order to avoid unacceptable jail terms, "made guys" began to testify in the prosecution of their associates in exchange for lighter sentencing. Over the years, high-profile headliners such as Al Capone, Paul Castellano and John Gotti provide a basis in reality for understanding Tony Soprano as a mob boss. While he pines for the bygone Golden Age, he lives with the realities of the modern mafia.

Old School

The reality of organized crime in twentieth century America blends with *The Sopranos* and provides authentic elements in the fictional story of north Jersey crime and Tony Soprano. The allure of the criminal life was powerful to the brothers Corrado Soprano Jr. and Giovanni "Johnny Boy" Soprano. They were accepted into the local crime family headed by Ercoli DiMeo.[1] Throughout the 1960s the two brothers honed their reputations as tough guys not to be trifled with. They made their money primarily from gambling and loan sharking.[2] Johnny branched out into other enterprises such as racetracks (dog and midget car) as well as the music recording industry with his friend Herman "Hesh" Rabkin.[3] Johnny Boy's loan sharking operation would often net him real estate or a small business when the proprietors got over their head in debt with no other method of payment. In this way Johnny became one of the principal owners of Satriale's Meat Market.[4] Corrado Jr. made money selling stolen cars to the Vittorio family in Italy from as early as 1961.[5] Later, with the help of his brother Johnny, Corrado developed the Executive Game, the high-stakes poker game which would only occur in limited engagements by strict invitation only.[6]

The DiMeo family was comprised of numerous notable individuals who made the family both feared and respected. Dickie Moltisanti was known for his swagger and viciousness. He also had a reputation for fierce loyalty and this character would be emulated as a role model by young Anthony Soprano.[7] Pat Blundetto, an uncle of Tony's, was known as a DiMeo tough guy. However, he was granted a rare early retirement on account of a year-long bout with the hiccups and ensuing suicide attempt.[8] Soldier Robert Baccalieri Sr. was a reliable hit man with a reputation as a "terminator."[9] Feech LaManna carried special significance because he was "made" in Italy, "on the other side." His operations were largely gambling and theft.[10] A young up-and-comer named Paulie Gaultieri attached himself to Johnny Boy and soon earned admission to his crew through demonstration of an ability to intimidate and the ability to act on that intimidation. Somewhere along the line he acquired the nickname "Walnuts." Paulie Walnuts made his bones around 1970 with the murder of Charles "Sonny" Pagano.[11] From there he developed his experience and reputation into one of the toughest thugs in north Jersey.

Men who participated in organized crime families share certain values and characteristics. Above all, the importance of loyalty to the Family is ingrained as their prime directive to which all else is subservient. This honor among thieves is their greatest tool in establishing long-term financial success. Anyone who betrays the trust of the Family signs their own death warrant. Each man's worth is demonstrated in their behavior in business and their personal lives. To be an honorable man, one is required to live the values of the Family. The traditions of the mother country Italy are valued as an important connection to the past but also as a means to continue into the future. Catholicism remains the required religious affiliation for acceptance into this elite group. Reverence for one's parents and the family unit are sacred. Strength and conviction are esteemed. A man who lives by these values is respected by his peers and respect is their most valuable commodity.

There is a consistent hypocrisy in the follow-through of these values, however. It is common practice for the men in these organized crime families to have extra-marital relationships. To varying degrees their wives understand and accept this. They preach the sanctity of the family and marriage but their actions don't reflect it. Catholic teachings are left unpracticed as they throw the Ten Commandments out the window; the Seven Deadly Sins are their bread and butter. This provides insight into the workings of a gangster's mind and conscience, which collate conflicting values and teachings.

The DiMeo family has been successful partly due to their business affiliation with the New York-based Lupertazzi family, headed by Carmine Lupertazzi, Sr. Lupertazzi was supported by Angelo Garepe, Phil Leotardo and John "Johnny Sack" Sacrimoni. The Lupertazzi family *consigliere*, the shrewd Angelo Garepe, contributed to Lupertazzi family success in the seventies but was incarcerated in the fallout of the RICO trials of the 1980s. Lupertazzi's primary enforcer, Phil Leotardo, had made a name for himself as a wiseguy capable of cold brutality. Unfortunately for the Lupertazzi family, Leotardo also fell victim in the RICO convictions and was sentenced to a twenty-year jail term.[12] Despite a certain condescension on the part of Carmine, the New York family worked out amicable business relations with the DiMeos and the Sopranos, ensuring profitability for decades.[13]

Johnny Boy was a major contributor to the DiMeo family's success and as Tony grew into young adulthood he began to express his intentions of following in his father's footsteps. The experiences of witnessing his father's physical violence (beating a man in the street and chopping off Mr. Satriale's pinky), rather than frightening and discouraging young Tony from pursuing that lifestyle, readied him for the dangerous and morally complicated operations of organized crime. The lesson that money is earned by preying on the weak seems to be cemented in his childhood. The hoodlum antics of his youth expanded into larger and larger enterprises. From selling stolen lobsters and taking joyrides, Tony developed his reputation with the help of his friends with similar criminal aspirations. His cousin Tony Blundetto, Jackie Aprile, Sal "Big Pussy" Bonpensiero, Silvio Dante and Ralph Cifaretto all provided a support structure that would give Tony Soprano the start that would allow him to go far in the world of north Jersey organized crime.

When Tony dropped out of college, it was a turning point in his life, a crossroads.[14] The robbery of Feech LaManna's card game was a pivotal event in determining the direction of Tony's journey.[15] Despite later claims that he did not have a choice, Tony finally committed fully to the life of crime, deciding to go into the Family business.[16] His high school football coach evaluated Tony as a natural leader.[17] This would prove to be true.

Tony was uniquely gifted for the business as he demonstrated time and again. His astute business sense supported gutsy ventures. His keen evaluations of opportunity combined with sound judgment for the greater good of the Family. After a few years of paying dues, Tony was given an opportunity which would solidify his future. By order of his own father, Tony was to make his bones by eliminating a Family problem — Willie Overall, the bookie. It was Labor Day 1982, and Paulie Walnuts was given the responsibility of escorting twenty-two-year-old Tony Soprano to carry out his first homicide. Together they assaulted Mr. Overall and locked him in the trunk of their car while they sought an appropriate location to finish the job. Once in the basement of Zi Pepine's house on Brantford Avenue, Tony took his first human life under Paulie's supervision. Together they buried him there in the basement. Johnny Boy had already encouraged a bond between Paulie and Tony with the familial euphemism of "uncle." As well as advancing Tony's career, the Willie Overall hit was a defining moment in his relationship with Paulie. Respected and admired by Tony, Paulie would be a pseudo-father figure to him in his younger years.[18]

In 1983 the DiMeo family experienced unrest. Tony's friend Pussy proved his dedication to the Family. In aiding Johnny Boy he took a giant step forward in his career and he was "made" as a result.[19] Tony and the rest of the crew were not far behind. Throughout the eighties they kept out of sight of the authorities but continued to move up in the Family. In the mid-eighties a Soprano family associate, Fabian "Febby" Petrullio, was "flipped" by the federal government. In exchange for testimony he went into the Witness Protection Program. This was particularly hurtful to Johnny Boy and Jackie Aprile, both of whom had trusted Petrullio as a friend. Years later Tony Soprano would gratefully exact revenge on behalf of the Family.[20]

When Johnny Boy Soprano died of emphysema in '86 it signaled a period of change for the DiMeo family. The structure of the family had Ercoli DiMeo supported by his *capos* Corrado Soprano Jr., Feech LaManna, Raymond Curto and Lawrence "Larry Boy" Barese, while the Soprano crew awaited the advent of Tony. Feech LaManna fell victim to the government's zealous prosecution, receiving a term of fifteen years, and in '89 Richie Aprile was also sent to prison.[21] At this point some of the Family associations had to be redrawn. With the opening created by LaManna's absence, DiMeo promoted Jackie Aprile to take over as *capo* of his crew. Ralph Cifaretto, who had made his bones in the early eighties, aligned himself with Jackie, becoming a top earner.

Later that same year, Tony's cousin, Tony Blundetto, was arrested for a truck hijacking. He was sentenced to seventeen years in prison on account of the prosecution's ability to attach the crime to a RICO predicate. Tony Soprano only narrowly avoided the same fate. Due to a panic attack brought on by an argument with his mother, Tony didn't make it to the truck job and unwittingly avoided arrest. He lied about the specifics of his absence, telling his associates that he had been mugged by two African-Americans. Tony Blundetto's jailing, in light of his own freedom, would be a source of great guilt for Tony Soprano that would persist for years.[22]

Tony moved on, though, carrying on his father's role in the business, and it wasn't long until he too was promoted to the position of *capo*. In addition to his crew of Silvio Dante and Pussy he inherited Paulie Walnuts from his father. Even though Paulie filled a father figure role for Tony, the reverse effect also came into play. So greatly did Paulie admire Johnny Boy that after his death Paulie directed that same dedication to Tony Soprano.

Business continued smoothly until 1995 when the Ercoli DiMeo was arraigned and convicted to life in prison.[23] Again, the power within the Family would shift. At DiMeo's direction, Jackie Aprile took on the role of acting boss of the Family. Jimmy Altieri was promoted to *capo* of Jackie's former crew, including Ralph Cifaretto who was pursuing family business opportunities in Miami. The naming of Jackie Aprile as acting boss caused Tony's Uncle Junior great a*gita*. He proceeded to let everyone know of his discontent through the passive aggressive move of hijacking one of Jackie's trucks. This caused a small ruckus but was cleared up with the aid of Big Pussy as a good will emissary between Junior and Jackie.[24] With bad blood behind them, the Family continued under the new arrangement of Jackie as acting boss supported by his capos Junior, Ray, Larry, Jimmy and Tony. Around this time Tony would begin to mentor young Christopher Moltisanti in the ways of the Family business. Christopher had a reputation for being a hot-headed kid with aspirations bigger than his station in life. However, Tony's great affection for Christopher allowed him to be a patient teacher of the business to the ambitious young man.

It would not be long until another unexpected tragedy would hit the Family when Jackie Aprile was diagnosed with stomach cancer.[25] Despite chemotherapy the damage was irreversible and he passed away in early 1999. This situation left Junior chomping at the bit to take the reins while the *capos* in the family preferred the more even-tempered and profitable leadership of Tony. In an inspired move, Tony acquiesced to Junior the title of boss (although technically acting boss, also known as "street boss").

However, in a secret arrangement with the *capos* it was agreed that their true leader would be Tony.[26] It wasn't long before Junior was arrested and Tony officially became the boss of the DiMeo Family which came to be known as the Soprano Family.[27]

The Modern New Jersey Family

Tony reigns as the boss of the Family with Silvio Dante as his *consigliere*. Not long after Junior's arrest he promoted Paulie Walnuts to the position of Underboss, which includes the responsibilities of *capo* of the Soprano crew. By late 1999 the other Family *capos* were Ray Curto and Larry Barese, though his brother Albert acted as *capo* while Larry awaited trial. Uncle Junior's crew was practically decimated by Tony and what little remained was run on the street by Bobby Baccalieri Jr., a Family soldier and son of the "old school" hit man.[28] After Jimmy Altieri left the Family with a bullet through his head, his crew was assigned to the recently released Richie Aprile, making it the Aprile crew once again. Paulie Walnuts would later assert that the Aprile crew was cursed due to its nine-year revolving door of *capos* suffering misfortune: Jackie Aprile Sr.'s death of stomach cancer; Jimmy Altieri's execution on suspicion of flipping; Richie Aprile shot to death by Janice Soprano; Gigi Cestone's heart attack on the toilet; Ralph Cifaretto killed by Tony in a fit of rage; Vito Spatafore's murder at the direction of Phil Leotardo; and Carlo Gervasi testifying for the government. Tony's nephew, Christopher Moltisanti, would become a *capo* some years later but it did not last long.

Some of the greatest lines and most fun storylines over the course of *The Sopranos* come from Tony's closest friends and business partners — "the guys." The guys' core consists of Christopher, Silvio and Paulie. Along Tony's journey they aggravate him, they commiserate with him, they make him laugh and they even make him cry. Without these characters brought to life by great writing and acting, Tony's world would not be as colorful and entertaining as it is.

First of all there is Christopher who holds a special place in Tony's heart due to their blood relation and Tony's reverence of Chris's late father, Dickie. Chris's Hollywood dreams and ongoing frustrations with Family business make him amusing and relatable. His struggles with chemical dependencies, most significantly heroin, make him pitiable and tragic. For years Tony pinned his hopes for the future of the Family on Christopher but he was to be disappointed in the end. Throughout the series, some of the funniest dialogue consistently involves Chris, usually with Paulie Walnuts or his girlfriend Adriana LaCerva. Chris's character is one of the most integral to Tony's journey and is discussed in detail in Chapter 6.

Over the course of his career in the Family business, Tony has had two contemporaries (both of whom have unique and somewhat comical hairstyles) at his side the whole time. The first of them is Silvio Dante. Interestingly, the character of Silvio is just as much a creation of actor Steven Van Zandt as David Chase. Chase chose Van Zandt based strictly on his appearance in Bruce Springsteen's E Street Band. Van Zandt then suggested to Chase the character of Silvio, the manager of a New Jersey club with a distinctive look defined by his caricature zoot suits and pompadour hair. The Bada Bing! Club was then written as a strip club that acts as one of two Soprano Family headquarters (the other being Satriale's). The Bing served as backdrop to business meetings and down-time but it contributed greatly in defining the look and feel of the show from the very first episode.

As part of Tony's crew, Silvio's early memorable moments consist of blowing up Vesuvio, working over a Hasidic motel manager and amusing his friends with his impressions and quotations from the *Godfather* trilogy. Even though he wears loud suits, Silvio is a man of few words. The only time Silvio is seen to lose his cool is when losing at poker. He earned his position as *consigliere* by being a smart, level-headed and bottom-line-oriented business man. In his responsibility for the staff of young women dancing at the Bing he occasionally reveals misogynistic tendencies when employing physical force as a management tool. This is also supported by the apparent satisfaction he takes in killing Adriana, perhaps his single most significant on-screen moment.

The toughness in those situations is contrasted by the conflict he experiences when the moment comes to execute his longtime friend, Pussy. He shows weakness in a moment when Tony needs him to be strong. His discomfort in this instance, though, shows that he has compassion and does not murder for pleasure but out of a necessity of business.[29] Because he is one of the more independent thinkers in Tony's business world, the two of them don't always see eye to eye. Silvio, like others, feels frustrated and marginalized when Tony makes Christopher acting *capo* of Paulie's crew. In a rare act of passive aggression, Silvio authorizes a heist directly against Tony's orders. Outraged, Tony sticks by his endorsement of Chris and confronts Sil with this. Sil pleads innocence and the two of them write it off as a misunderstanding, Sil having registered his complaint and Tony tacitly understanding this.[30]

Silvio is exceptionally perceptive about the nuances of mafia management. Of equal importance, though, he understands when to speak and when not to. He knows which questions to ask and which questions not to. A good example is his restraint in addressing concerns about the disappearance of Ralph Cifaretto. Though Silvio would never ask for confirmation, it is likely he senses Tony's role in this problem. He toes the party line without losing the trust of the other made guys.[31] After AJ's suicide attempt he lets Tony say his piece, then diplomatically closes the topic among the crew. Silvio is skilled at not rocking the boat.[32]

In season five Silvio earns his pay by confronting Tony about his management of the conflict with Johnny Sack in regards to Tony Blundetto. While Tony delays the inevitable unpleasant resolution, Sil forces him to consider that he is deluding himself into believing his motivations are based in business or family loyalty. Sil bravely suggests to Tony that he has a problem with authority and his pride is getting in the way. Tony callously, though not without merit, accuses Sil of lacking comprehension of the full weight of responsibility of a boss. They agree to disagree but more importantly Silvio dutifully fulfills the role of an analytical and honest *consigliere*.[33]

Silvio's greatest test comes when he must fill in as acting boss while Tony is in a coma. His wife encourages him to consider loftier, long-term possibilities in contrast to his own view of the situation as a temporary but necessary call to duty. However, any big ideas are quickly dispelled as delusions of grandeur when he physically breaks down under the intense pressure from and responsibility to the crew, specifically in resolving internal disputes. True to his evaluative skills, his original estimation of himself being ideal for the position of second-in-command is proven correct. Silvio is a "Number Two" and is content in that role without any greater ambition.[34]

If Silvio is Tony's right-hand man on this journey, then close at his other hand is the longest standing active member of the Soprano Family, Paulie "Walnuts" Gualtieri. Paulie is old school, having risen from a lowly associate of Johnny Boy Soprano in the '50s to the position of Underboss in the new millennium. In their youth, Tony and his friends looked up to Paulie as the toughest guy around. Possessing the face and demeanor of a bulldog, Paulie can intimidate with his half-deranged glare or take pleasure in putting his muscle to good use as an outlet for his frustrations. His skill as an enforcer and button man were a great asset to the Family in the '70s and '80s. Paulie is a violent psychopath capable of impulsive brutality like throwing hot oil on a stranger for a verbal insult or gruesomely suffocating an elderly friend of his mother's when caught robbing her.[35]

As a child, Paulie was raised as a strict Catholic, serving as an altar boy for a time.[36] His mother, Nucci Gualtieri, never wavered in her love for and loyalty to him even as he strayed from the teachings of the church. Whenever young Paulie ended up in the principal's office or ran afoul of the law, Nucci always did everything she could to defend and help her son. For this he felt he owed her an eternal debt of gratitude and doted on her at every opportunity.[37] Paulie has girlfriends but never for long and he never married, a rarity in his circle of friends.

Paulie and Christopher have been through a lot together, most memorably their adventure with the Russian in the snowy New Jersey Pine Barrens. Paulie constantly gives Chris a hard time by "breakin' his balls" and Chris bristles with frustration. When conflict erupts between them, Paulie is usually the one at fault, whether he's sniffing Adriana's panties or scamming Chris's father-in-law.[38] They always make up in the end, though, with remarkably honest expressions of apology and love. After Chris's death, Paulie shows regret for not being a better friend to him and will always have a special place in his heart for Christopher.

Paulie Walnuts has more than his fair share of quirks. His old-school mentality has cemented in him the value of loyalty and he lives in anger at betrayal in any form. This is introduced when one of his closest friends, Pussy, is flipped by the FBI. Paulie takes this quite personally as he does in other instances, great or small: Italians not enthusiastically embracing him as their country's son; Tony not visiting him in jail; Johnny Sack inveigling him with empty rhetoric; the discovery of his true parentage; Vito's homosexuality. Paulie's philosophy of snakes' asexuality being indicative of their untrustworthiness hilariously summarizes his eccentric, though not unfounded, obsession with betrayal.[39]

Paulie's fears often manifest themselves in preoccupations with superstition and the belief that the worst will happen to him. These often have roots in his peculiar interpretations of the Catholic teachings of his youth. Paulie fixates on Chris's comatose vision of Hell and the implications of three o'clock. He takes it as an omen regarding his own sin and potential after-life. His consultation of a psychic only encourages his fears and similar thought processes are seen years later in regards to a cat that habitually stares at a photograph of the deceased Christopher.[40] After the discovery that his mother is actually his aunt and vice versa, Paulie sees a vision of the Virgin Mary hovering above the stage of the Bing. This vision frightens him but also encourages him to make amends to the woman who raised him.[41] Paulie's superstition translates to health concerns as well: He immediately assumes the worst when being tested for cancer; he is dismayed at aging and the loss of his youthful vigor; and his germophobia classically demonstrates his paranoia and groundless fears.

Despite his self-involvement, fears and psychopathy, Paulie is a loyal wiseguy. After his inflated ambitions planted by Johnny Sack are popped, Paulie's feelings of guilt cause him to appreciate anew that he is in the right line of work with a good Family. He is not known for his brain but his muscle and he deeply respects Tony like a general for whom Paulie lives to serve.

Where's the Money?

The DiMeo Family owed much of its early profitability to its interests in the waste management business. With fronts such as Barone Sanitation and the Zanone Brothers, the family is able to charge inflated rates, cut corners and "cook the books," leaving vast amounts of income undeclared. The success of the Soprano Family is the result of a diversified business model, extended far beyond the limits of waste management. Between the *capos* and their innovative boss, they manage to find a nearly limitless number of income streams.

Simple theft of money and goods provides the Sopranos with consistent revenue. Once stolen, goods are sold (or "fenced") to criminal associates in a position to easily redistribute them for profit. The size of a score ranges from as small as antique watches (filched from an open Federal Express truck) to whole international shipping containers. Opportunity dictates that if a family associate *could* jack goods, they would. Fine Italian suits, DVD players, computers, Gucci bags, imported provolone, Pokemon cards, Vespa scooters, Mexican ceiling tile, luggage, cigarettes, Jimmy Choo shoes, air mattresses, pool toys, air bags, fiber optic cable, Harry Potter books, sheet rock, vitamins, Easter baskets, assault rifles and Thanksgiving turkeys are just some of the goods the Soprano family has found itself in the position of moving and profiting from. Stolen automobiles are sold to the Sopranos' Italian connection or "chopped" for part resale. In addition to commercial theft, cat burglary is also a common practice for those looking to work their way up in the organization.

Extortion and racketeering are foundational aspects of the Business. In a racket, the Family creates a situation in which their services are required. The most common form of racketeering is protection, an arrangement in which they refrain from inflicting personal or property damage in exchange for a fee. Insurance fraud provides occasional boosts in income. Arson is one way to turn a profit out of a situation which has passed its earning potential and the Sopranos make use of a specialist when such a course of action is deemed necessary. Artie Bucco's restaurant and the horse Pie O My's stable were both incinerated by this practice.[42] In '99 Tony hit upon new opportunity in insurance fraud by exploiting a delinquent debtor in the managed care field. By having their front man file fraudulent claims, the Sopranos were able to collect hundreds of thousands of dollars.[43]

Construction has been perhaps the single most profitable branch of the family business. Through their connections and influence the Sopranos have been able to fix job bids so that the lucrative ventures were steered in their direction. The incentive for opportunistic officials is a healthy kick-back. Influential union bosses on the Family payroll (paving, electrical, joint-fitters, pipe-fitters, carpenters) skim money and funnel it out by means of paychecks for fraudulent jobs called "no work" or "no-shows." At times it has been necessary to resort to threats of physical violence to insure that the unions voted for individuals who were willing to play ball. In his earlier years Tony had experience in the construction business and preaches maximum value. Every nickel is extracted on demolition sites whether it's in the form of copper piping, wall sconces or anything else that makes money. The development of the city of Newark's esplanade along with the Museum of Science and Trucking is a huge windfall for Tony Soprano thanks to his connections to Assemblyman Ronald Zellman, who worked with both the Soprano and Lupertazzi families. Zellman has also opened up business opportunities in real estate with his inside knowledge of development plans, tipping off Tony regarding favorable changes in property values. Tony buys low and after the construction plans become public knowledge he sells high. Zellman also collaborated with the Sopranos on a scam of the federally funded program Housing and Urban Development. Along with the assistance of willing front-men and a licensed appraiser on the Family payroll, Tony and company were able to net hundreds of thousands of dollars in defrauding the United States government.[44]

Fraud takes many forms in organized crime and the Sopranos are no exception. The sale of defective goods creates valuable revenue. Stolen phone cards have been sold at cut-rate prices only for the dupe to later find out that the cards have no value. Previously deployed air bags are resold as new. Expired prescription medications from Canada became more profitable as the growing expense of American pharmaceuticals drove consumers to seek alternative sources. Stock frauds called "pump and dump" operations are another boon to the Family. In these operations a bunk stock is heavily promoted and sold to unwitting seniors and then unloaded at their loss and the Family's gain. Credit card numbers are frequently stolen and then sold to associates who make fraudulent purchases on the Internet or actually mint new plastic and sell them.

Servicing of vices is a traditional endeavor in illegal commerce and contributes to the Family wealth. Prostitution is a reliable source of income. Virtually all of the crime families include it in their operations whether in massage parlors or in conjunction with places like the Bada Bing! Club, where services are rendered to a more elite clientele for larger fees.

The trafficking of drugs is a necessary and profitable arm of the business. Though marijuana trafficking is reliable, it is a relatively low earner. Cocaine has long been a steady business for Junior, especially with the help of Richie Aprile. Ralph Cifaretto is no stranger to the drug trade. His involvement even extended to a coke habit which he would later fault for his rage in the killing of the young dancer, Tracee. Ralph also had connection to MDMA, more commonly known as ecstasy, and offered to supply Jackie Aprile Jr. Though heroin had its heyday as far as a lucrative venture, new federal sentencing guidelines made it a liability for any Family and involvement is strongly discouraged. The quintessential cautionary tale is Pussy Bonpensiero who, in the '90s, got involved in heroin trafficking because he needed a cash injection to meet his financial responsibilities to put his kids through college. Tony and Jackie Aprile Sr. both strongly advised him to discontinue the practice.[45] Pussy disregarded their advice and was eventually arrested for major heroin dealing and was faced with the possibility of a life sentence. He was caught in a no-win situation and for this reason Pussy turned against his Family. In a similar turn, *capo* Carlo Gervasi gave testimony to protect his son who was arrested for dealing ecstasy. A change in the drug playing field required the Soprano family to develop interests in crystal meth, an aspect of the family business which Vito Spatafore ran until his demise.

Gambling, in its many forms, represents another large source of income to the Family. The simplest form is the traditional neighborhood card game. Casino operations are on a higher tier where the added attraction of blackjack, roulette, craps and the like are offered. At least one Soprano casino is run above the front of Mancuso Hardware. Betting on professional sports is the other part of the Family's interests in illegal gambling. Horse racing, college and professional basketball and baseball are all popular betting forums. None, however, tops the earning potential of football. Football season is synonymous with Tony's "busy season" because of the voracious appetite for gambling on America's favorite game. The single biggest sporting event, the Super Bowl, is the crowning event, so large that its success or failure has a financial impact on the entire off-season. A sad example of its power and influence is the poor turnout for Jackie Aprile Jr.'s funeral, resulting from the necessary allocation of Family manpower to handle the peak volume of bettors.

A business corollary to gambling is loan sharking. Gambling remains successful because of the addictive nature of the endeavor. When a gambler is winning he experiences an extreme feeling of elation. So powerful is this feeling that gamblers continually attempt to recreate the high but the odds are against them and the bookies know this. When the losing sets in, a player will usually want to continue to satisfy two things — the requirement of paying off their losses, but also their desire for the rush. A bookie takes on the role of loan shark by lending the gambler money with interest, commonly known as a *vig*. The longer it takes for a debtor to repay, the more money earned by the shark on the loan. If there comes a point that repayment is beyond a debtor's means, a loan shark will take other methods of remuneration, other assets such as personal property or favors. If the debtor is a business owner, it is common practice for them to be "busted out." In a bust-out the shark has the debtor proprietor order goods on credit. An example would be Davey Scatino ordering huge quantities of Ramlosa Spring Water and picnic coolers.[46] The shark then fences the goods through his various connections, keeping the profit for himself. This process is continued until the debtor's credit runs out and he is left bankrupt while the shark has made significant earnings on a simple loan. Another option is for the debtor to make payment with the business itself, as Mr. Satriale did with his pork store in payment to Johnny Boy Soprano.[47]

This is just a brief summary of the business of the Soprano family. The creative team behind *The Sopranos* bases their writing on extensive research of real-life mafia operations. In translating these details to the television screen, they provide a window on a world that frightens and fascinates their audience. Regardless of his lovable and sympathetic qualities, the criminal enterprise is Tony Soprano's bread and butter.

Some Friends of Ours

The Soprano crime family operates with the help of many business partners and associates, euphemistically referred to as "friends of ours."

The Sopranos' longevity and success is due in part to their partners in other crime families and legitimate institutions. The longest standing of these partners is Herman "Hesh" Rabkin. Hesh has been a high level associate of the Family, working with Johnny Boy Soprano since the '50s and continuing that relationship with Tony after Johnny's death.[48] Hesh is an investor in Family enterprises and acts as facilitator and liaison with his extensive connections in the business. His wealth affords him unique influence but he relies on Tony Soprano as a business partner and protector.

Apart from New York, the Sopranos have connections to organized crime in other parts of the country. They work with a Philadelphia-based family on gambling.[49] Atlantic City is a natural hub of successful operation where the Sopranos are known to be involved in prostitution, drugs and of course gambling.[50] Florida is another long-standing outpost for Family business. Its exceptional geographical position for shipping makes it an excellent port for smuggling and heists. Ralph Cifaretto and Carmine Lupertazzi Jr. both had extensive business there.[51] Peter "Beansie" Gaeta has been the Soprano family ambassador in Miami ever since his rehabilitation in living with the paraplegia he suffered at the hands of Richie Aprile.[52]

Soprano connections extend internationally as well. Tony has worked with a Russian crime family through their point man in New Jersey, Slava Malevska. Slava helps Tony with the laundering of money through offshore accounts.[53] The Sopranos also maintain their ties to the Vittorio family in Naples. Now headed by the daughter of the mentally ailing don, the Vittorios remain a good partner in the car business and also the occasional use of muscle.[54] Furio Giunta stayed stateside for nearly three years acting as an enforcer for the Sopranos. Occasionally circumstances required absolute deniability in carrying out significant hits. The Vittorios provided two assassins for the execution of Rusty Millio and the failed attempt of Phil Leotardo.[55]

Although police and law enforcement are the Soprano family archenemy, there are those within those organizations who can be persuaded with the appropriate financial compensation. On *The Sopranos*, police are typically portrayed as corrupt, but in a jovial manner. Cooperation from law enforcement authorities can be as simple as looking the other way for a bribe to the role of accomplice. Paulie Gaultieri regularly pays off an officer to avoid any disruption of the Executive Game.[56] He also carries a Newark Police Department sergeant on the payroll to provide inside information of police activity.[57] The Soprano Family maintains a parole officer in its pocket as well, seen sending Feech LaManna back to jail in

'04 to relieve Tony of another headache.[58] Patsy Parisi is known to associate with an officer in Fairfield.[59] Bobby Baccalieri is the primary contact to a woman in the courthouse with access to high level information.[60]
Barry Haydu, although allegedly responsible for the death of Dickie
Moltisanti, was allowed to live in return for services to the Family.[61] The
most memorable law enforcer "on the take," Detective Vin Makazian
worked directly with Tony Soprano in the late '90s. Although their relationship was fundamentally based on Tony providing an outlet for Makazian's gambling needs and Makazian's ability to give Tony inside
information, they ultimately found a level of mutual respect. Makazian's
suicide left more questions than answers regarding suspicions of Pussy
being a cooperator with the FBI.

Crime families have long ago learned that it is worth the investment
to find a highly skilled and sympathetic legal counsel. Tony's lawyer, Neil
Mink, has proven his worth on various occasions. Whether knocking down
a flimsy weapons charge or counseling Tony on how to insulate himself
from possible prosecution, Mink has helped Tony avoid conviction. Uncle
Junior was forced into a long and expensive legal battle when he was
arrested and brought to trial. Junior's defense reportedly cost in excess of
a million dollars, and even then he remained under house arrest pending
retrial. The skill of his lawyer Harold Melvoin in prolonging the proceedings allowed Soprano Family members to extract a mistrial through the
threat of physical violence toward one of the jurors.[62]

Organized crime has found that most people in a position to help
them have a price. From fellow Families, both continental and international, to cops to lawyers — Tony Soprano gets by with a little help from
Some Friends of Ours.

The Boss of This Family

Tony Soprano is a businessman. He demonstrates all the skills that
would be seen in a successful CEO of a legitimate business. Tony is a brilliant problem solver, weighing a vast number of variables and making difficult decisions. He manages individuals, organizing them to work as a team
for the good of the Family and themselves. Tony sees market trends and
has reliable instincts on how to adapt and grow the business with changing conditions. He remains focused on the bottom line — making money.
Tony came to his position as boss for all these reasons but also from an
intangible sixth sense that differentiates him from the others in his field.

In examining these factors in detail, Tony's internal processes regarding business and personal life can be better understood.

Whereas CEOs work in offices or boardrooms, Tony's centers of operation are a pork store and a strip club, occasionally meeting in unobtrusive locales like OfficeMax or a diner. His staff consists of thugs, thieves, psychopaths and murderers. To make the organization work with such deceitful and volatile individuals is a testament to Tony's managerial skill. His people have human qualities though and they respond to Tony's keen understanding of human behavior and motivation. The familial model of the organization is reinforced with greetings of a kiss on the cheek and deals sealed with a warm embrace. Tony is tough but he can also show compassion by sympathizing, offering advice or helping his guys with their problems. The result is a combination of strictly-business indebtedness but also heartfelt gratitude on the part of his *capos* and soldiers. Tony will sometimes even go above the reasonable call of duty, such as rescuing Chris and Paulie from the Pine Barrens or supporting Silvio in his public relation battle regarding Christopher Columbus. At various times Tony acts as a friend, a brother or even a father to his men. He is able to fulfill these roles without losing his authority as a leader and his men love and respect him in return. Tony works to keep his people happy for their own sake but also because the alternative is bad for business.

Occasionally members of Tony's family are unhappy and cause trouble, impacting his stress level and the Family's bottom line. Whether their beef is with Tony or another associate, it is part of Tony's job to make sure it gets solved. Tony knows the value of nipping problems in the bud before they become major headaches. Signs of disrespect, no matter how small, are a clear indication of potential problems and Tony deals with them immediately and head-on. He is skilled at tailoring his response to suit the message and makes it clear to the offender and everyone else involved that such disrespect will not be tolerated. It may be as a verbal reprimand, demanding payment of a tribute, or worse. When Richie Aprile defies Tony's orders not to sell cocaine on union garbage routes, Tony sees it as part of a larger pattern of negative behavior.[63] When Christopher openly questions Tony's judgment, he gets forcefully put in his place.[64] When Ralph Cifaretto refuses his offer of a drink, Tony makes Ralph crawl to him for forgiveness.[65] When Jackie Jr. disrespects Tony's lunch invitation, Tony bends Jackie to his will.[66] When Feech LaManna's frustration with Tony appears irreversible, Tony sends Feech back to jail.[67] These and others have paid the price for not showing Tony the proper respect.

Conflict arises when the small issues of made guys become larger problems. Tony acts as a moderator and judge in such cases, whether at his discretion or in response to a request for a sit-down. His business acumen is seen in an early sit-down to resolve Junior's taxation of Hesh. In this instance Tony cleverly solves Hesh's problem while stroking Junior's ego and establishing his own new leadership role.[68] Tony mediates conflicts between Paulie and Chris, Richie and Beansie, Paulie and Ralph, Ralph and Johnny Sack, Paulie and Vito and others. Tony takes these opportunities to offer guidance as a teacher or mentor, exhorting his men to exercise impulse control. He does so with consideration for the individual while reinforcing the hierarchical chain of command in their paramilitary organization.

Regardless of the specifics, the bottom line is the ultimate guide in Tony's business decisions. When conflicts arise, Tony negotiates a compromise. There is a strategy of give-and-take which evens out over the long run to insure the Family's financial success. In considering his people, Tony often defines them as earners. Each man is only as good as this week's envelope. When revenue diminishes he calls a meeting with his *capos* to express his extreme dissatisfaction and make clear his expectation of results in actively addressing the matter.[69] Tony is always on the lookout for new opportunities. This instinct has led him to successes with HMO fraud, HUD scams, MRI operations and others. When sympathizing with Davey Scatino on the bust-out of his sporting goods store, Tony shows poignant openness about his own nature for plundering those weaker than himself, like a scorpion preying upon a frog.[70] In aid of the bottom line, one of Tony's top concerns is the maintenance of a low profile, both for himself personally and the Family. He discourages risky operations and overt public violence that draw attention to them, whether from the citizenry or the law. When they're under scrutiny and pressure or at war with each other they can't earn. This puts the Family and Tony himself in jeopardy. Therefore the welfare of the bottom line is an effective guiding principle as Tony leads the Family.

Just as anyone in a demanding leadership position, Tony has occasionally shown himself to be imperfect. His decision to make Gigi Cestone *capo* of the Aprile crew was a flawed one. Gigi was not respected by those of whom he was put in charge. This selection was influenced by Tony's personal feelings rather than based strictly on business considerations. Tony's dislike of Ralph Cifaretto came into play on the Gigi decision and other instances as well. When Tony hit Ralph in response to his fatal beating of the dancer Tracee, it made the situation worse.[71] Tony's emotions got the better of him and in hitting Ralph he violated a code among made guys. The resultant rancor between them would never be fully put to bed. Later, Tony's temper would drive him to kill Ralph for his apparent murder of Pie O My, a horse. Tony's anger was understandable but the cost of his vengeful act was a new suspicion and loss of confidence in him on the part of some of his subordinates.[72] A similar fallout occurred when Tony delayed his decision to whack Vito Spatafore for his homosexuality. Even though Tony had a moral basis for sparing Vito, some of his key men were disenchanted with Tony's hesitation to act. When Tony finally did decide to have Vito killed, it was when it became clear that the Family would avoid conflict with New York and make more money by placating Phil Leotardo rather than give Vito a pass.[73]

Tony admits the greatest blunder of his career was the grooming of his nephew Christopher to be his successor. Their personal relationship clouded Tony's judgment. He allowed his love of Chris, his feelings toward Dickie Moltisanti, his need for a plan of succession and a misguided faith in blood relation to blind him to Chris's hopeless drug abuse. Tony is shown to be totally oblivious to Chris's problems at times and willfully self-delusional at others. It takes Christopher's movie, *Cleaver*, an admission of relapse in his battle with addiction and a half-fatal car crash to supersede Tony's fatherly sensibilities. Tony takes Chris the other half of the way for the greater good of the Family business.[74]

Tony's mistakes are part of his learning process and his journey. Along with his conflict resolution and bottom-line orientation, his continued success can be credited to his efforts at self-improvement in his work. From varied sources he applies lessons to his business world, giving him the ability to adapt and survive when new challenges arise. Tony seizes upon Melfi's mention of Sun Tzu's *The Art of War* as a strategy guide, finding it superior to Machiavelli Cliff's Notes. From the beginning of the series Tony is shown to be a fan of the History Channel. He knows the value of learning from history and sees applications to his gangland problems in World War II documentaries. An example of Tony's approach can be seen in his coaching Uncle Junior in generosity by citing Augustus Caesar.[75] Even with his faults, Uncle Junior is another valuable tactical adviser to Tony. Despite his failing mental health in later years, Uncle Junior demonstrates moments of astute business evaluations. He learned how to split his enemies from Joe Profaci.[76] Junior advised Tony to eliminate Chris *five years* before Tony finally accepted the wisdom of it.[77] In counseling Tony regarding Ralph, Junior showed an awareness of the many variables involved. As a result of Junior's first attempt on Tony's life they were estranged for a time, but Tony recognized that this was a strictly-business decision. Junior summarized his philosophy on leadership with the assertion that there are not always answers to problems, a boss does the best he can and finds simple pleasures in the meantime.[78] Tony's success owes credit to such valuable lessons as this throughout his experiences.

One asset contributing to Tony's success as a boss is an unquantifiable, ethereal instinct about problem-solving. Tony is known, by his *consigliere* no less, to have his own unique process of evaluating all the facets of a problem and hitting upon a unique solution. It is most pointedly explained to the audience in the context of a History Channel documentary on the World War II German General Rommel who is described as having *Fingerspitzengefühl*— a sixth sense of sizing up a situation. This can be seen in Tony on numerous occasions. The direct context of the documentary is in regards to the Tony B. problem. Tony S. is faced with a complicated situation: New York wants the cousin handed over to them to torture and Tony feels compelled to protect his cousin, despite his grievous affronts. Tony takes none-of-the-above action by, himself, killing Tony B. With no good options presented to him, Tony hits upon a slightly less disgusting one that serves the greatest good, short-cutting to Tony B.'s inevitable demise, satisfying his own Family and New York boss Johnny Sack.[79]

Tony's *Fingerspitzengefühl* contributes to the Tony B. solution in a dream which revolves around his cousin and prompts Tony to take a proactive course. Tony's dreams play a critical role in his realization that Pussy had been flipped, another subconsciously derived solution to a business problem.[80] Similarly, Tony's *Fingerspitzengefühl* is at work when he hallucinates a young woman named Isabella. This experience is a subconscious awareness of Livia's toxicity. All of her absent maternal qualities are embodied in this figment of Tony's imagination. Tony's unusual process is seen when he considers the possibility that construction associate Jack Massarone may be cooperating with the FBI. To meditate on this, Tony spends an evening alone, drinking heavily and contemplating Massarone's ambiguous gift, a portrait of Frank Sinatra, Dean Martin and Sammy Davis Jr.— the Rat Pack. This process in conjunction with a perceptive consideration of one of Massarone's empty compliments allows Tony to see the truth of Massarone's betrayal.[81] Tony is not always consciously aware of his *Fingerspitzengefühl* and neither is the audience. Camera shots which may seem out of keeping with the flow of a scene are later shown to have hidden meaning. Awareness of Pussy's betrayal is foreshadowed twelve episodes previous with a simple slow-motion portrait of his friend from Tony's point of view. He knows there's something there but it takes the entire second season for his subconscious instinct to puzzle it out.[82] When Carmela recounts a tragic story of an infant drowning in a pool, Tony does not know why he can't get the story out of his mind. As it turns out, it is his *Fingerspitzengefühl* at work, trying to warn him of AJ's imminent suicide attempt in their own pool.

Again and again, with his ability to manage people, attention to the bottom line, continuous evolution and unique instinct, Tony shows he deserves to be the Boss of his Family.

David Chase and company do a wonderful job at creating a fascinating world that satisfies its audience's voyeuristic inclinations, informed by realistic operational details of modern organized crime. The history of the New Jersey Soprano Family is rich in detail and the colorful cast of characters serves to entertain and caution. Leading them is Tony Soprano, an imperfect but incomparably effective boss, served by his charismatic personality and exceptional business sense. At the helm he has successfully guided his Family into the twenty-first century.

4

The Taste of Brylcreem

The Soprano Family is not without its enemies and none is greater than the Federal Bureau of Investigation. Just like an organized crime family, the FBI is a business. The federal government invests millions of dollars in evidence collection and prosecution of professional criminals and the taxpayers expect a return on their investment. The FBI has been portrayed in a non-traditional manner on *The Sopranos,* deserving little more sympathy or respect than the Soprano Family. The FBI's strongest tool is the capture and recruitment of pliable individuals, coercing them to betray their Family. This phenomenon is the greatest threat to organized crime. With incomparable resources, the FBI and their rats are...

Private Enemy Number One

When Tony acquiesces to Junior, allowing him to assume the role of Family boss, it preempts conflict or, even worse, war. It also provides the benefit of a buffer between Tony and the possibility of action on the part of the Federal Bureau of Investigation. The Bureau is gradually introduced as a character in its own right, exhibiting many of the characteristics that define a Family. They have a hierarchical structure, work for a common cause, and most agents on *The Sopranos* are Italian-American. This family, however, is on the other side of the law — the "right" side.

In the context of *The Sopranos,* the FBI is introduced in a passing mention between Family associates. The tone suggests indignance combined with real fear, as if the Feds are the bogeymen to wiseguys everywhere. Dear friends of the Family have been taken away by the Federal government and they are reviled for their interference in This Thing of Ours. The presentation by the show's writers proceeds on the basis that their audience is familiar, in concept, with some basic surveillance techniques. Soprano Family members make use of public phones to avoid any wiretaps. Chris and Georgie conduct regular sweeps of the Bing to insure there are no "bugs." Verbal code is an especially interesting phenomenon. Understanding that any business details overheard by the wrong party could cause major problems, legal or otherwise, members and associates of the Family develop certain mannerisms of speech. When in public or a potentially surveilled locale, specifics are rarely mentioned in preference for vague generalities. The expectation is that the second party is already familiar with the details and retreading this ground only creates possible liability. A question as simple as "Did you see that guy about the thing?" could carry life-or-death implications. A certain foundational understanding between two associates is necessary but this code, if overheard by a third party, means nothing and cannot have any weight in a court of law.

The gradual introduction of the FBI continues when they are first seen taking surveillance photographs from afar at Jackie Aprile Sr.'s funeral. The situation is meant to illustrate AJ's awareness of his father's other Family but it also serves to introduce the Family's arch-nemesis.[1] The next encounter with the FBI is much more invasive when they conduct a search of the Soprano household with Tony, Carmela and the children present. It is here that the audience is introduced to Agent Harris, who would come to be the FBI's point person in dealing with Tony Soprano. Tony repudiates the agents with ridicule and bullying while they remain professional, with the exception of Agent Grasso who rises to Tony's taunts. The contrast in attitude between Tony and the FBI informs our understanding of the ongoing battle between them. Later Tony and Carmela spin the incident as unfounded persecution of an honest businessman for his Italian heritage. This rationalization is primarily for the benefit of Meadow and AJ but there is also a degree of self-deception on their part.[2] Over the course of the first season and throughout the series, the danger of consequences at the hands of the FBI is conveyed to the audience in pieces until the reality of possible legal repercussions looms very large. The audience is subtly put in Tony's shoes and given a sense of impending doom.

Junior's reign as boss is brief. His major actions as head of the Family are the unintentional maintenance of his reputation as a greedy individual and a failed hit on his nephew Tony. It does not take long for Junior to unwittingly fulfill his role as a safety measure and fall guy for Tony and the rest of the Family. Later the very same year, the FBI completes their preparations in the arrest and prosecution of numerous Family members and associates. Junior, Larry Barese, and others are arrested and arraigned on several RICO statute crimes. With Junior imprisoned and under indictment, Tony steps up to the position of boss of the family, in name and in everything.[3] Junior is further ensnared by the Feds when they plant an undercover agent in his doctor's office.[4] Junior sums up the overwhelming might of federal pursuit with the simile of marshals so far up his backside he can taste Brylcreem. However, after nearly a year and a half of legal proceedings, Junior's conviction is averted by threats of violence to a susceptible juror and his family.[5]

The FBI's surveillance methods leave no stone unturned, demonstrated when it is discovered that they wire the retirement home of Livia Soprano. The unlikely source for information yields fascinating results because of the conversations between Livia and Junior. Because Junior looks to Livia as a *semi-consigliere*, sensitive topics are leaked to the FBI. Their plan of attack is to approach Tony with the information in hopes of intimidating him into cooperation, but their bluff fails.[6] This has the effect of further sensitizing Tony to federal surveillance possibilities and numerous instances are seen in which he takes precautions to avoid detection. He has Gigi log-off his computer before discussing sensitive topics because cookies make him nervous.[7] Tony mentions to his Cadillac dealer that he removed the global positioning system from his Escalade, the implication being that he could be tracked in such a manner.[8] His vehicle precaution extends even to routine servicing, immediately after which he will not discuss business specifics in his car for fear of microphones.[9] In determining placement of a fabricated lamp with a concealed transmitter, the FBI considers the tidbit that Tony fears parabolic microphones potentially directed to his backyard and thus is reluctant to discuss business there.[10] A common practice to avoid surveillance is to meet in public places not likely to be watched. Tony conducts meetings at the mall, at Office Depot, diners and elsewhere. Once Tony reaches a certain level of prominence, specifically when Junior is taken out of the spotlight, sensitive discussions are rarely conducted directly with Tony and the location is never in such an obvious locale as Satriale's patio. Tony's plan of ascension for Christopher is also motivated by the additional buffer between himself and potentially incriminating conversations.

The personal portraits of the federal agents in the first season are straightforward. They are not overbearing or violent. They are even-tempered and business-like. In season three the FBI picks up the intensity of their pursuit of Tony Soprano by infiltrating his home to place a bugged lamp. The operation is depicted as a precision, almost militaristic execution accompanied by a unique blending of the *Peter Gunn* theme and "Every Step You Take" by the Police. In this episode, more of the FBI operational details are shown. The Feds give cute nicknames to each of the Soprano family, creating an odd mix of business and humor. Due to the invasive nature of the FBI's lamp operation, they come off to the audience as the offenders, the wrong-doers. Even though it's clear that Tony is a criminal, the audience, to a degree, roots for Tony to come home and catch the Feds in the act. Actor Frank Pando, who plays Agent Harris, recounts that while *The Sopranos* was airing, random citizens on the street would tell him to "Leave Tony Soprano alone!"[11]

The FBI agents are given a less sympathetic portrayal, especially beginning with the lamp operation. Bureau Chief Cubitoso is the low-key administrator of the ongoing Soprano investigation, the equivalent of a *capo* in his federal family. Tony has a sense of humor in his relationship with Cubitoso, enough to send an elaborate fruit basket on holidays and special occasions. The one time Cubitoso is shown to lose his temper is with Christopher's pitiable fiancée, Adriana LaCerva. Cubitoso is able to coerce greater cooperation from her with threats and rage, leaving the audience feeling for Adriana as an innocent victim.[12]

Agent Dwight Harris is Tony's point of primary contact with the FBI. Historically, Agent Harris fits the "good cop" role while his colleagues and subordinates are shown to be witless and two-dimensional, his superiors to be vain and vindictive. Tony and Harris have an established rapport illustrated by their cordial exchanges about basketball, the weather and mortadella. Harris is eventually reassigned to anti-terrorism and this adds a realistic credibility to the tapestry of the show. This turn of events enhances its contemporaneous quality, reflecting the re-allocation of federal resources in response to new priorities post-9/11. It serves to show that the FBI hasn't taken their eye off Tony but they have other fish to fry. Harris shows new concern and generosity when he tips off Tony to the possibility of the New York Family whacking someone high up in the Soprano Family.[13] This leads to a surprising turn of events in which Tony gives Harris information about two Middle Eastern associates of the Family, with the promise of consideration of such cooperation if ever Tony were to be convicted of a crime.[14] Tony not only wants that carrot but he also believes in returning a favor. Tony cooperates and as he does so it feels like a betrayal, especially when only two episodes previous Tony reasserted that such an act would qualify him as a rat. As the final episodes play out, it appears that Tony's *Fingerspitzengefühl* may have been at work when Harris breaches all FBI regulations by reciprocating further and giving Tony crucial intelligence that wins for Tony the brief war with Phil Leotardo. Harris is ultimately depicted as a partisan cheerleader of Tony Soprano.[15] They are on different teams but they respect each other as veterans of the same game. Harris is a peer to Tony, which is a rarity, and his role in Tony's fate is immeasurable and unforgettable.

Harris's fellow agents are less sympathetic toward Tony Soprano and his Family. Agent Grasso has been working on the Soprano case for nearly as long as Harris. His initial claim to fame is the accidental shattering of Carmela's glass bowl while conducting a search of the Soprano home. Grasso's function in the story is to give Tony an opportunity to express his disgust for someone of Italian descent working for the federal government. Tony tells his children that such a person is betraying his own people. This also creates a dichotomy in Tony's world with law-abiding Italians in opposition to those in the Family.[16] In kind, Grasso has only disparaging remarks about Tony through the remainder of the series.

Agent Skip Lipari, Pussy's handler, is portrayed as a more likable "every-guy." He's overweight, balding, speaks with a thick Jersey accent and he gripes about his job. With Pussy, Skip walks the line between authoritarian and friend. The two of them develop a relationship as peers who can share each other's problems over a cup of coffee. However, where Pussy perhaps misinterprets the extent of their friendship, Lipari keeps in sight that when the assignment's done Pussy will be doing serious jail time. Unlike Harris, Lipari does not waver from the black-and-white perspective that the wiseguys they pursue are no more than criminals.

Agent Deborah Ciccerone is assigned to work undercover by embedding herself as the new best friend of Adriana. At the beginning of season four, Agent Ciccerone is re-introduced in a scene in which she teases her hair and appearance to fit Adriana's sensibilities. While she transforms herself the audience is given a glimpse into her family life. She has a husband and also a baby and this simple portrait is one with which an audience can respect and appreciate.[17] This image fades, though, and her duplicity returns to the forefront. This deception on the part of Agent Ciccerone is in the line of duty but seems even fouler when Adriana shares the deep, personal secret about possible reproductive complications resultant from an abortion in her past, something which she had never told anyone.[18]

When Chris sabotages the FBI's plan by disrupting the friendship, the Feds change their approach by arresting Adriana, confronting her with the ruse of which she has been the victim for the last four months. Adriana feels wounded by treachery at the hands of someone whom she trusted like a sister. There is no sensitivity to this on the part of the FBI and Adriana is treated like a commodity to be manipulated for their own benefit. Little human consideration is given and her emotional state is essentially disregarded. Of course the Feds feel justification in her complicity to organized crime, a perspective that is not without merit. However, the audience feels Adriana's pain of betrayal rather than satisfaction of justice pursued. The Feds facilitate Adriana's servitude with threats of repercussions, either from them or from the Soprano Family, for being taken in by the bureau's deception. They coerce Adriana's cooperation and create for her a tormented existence of guilt and fear.

Once drafted by the Feds, Adriana meets her new handler, Agent Robyn Sanseverino. Sanseverino is depicted as cold and detached. She exhibits little empathy for Adriana's distress. Adriana, in need of someone to talk to, makes numerous attempts to share her feelings with Sanseverino and is consistently rebuffed. Just as Ciccerone was given a brief matronly portrait, so too is Sanseverino. Her demeanor with her ten-year-old daughter, though, is consistent with her businesslike, controlling approach to Adriana. When in the company of her fellow agents, Sanseverino is disparaging, condescending and even cruel in her remarks behind Adriana's back. She belittles Adriana's intelligence and sensibilities. These comments go a long way in distancing the audience from Sanseverino and her associates. The greatest personal insight into Sanseverino's character comes from the details that inspired her to become a federal agent — the tragic death of her sister. The story is touching and human but its impact is washed away when she spins it with patriotic jingoism into a propagandistic justification of the federal coercion of Adriana's cooperation. Sanseverino does present some genuine concern for Adriana's wellbeing when Ade is forced to seriously consider her cooperational commitment and the possibility of escaping into the witness protection program. When Adriana is lost to the Feds, Sanseverino is naïve in her belief that Ade may have simply run off while Cubitoso and Harris are more realistic.

Over the course of *The Sopranos*, the Federal Bureau of Investigation is depicted with the same neutral tone as the Soprano Family members. They are not put up on pedestals as heroes of American justice, just as the Family is not shown to be straightforwardly evil. They do not fit into traditional presentations of "good guys." The federal agents have favorable and unfavorable qualities. They are just as human as Tony and his associates. It is up to each viewer to weigh the positives and the negatives and decide for themselves how they feel about the agents just as they must consider the "bad guys."

The Rat Pack

The Federal Bureau of Investigation invests large quantities of time and money in accumulating evidence against organized crime. The intent is to amass enough evidence that, when brought to trial, they are confident of a conviction. To build a successful case takes years of surveillance, data collection and collaboration. It takes six seasons for the Feds to have sufficient evidence to consider mounting a trial against Tony. The greatest weapon that the FBI has in organized crime prosecution is a witness with direct ties to the organized crime family. When a Family member violates their vow of *omertà* and cooperates with the federal government, they are branded a "rat." There is no one more reviled in organized crime because of the extremity of their betrayal, forsaking the cornerstone of the Family relationship. There have been numerous examples of rats in the Soprano family and each of their stories has been tragic.

The first rat seen in *The Sopranos* came in the popular episode, "College." While visiting prospective colleges with Meadow, Tony spots an old associate of the family, Febby Petrullio, who was busted for selling heroin in the mid-eighties. Petrullio entered the witness protection program but was later kicked out and became a public speaker on the mafia. The depth of Tony's commitment to *omertà* is demonstrated when he garrotes Petrullio in his first on-screen murder, a particularly vicious and graphic one at that. David Chase has recounted the reticence of HBO for Tony to be portrayed in this graphically violent manner, afraid to lose his likeability with the audience. However, Chase felt strongly that the audience would lose respect for Tony if he *didn't* kill Petrullio.[19] He was right. It also hammered home the life-or-death stakes with which the characters in this universe deal.

Later in the first season the shadow of suspicion falls on current members of the Family. First, Pussy is identified by Detective Makazian as a cooperator. The distress and anxiety Tony and his associates feel after receiving this news is weighty.[20] It then appears that the rat is Jimmy Altieri and not Pussy. The crew deal swiftly with Altieri, luring him to a hotel where Silvio shoots him in the back of the head.[21] The message is clear that those who deal with the government have kissed tomorrow goodbye. Knowing this and sensitive to the suspicion cast on him, Pussy disappears.

The psychology of mob informant contributes a fascinating story to *The Sopranos*. The portrayal of Pussy is one of the main arcs through the second season and has implications through the entire series. After returning and dispelling suspicion in the Family, his cooperation with the federal government is confirmed to the audience. It is additionally tragic that his situation resulted from an arrest for involvement with heroin, which Tony and Jackie Aprile specifically warned him against in the past.[22] The introduction of his FBI handler, Lipari, provides greater insight into the functioning relationship between informant and the Feds. Pussy is seen to deal only with Skip and their interactions range from genial to hostile. At times they commiserate over the stresses in their lives such as being passed over for promotion. Over time, Pussy's demeanor changes. Initially he bristles under Skip's coercion of him. It becomes apparent that Pussy is not totally forthcoming in his information in an attempt to stall for time, perhaps in the hope of eventual escape from his predicament. However, it slowly becomes apparent that there is no light at the end of the tunnel for Pussy. We see his descent take a sharp dive when he murders an unsuspecting Elvis-impersonating associate out of paranoid fear of being discovered. His relationship with his family at home suffers when he becomes so preoccupied with his impossible situation that he is unresponsive when his wife, Angie, deals with the possibility of a cancer diagnosis. He is no longer the man she married and she resolves herself to divorce.[23] Pussy reaches his breaking point when he is forced to wear a wire to AJ's confirmation party. When his surveillance paraphernalia is almost discovered by Angie, he reacts like an animal backed into a corner, to the point of physical violence upon her witnessed by their horrified son. Pussy's despair is painfully rendered as he is shown weeping tears of anguish, consumed with grief over his irreversible course.[24] His family, which he strove to protect, is being destroyed under the pressure of his divided loyalties. He is betraying his friends whom he's known his entire life. Pussy realizes that he will ultimately be left with nothing.

From that moment, reckless, self-deluded, self-destructive behavior is seen as Pussy changes his tune entirely and becomes a willing, enthusiastic cooperator. With professed aspirations of becoming a law enforcement operative himself, he eagerly provides Lipari with any and all scraps of information. Lipari evaluates this the equivalent of Stockholm Syndrome, a situation in which a kidnapping victim becomes sympathetic to the kidnapper.[25] Pussy certainly demonstrates symptoms of new allegiance but it is the beginning of the end. It seems unlikely that Pussy actually believed he might reform and work on the side of the law. Rather, this was an artifice, a lie he told himself so he could survive without totally cracking under the enormous strain of his predicament. When Pussy is ultimately discovered for his betrayal of the Family, he is executed by his closest friends — Tony, Paulie and Silvio.[26] Despite the deep love these men feel for Pussy, it is their duty to the Family and their own rules to exact the absolute punishment, putting an end to Pussy's sad story.

Despite the demise of Pussy it is illustrated that the threat of betrayal to the federal government is constant. Ray Curto, one of Tony's *capos*, is shown to be working with the FBI. In the presentation of Curto's cooperation it appears that is their relationship has some tenure as he is accustomed to the expectations of the FBI and graciously cooperates. Ray is an example of loyalty to himself. He does not show the compunction about wearing a wire into Tony's home and he is not coy in requesting financial reimbursement from the FBI for expenses tenuously incurred in his activities in data collection.[27] He works all angles to give himself the greatest advantage. Ray continues to be a cooperator until his untimely (or timely, from Tony's perspective) natural death in 2006.[28] This is a classic example of David Chase's storytelling. For five years this threat was known to the audience, not Tony, planting seeds of fear of Family downfall. When Ray dies of a heart attack, the threat fizzles out in a mundane though realistic turn of events and the audience is left to re-evaluate their expectations of the *Sopranos* storytelling once again. In practical terms it is probable that much of Ray's evidence will be rolled into the prosecution of Tony Soprano, if and when that comes to fruition. The irony lies in the praise and respect Ray's business associates pay him at his wake, entirely ignorant of his betrayal. Chase and company create in the audience a real paranoia that such betrayal could be going on at any time with anybody without knowing until it's too late or never, just as Tony must feel. In this way the audience is brought closer into the Family experience in living with the suspicion and fear which leads them to trust no one.

The FBI takes a different approach in 2001 by concentrating upon Adriana LaCerva. Adriana, though complicit in Christopher's crime, is portrayed as an innocent without any direct knowledge of the Family business. The deception of Adriana is necessary from the law enforcement perspective but audience sympathies lie with her. The allegiance to Adriana stems from the peripheral nature of her connection with the Family. Even though she is aware of Chris's Family involvement, even encourages it and reaps rewards from it, she is never directly involved. Her unsophisticated nature seems innocent in contrast to Chris and his associates. The audience comes to know Ade as a person and not the criminal accomplice the

FBI considers her to be. Chase and company create another fascinating scenario in which the audience roots against the law. In Ade's embrace of the duplicitous friendship of Agent Ciccerone, the audience understands the deep connection and support she seeks while knowing her hopes will eventually be dashed. Adriana is taken in completely by the FBI charade, sharing painful personal secrets in the belief that she has a new best friend. The FBI's treatment of her is shown to be cold, condescending and bullying. By instilling fear of retribution at the hands of Chris or even Tony, they coerce Adriana into cooperating.

In the ensuing months Adriana ails under the stress of being put into the position of betraying the man she loves and his Family. She is desperate to find a way out of her dilemma. All of her friends are Family associates so, with no one to talk to, her stress soon manifests itself in the physicality of bowel dysfunction. There is a correlation of physical symptoms to emotional conflict throughout *The Sopranos*. Similar to Pussy suffering back pain from the weight of guilt, Adriana is torn up inside over her predicament. The death of Adriana must be laid at the doorstep of the Soprano family but the FBI is not without their share of guilt. Their primary concern is not the safety of this relatively innocent person and Adriana slipped through the cracks like so many who are peripherally involved in organized crime. Adriana's story is one of the great tragedies of *The Sopranos*.

There are a few other instances of FBI informants in the series including Jack Massarone, a Soprano family construction associate, and Jimmy Petrile of the Lupertazzi family. The Soprano *capo* Carlo Gervasi is the final rat, flipped supposedly in response to the threat of prosecution of his son who is caught selling ecstasy. In twenty-twenty hindsight Carlo's behavior in the preceding months is odd. On several occasions he appears tense, preoccupied, uneasy (perhaps some bowel issues, to boot), and exhibits a new fixation on *The Twilight Zone* instead of earning. Eugene Pontecorvo is an especially sad case. The tragedy of the Gene and his wife lies in the miraculous glimpse of freedom they get when they inherit two million dollars by completely legitimate circumstances. They rejoice in a fleeting hope of leaving the Soprano Family to start a new life for themselves and their children. However, Gene is too deeply entrenched. Tony will not allow his retirement and neither will the FBI because they want him for continued evidence-gathering. Another sympathetic character squirms under the pressure of the Feds, who come across as "bad guys" once again. When Gene hangs himself it is just as much a result of the pressure put upon him by the Feds as the Family, but he knows that the ultimate culpability is his own.

Even though it is painful to see Pussy, Adriana and Eugene in such great despair, it must be acknowledged that these are strictly consequences of their own decisions and actions. The tacitly understood rules of Family involvement state that everyone who chooses to participate knows the stakes going in and by committing to the Family relationship they agree to accept the possible consequences. The portrayal of FBI informants in *The Sopranos* does not give the audience a black-and-white message of what's right and wrong. If there is a clear lesson it is that human beings who open themselves up to the risk of comeuppance will sometimes be called to make good on their debt. Those who are caught find themselves in a no-win situation. Underneath the macho veneer of these connected guys, they have genuine fear of this possible fate. The Federal Bureau of Investigation knows it and exploits it in the ongoing battle between "good and evil." The ambiguity lies in the definition of those terms.

5

Carmela Soprano, Queen of the Mob Women

Tony has chosen the Family business with all of its wiseguys and associates as his partners. In his personal life, Tony has Carmela as his partner. They have raised two children, making a family of which they can be proud. Although their relationship is at times turbulent, Tony and Carmela uniquely complement each other. Carmela understands Tony better than anyone and Tony finds in her that which supports him without letting him be totally consumed by his criminal life. They frequently lock horns but they are better off with each other than without. They each have personal issues with which to come to terms. The conflicts seen over the course of six seasons are the growing pains they experience as they struggle to find and accept their personal and joint identities.

Behind the Primped Hair, Manicured Nails and Gold Crucifix

To anyone oblivious to Tony's profession, Carmela Soprano would seem to be an average upper-middle-class suburban housewife. She is a loving mother, she gets dinner on the table, goes to church and socializes with the wives of Tony's associates. Carmela is college-educated in business administration but left her studies without graduating. She is equally informed by the Catholic Church. Like many people in Tony's circle, she is not especially intellectual but she possesses formidable survival instincts and is skilled at manipulating others to her will. Carmela takes great pride making a beautiful home for her husband and children, but most of all herself. She loves opportunities to flaunt her taste and affluence by hostessing Sunday dinner or the occasional social event. She feigns modesty but is happy to bask in compliments on a $3000 Lladro figurine or the *loggia* she contributed to the design of their great-room.

Despite outward appearances of a simple and innocent domestic existence, Carmela is fully complicit in Tony's crimes, more than anyone else. In a rare one-on-one discussion with Dr. Melfi, she recounts Tony's courtship of her. On their second date, the teenage Tony gifted Carmela and her mother a dozen roses each while he gave her father a $200 power drill.[1] This story serves to illustrate Carmela's awareness of Tony's illegal activities from the very beginning of their long relationship. When it comes to Tony's business, Carmela knows not to ask questions and rarely speaks of it to him but there are a few instances that remind the audience of her awareness. She asks Tony to have Pussy use his connections to recover the stolen car of AJ's science teacher[2]; she helps Tony hide guns and money when the Feds appear to be closing in[3]; she tacitly understands Tony's revenge murder of Matt Bevilaqua[4]; she knows Tony has large quantities of money secreted away; she recognizes deeper implications of concerning demeanor in Paulie and Vito in paying her tribute[5]; she knows the drill when Tony goes on the lam; and, just like Tony, she lives in constant fear of "It"—federal indictment.[6] When Christopher is near death in season two, Carmela prays to God. While seeking mercy for Chris she acknowledges that he and everyone else in the Family have chosen the criminal life, fully aware of the consequences of their sin.[7] In marriage to Tony, Carmela is just as much a part of his crime Family as she is his blood family. Carmela's conflict arises from the acceptance of Family consequences. This goes much deeper than living with intense guilt or the possibility of eternal damnation in the after-life. It is about her own journey of self-acceptance.

Carmela is provided for, has a beautiful home, children and husband, but she is not happy. At the beginning of the series she claims to have moral superiority about the work Tony does. Because she professes to be a devout Catholic she reminds him that Biblical teaching says he will be damned to hell.[8] Carmela disconnects her own responsibility in his crimes despite her acceptance of their benefits. She is also unhappy that Tony also indulges in girlfriends but she understands that it goes with the territory of marrying a made man. As much as Carmela enjoys being the queen of the castle she is also like a princess locked in the tower. In accordance with cultural traditions, Tony's role in the family is to take care of the money and Carmela's is to take care of the house. The wife of a man in the Family is strongly discouraged from working. For a long time Carmela is content with this situation, satisfied to be a mother and have the creature comforts that Tony's work provides. Once her children reach maturity, though, Carmela struggles with a nagging sense of emptiness. Family limitations imposed on her career aspirations coupled with expectations of her subservience lead Carmela to feel like a secondary component in Tony's world rather than the leader of her own life. She also begins to feel, more acutely, a sense of helplessness as a result of her dependence on Tony for financial stability.

This predicament is forced into the spotlight with her consultation with a psychologist, Dr. Krakower, who does not mince words. He holds up a mirror to show Carmela that she is complicit in Tony's crimes which earn them blood money. She cannot excuse herself with a plea of no direct involvement. She cooks his meals for him — she is an enabler. Krakower gives Carmela the blunt advice to leave Tony, taking the children with her. She is faced with the fact that, were she to take that course of action, she would no longer have the means to provide for the children in the manner she would like. This is characterized by her recent commitment of $50,000 to Columbia University. After some time wrapped in a warm down comforter on the couch, contemplating Krakower's words, she reconciles herself as best she can with the situation.[9] The sacrifice that Carmela makes for her children is the continued endurance of her situation of internal conflict — her and the children's dependence on Tony and blood money. This is consistent with a common survival function of theses characters — a vertical split. This is a condition in which an individual internally separates conflicting thoughts or behaviors to remain functional.[10] Tony is a perfect example because he separates his behaviors as a loving father from those of a necessarily amoral mob boss. Carmela has her own vertical split in that she chooses to continue an existence of denial so that her children might one day escape from it.

The only thing that Carmela puts more energy into than her home is her children. Tony largely leaves the child-rearing to Carmela, in keeping with traditional roles of husband and wife encouraged by their parents and the Family. Carmela's fervor and drive for her children's success exhibits itself in very non-traditional ways. There is the infamous incident in which she uses a ricotta pie to extort a college recommendation letter from Joan Cusamano.[11] When AJ's college prospects are in crisis, she even goes so far as to sleep with his English teacher.[12] As she takes these unusual measures, she deceives herself about her own sense of ethics.

Carmela loves her children and wants them to have happy lives but sometimes she uses them as outlets for her own issues. For example, the $50,000 donation to Columbia. Tony is not receptive to the idea of a large contribution and around the same time he is absent from a scheduled joint session with Melfi. Also, she learns that Tony gives Pussy's widow, Angie, money as a business expense.[13] Carmela's concern is twofold — that Tony appears to prioritize Angie over Meadow and that he is not working on mending his relationship with Carmela. She doesn't feel that Tony is living up to his responsibilities as a father or as a husband but she uses Meadow's scholastic security as the surface issue. This is typical of Carmela's frequent use of subterfuge in addressing an issue. She says one thing and means another. This is consistent with Carmela's vertical split which requires her to deceive herself, to allow plausible deniability to even herself. This denial causes her delay in recognizing and accepting her true identity.

As Carmela struggles with her own identity, so do her children. When these struggles intersect, there is heated friction. Carmela holds Meadow accountable for breaking curfew, chastises her for lapses in work ethic and cautions her about secrecy of the Family business. Meadow butts heads with her mother regarding her judgment of hypocrisy in Carmela. She feels that Carmela does not practice what she preaches, aware of her complicity in Tony's work. Carmela also has a difficult time coming to terms with Meadow's need to differentiate herself. Meadow's choices of college, boyfriends, or career cause Carmela to wrestle with her own values and how she is living them. Where Carmela may compromise herself for Tony and family, Meadow asserts her independence. Whatever the specifics of the situation, Carmela's feelings about Meadow indicate her feelings about herself.

Carmela's frustration with AJ stems from rebellion as well. She feels helpless when he questions the meaning of life.[14] Unsure of how to handle this, she sweeps the issue under the rug, leaving it unaddressed. When AJ attempts suicide years later, she expresses shock, thinking that AJ was always a happy little boy.[15] This is clearly not an accurate assessment when considering his history, especially his egregious disrespect of Carmela during the time she was separated from Tony. This is another example of how she deceives herself about her problems. Her unwillingness to deal with the difficult questions that AJ poses as a confused teenager reflect her aversion to dealing with the hard questions in her own life.

When ignoring issues with her children and herself, Carmela displaces her resultant guilt. In family therapy after AJ's failed suicide attempt, Carmela expresses concern about the influence on AJ's actions of the W.B. Yeats poem "The Second Coming." Carmela suggests that the dark tone of the poem may have encouraged AJ's suicidal thoughts.[16] It is likely that she has been guided by her church of which certain passionate affiliates have crusaded against rock 'n' roll and rap with the justification of protecting American youth from evil influences. Such beliefs would have been informative and influential on Carmela as a result of her devotion to the church but also from a natural mother instinct to protect her children. Carmela's frustration at AJ's suicide attempt manifests itself in misdirected anger at the Yeats poem when her hidden concern is that it might have been her own fault, with some share given to Tony.

Carmela's most open and direct acknowledgment of personal responsibility for the children's fate comes in a discussion with Dr. Melfi.[17] She expresses an acceptance of the consequences of her choices but she fears that there are repercussions for Meadow and AJ, who had no say in such decision. Not only is Carmela concerned that she and Tony may be limiting their children's options but she is worried that they too become complicit in the crimes of the Family. Like Tony, Carmela does not want the Family life for her children. She wants them to escape but for this to happen she must lose them in certain ways and this frightens her. Carmela tries to balance these considerations which impact who her children will become. As she does so, she also defines who she, herself, is.

Meadow and AJ's rebellion is a trait of their mother's as can be seen in Carmela's relationship with her parents. Mary DeAngelis has difficulty fully embracing Tony and her daughter's marriage to him. She often recalls Carmela's rebuffed high school suitor who later became a successful business owner. Mary's comments are laced with self-loathing whether it's distaste at the complexion of newborn Meadow or defense of insults directed at Tony's criminality.[18] Carmela's father, Hugh, accepts the benefits of Tony's influence but refuses to acknowledge it. Both Hugh and Mary blame Livia for years of estrangement from their daughter while denying any responsibility for themselves. Carmela tries to strike out in a different direction, away from her parents' unhealthy behaviors, and her children do the same in regards to her.

As she strives for happiness, Carmela must come to terms with who she is. She does so in her relationships with Tony, her children, her parents and also her peers. Carmela deals with guilt, frustration and great inner conflict as she slowly learns and accepts her true identity.

Mob Wives

Carmela Soprano is a member of an elite group of women — mob wives. Mob wives play a critical role in the lives of their husbands. They serve to legitimize them by providing children in accordance with the venerated family values handed down through the generations. They support their husbands as accomplices. However, they are never privy to all the details of their husbands' work. The necessity of being kept in the dark regarding the specifics is frustrating at times and can result in behavior counter-productive to aiding their husbands. A better understanding of Carmela's journey can be gained by examining the spectrum of mob wives and the married mob couple dynamic on *The Sopranos*.

The matriarch and historical model of mob wives is Tony's own mother, wife to Johnny Boy Soprano, the acerbic Livia Soprano. Livia's knowledge of the Family business is established in her discussion with Junior from the very first episode. She seems to have honed her manipulative skill on Johnny but also from watching and learning from his business. Livia reaped the rewards of being married to a top made guy but showed little gratitude. Tony and Melfi speculate that the only sexual attention she gave Johnny Boy was in reciprocation for free meat and produce for their family. Considering this situation, it is understandable, though not necessarily excusable, that her husband sought comfort in other women. Livia's antisocial personality didn't allow her to support Johnny in his aspirations, bringing a cloud to permanently hang over their household. She nagged and belittled her husband until the day he died, after which she preached his sainthood. Livia's idea of mothering was tough love, weighted to the tough side of the equation. Livia once characterized children as animals to be trained.[19] Her caustic maternal approach was to have her children develop a thick skin for what she perceived as the harsh adversity and disappointment that life would throw at them. The silver lining in this hostile mothering is that her children would grow up tough enough to survive in the most antagonistic of environments. The obvious downside is the severe self-esteem issues the children lived with for the rest of their lives.

There is a cast of contemporary mob wives, peers of Carmela's, who broaden the understanding of what it's like being married to the mafia. Rosalie Aprile, Jackie Aprile Sr.'s widow, is Carmela's closest friend. She is like a former first lady of the Family and acts as a pseudo-*consigliere* to Carmela. Rosalie understands the business and, just as importantly, knows where not to stick her nose in. She wisely counsels Carmela not to get involved with Furio. The death of her son Jackie Jr. causes Carmela and Tony to more deeply appreciate AJ and safeguard his future. Rosalie touchingly advises Carmela on her approach with AJ, based on the hard lessons learned from her personal tragedy with her own son. Upon their trip to Paris, it seems that Carmela changes, perhaps outgrowing Rosalie in some ways with a more philosophical perspective of their lives.[20]

Silvio's wife, Gabriella, is another in Carmela's close circle of friends. Though generally unobtrusive, Gab's most memorable turn came during Tony's coma, when she plants delusions of grandeur in Silvio during his stint as acting boss. Rather than leave Silvio to handle his job as he sees fit, she pushes her own ambition on him like Lady Macbeth. This demonstrates a gap in understanding of the business on the part of some mob wives. In Silvio's case it leads to problems when he physically breaks down under the pressure of trying to be a boss when he knows he is not cut out for it.[21] The same behavior can be seen in Patty Leotardo who relentlessly pesters her husband Phil into redressing Vito Spatafore's homosexuality in accordance with church doctrine.[22] Phil is torn between satisfying the demands of his crew and his wife in opposition to Tony. This mob wife's protestations lead her husband down an irreversible path and contribute to his ultimate demise.

Angie Bonpensiero serves as a cautionary example for Carmela. When Angie openly shares her marital frustrations and pursues divorce, Carmela discourages it but she is secretly envious of her friend's bravery and proactive approach to solving her problem.[23] After Pussy's disappearance, Carmela spots Angie handing out free Polish sausage samples at the local grocery store.[24] Rather than concern for Angie's loss of financial stability, Carmela is concerned that the same fate could be in store for her. It is shared with the audience that as part of his responsibility as boss, Tony helps support Angie financially when Pussy is gone. At Carmela's recommendation, Tony goes to talk with Angie, and is unsympathetic when he sees that she is trying to milk this system. In a similar situation, Marie Spatafore requests a tribute of $100,000 to relocate in the aftermath of Vito's death. There is a silent understanding on the part of the mob widows that their husbands were taken from them as a result of their work. It is a common practice of mob widows to receive a retainer for their sorrow, and hardship — and to insure that they don't become a problem for the boss and his Family. The mob widows are frequently left to fall through the cracks, as happened with Ginny Sacrimoni. Arguably the least guileful of the wives, Ginny was blessed with the rarity of a faithful and loving husband. Unfortunately, she is left destitute when her husband passes away in prison.

Supporting a widow puts a dent in the bottom line and historically is not worth the investment. Tony apparently turns his deficit with Angie around when he responds to her request to take over the body shop that was once run by Pussy. This leads her to financial stability but also involves her in criminal enterprise with the Family, another revenue stream for Tony. When Carmela learns this, she is intrigued by this feminine model of independence but is also aware of a certain toxic effect the business seems to have. Angie makes Carmela consider possibilities of autonomy.

Adriana, though not married to Christopher, is practically a mob wife. Her delight in the fruits of Chris's crime do not outweigh her desire for a happy life for her and Chris. Her possible inability to bear children nearly precludes marriage but Chris finally accepts it. Ade is supportive of Chris in a healthy, if naïve, way. She encourages him to follow his Hollywood dreams by way of his screenplay efforts. When Chris vents his job frustration to her, she proposes the possibility of a new life away from the Family. Her intentions are pure but she does not fully comprehend Chris's fundamental commitment as a soldier in Tony Soprano's army.

There is a parallel to this in Deanne Pontecorvo. When Deanne and her wiseguy husband, Eugene, inherit two million dollars, they see it as a chance to leave the Family. After Tony disallows it, Deanne persists and castigates Eugene for his fealty to his boss above his wife. Deanne does not understand the permanence of Family commitment and her entreaties to escape only serve to worsen his situation. Eugene's loyalties are torn further asunder by his cooperation with the FBI. Consumed by a sense of absolute failure without any hope of escape, Eugene hangs himself.[25] Entreaties such as Adriana's or Deanne's only complicate a made man's world and force him choose between his two families. And the Family always wins out.

Finally, there is Janice Soprano, the queen gold-digger. After twenty years of running away, Janice returns to New Jersey and the Family when she grows tired of trying to make her way in the world. She opts, instead, to find a made man who will provide the easy life for her. Thanks to her father and Tony, Janice has first-hand knowledge of Family business and this allows her to avoid many of the pitfalls of her contemporary mob wives. Janice and Lady Macbeth were cut from the same cloth as can be seen when she reunites with her high school boyfriend, Richie. She goads Richie into anger and encourages him to move against Tony with thoughts of being the boss. Richie is reticent to act so boldly but Janice easily manipulates him to her will. Just like her mother did previously, Janice conspires against Tony. However, Richie shows himself to be too much of a loose cannon. When he punches Janice in the mouth for suggesting his son might be homosexual she realizes that the relationship will be untenable. She shoots him in an instant.[26] Her trauma and Tony's ability to come to her rescue by disposing of the body and covering her tracks dispels any ambition of usurping Tony's position.

Janice sets her sights on her next prospect and unscrupulously steals Rosalie's man, Ralph Cifaretto, likely selected for his position as a top earner. Tony chastises Janice for her choice and she asserts her right to pick her mate, believing Tony's disapproval comes from his frustration at her happiness. She has Ralph wrapped around her finger and she can dominate him in more ways than one. The two of them would have been a dangerous combination. However, when Janice compares him to the recent widower Bobby Baccalieri, she decides she can stomach Ralph no longer and ends the relationship.[27] She cattily seizes Bobby from the clutches of fellow mob widow JoJo Palmice. Janice helps Bobby and his children through the mourning period for his deceased wife, Karen. In Bobby, Janice finally finds a wiseguy for whom she has some level of respect while still being in control. She is very direct in discussing Family business, convincing him of the necessity to soldier on in his work. With a new life together taking shape, the two of them marry.

Janice becomes a mother to Bobby's children, though partly motivated by his consequent indebtedness to her. She and Bobby have a baby girl and Janice seeks to make right through little Domenica what she got wrong with her estranged son, Harpo. Despite claims to the contrary, Janice still possesses her share of Livia's warped habits. She has anger management issues and tries to pass them off as mothering. With no other maternal role model, she employs Livia's practice of tough love. She prioritizes the child of her own womb over what she comes to see as Bobby's brats. In addition, she is an infamously bad cook which symbolizes her maternal unfitness. As a breadwinner, Bobby is somewhat disappointing to Janice, dedicating energy to his toy trains when he could be earning more money for Janice's comfort. She addresses this by using her influence with Tony to advance Bobby's career. Tony initially responds by paying her off with a house but later puts Bobby to work once he demonstrates his renewed commitment and initiative. Janice's push for Bobby's career is partly responsible for putting him in the position to be whacked when war with New York comes. No doubt, Janice will survive as is her internal imperative. She learned from Livia that wildflowers bloom best among rocks and she lives this lesson throughout her life.

The typical mob wife is to varying degrees cunning, perceptive, shallow, frustrated, tragic and resilient. The lives of made guys and their wives are often turbulent and occasionally peaceful. They try to love and support each other but they also engage in behaviors detrimental to those ends. The secret nature of the Family makes it difficult for the mob wives to understand what their husbands go through and how to help them. The men devalue the role their wives play as their single most important partner in crime. These connected women are trying to survive and find happiness in a man's world and they have a great impact on the fates of their made men.

The Spiritually Thirsty Carmela

Carmela's frustration with Tony and her own identity is explored through a series of extra-marital romantic flirtations in which she tries to satisfy her thirsty soul. In the first season, Carmela pursues answers to her questions in Catholicism. She seeks the guidance of Father Phil Intintole as a spiritual mentor but it becomes apparent that she has developed carnal inclinations. Carmela and Fr. Phil talk about the possibility of Tony's salvation and redemption but in doing so Carmela's hidden desire for escape from Tony is unveiled. She is disillusioned and feels used when she comes to see Fr. Phil's affection for her as self-interested satisfaction of his vices of fine food, wine and platonic sexual tension. Carmela learns the hard lesson that her salvation lies elsewhere.

She continues to rely on church doctrine in the second season when counseling Angie Bonpensiero against divorce. Despite Pussy's despicable behavior, Carmela encourages Angie to soldier on in fulfillment of her marriage vows. As Carmela tries to convince Angie of the validity of this argument, she is actually trying to convince herself. Her own relationship with Tony has reached another low point. However, her fear of drastic action leads Carmela to talk herself out of consideration of divorce as the solution to her problems. Shortly after, she feels a reprieve from her sense of drowning when she meets Victor Musto. Vic is a wallpaperer whom she employs for a little home improvement, itself a metaphor for Carmela's internal state. With Vic, Carmela moves the boundary of romantic exploration by briefly succumbing to unspoken desires with a passionate kiss in the powder room. It appears that their relationship will go even further until Vic demurs upon learning of his brother-in-law's bankruptcy and Tony's role in it.[28] Carmela is heartbroken at the evaporation of another possibility of relief from her unhappy existence. She is additionally dismayed when Gab Dante informs her that Vic's absence is motivated by fear of Tony.[29] Carmela is confronted with the consideration that not only was Victor less than a white knight in shining armor but Tony, that from which she strives to escape, is once again the root of her continued imprisonment.

Carmela's building anxiety expresses itself in legitimate concern over the financial security of herself and the kids. She takes an interest in the stock market and goes so far as to steal $40,000 from Tony, which she invests. Tony is adamantly opposed to her handling of the family finances as a result of his conviction that husbands take care of the money and wives take care of the house and children. Tony credits Carmela with being a smart woman and it's possible he is concerned that stock success would change their respective roles. If Carmela were to bring home some bacon, she would gain independence. Tony is defending his concept of marriage but also keeping himself from being usurped and possibly abandoned by Carmela, which Melfi acknowledges to be a possibility. He keeps Carmela under his thumb out of his own selfish desire to present, to himself and his subordinates, the image of fulfillment of the Italian-American Dream. In this way, Tony uses Carmela to maintain his power with the assertion of his alpha male status.

Carmela is increasingly disenchanted and impatient with what she perceives as Tony's lack of consideration for her feelings. Her next flirtation is with Furio, whose tenderness and sensitivity appeal to her. Though their emotions are never expressed explicitly, Carmela and Furio feel an intense connection to one another. Once again the promise of happiness is dashed when Furio recognizes his only options are to kill his feelings for Carmela or kill Tony. He chooses the former and retreats to Naples. Carmela is in absolute shock when she learns of this, from Tony no less. Consistent with past frustrations, Carmela's feelings of loss and disappointment find a tangential outlet, this time Herman Melville's *Billy Budd*. At a dinner table of mixed company, Carmela's feelings regarding this novel are quite out of proportion to the discussion. Her vociferous persistence that *Billy Budd* does not have homosexual themes is not the result of a considered analysis of the literature but her displaced sorrow about Furio's flight.[30] Her real frustration stems from her deep dismay at Furio's exodus. She feels lost and doomed. Just like her feelings of angst about her mothering in respect to AJ's suicide attempt and "The Second Coming," Carmela lashes out at her company and *Billy Budd* rather than acknowledging her feelings of loss, desertion and hopelessness.

As she continues to despair, there is greater fallout from Furio's abandonment of Carmela. AJ later answers a phone call from one of Tony's former *goomahs,* Irina. Irina rubs Carmela's nose in Tony's infidelity and it is the straw that breaks the camel's back. Carmela is outraged at Tony's indiscretions coming home to haunt their children but her reaction is also the result of her highly emotional state from the recent turn of events with Furio. For the third time she glimpsed the possibility of a brighter future beyond the control of Tony Soprano and freedom from the weight of self-implicating moral questions that come with being his wife. For the third time the lifeline is snatched away from her. The cumulative impact of Tony's misdeeds and her own unaddressed complicity force Carmela into the act of throwing Tony out of their home.[31] It is a desperate attempt to force a solution to her chronic discontent. Carmela's bitterness and anger, both at Tony and herself, well up and explode. The depiction of Carmela's bitterness and hate during this "had-enough" period draws comparisons to Livia. It begs the consideration that some of Livia's behavior may have been the result of similar difficulties: her husband's chronic infidelity and personal sense of guilt.

Once Carmela has successfully facilitated a separation from Tony, she experiences freedom from him for the first time in more than twenty years. She exercises her newfound independence with AJ's English teacher, Robert Wegler (interestingly, the same one who assigned him *Billy Budd*). Carmela is captivated by Wegler's intellectual and gentlemanly nature. Their acquaintance soon turns romantic and Carmela reveals that he is her first sexual partner apart from Tony. Carmela is invigorated and enchanted at this new world of possibility before her but it is predictably short-lived. Once she persuades Wegler to exert his influence to help AJ's English grade, it seems she may be more motivated by securing her son's future than cultivating a relationship. Guilt-stricken, Wegler ends the affair and accuses Carmela of being a user. She has difficulty understanding Wegler's allegation and continues to misidentify the problem as guilt by associa-tion with Tony. She shares her pain with her father who is speechless — unable or unwilling force Carmela to consider her own role.[32] Carmela refuses to see that Wegler's appraisal is more accurately an indictment of herself. In examining her past, Wegler's assessment rings painfully true. She has a history of viewing others as tools to get what she wants. She uses Tony to get security for their children but also the creature comforts she desires (fur coats, jewelry, cars and of course their home). She uses Joan Cusamano to advance her cause of Georgetown admission for her daugh-ter over Meadow's preference of Berkeley. Carmela uses Charmaine Bucco to cater her party under the veneer of equality and friendship when her behavior reflects an attitude of superiority stereotypical of an employer-employee relationship. This is Carmela's modus operandi: She gets what she wants under the guise of amiability. The reason that this confuses Carmela is because she is blind to its validity. To her it's baseless because in her mind her actions are all wholesomely motivated and likewise pursued. She mutates the accusation of herself into an indictment of Tony and his curse befallen her. Thus she tearfully deceives herself, refusing to consider her own fault. The truth is that she is motivated by self-interest and survival, and simply refuses to see it. Just as Tony's nature is instinctual and subconsciously calculating, so too is Carmela's. As Carmela seeks escape from Tony in the arms of other men, she learns about herself the scary truth of her nature and identity which she desperately tries to deny.

Goomahs

Along with the criminal life comes money and indulgences in vice such as extra-marital relationships. This may be in the form of a brief encounter with a prostitute or a relationship with a *goomah*. It is part of the wiseguy tradition to have girlfriends in addition to wives. Some made guys maintain long-term relationship with *goomahs,* as if they were a second wife. *Goomahs* are the alternative mob wives, without the status or respect but nevertheless an ubiquitous feminine identity in the lives of these made men. By comparison to Carmela's romantic explorations, Tony's infidelity is much more overt. Tony and Carmela employ a don't-ask-don't-tell policy. Tony repeatedly pleads absolute faithfulness to Carmela until she finds out otherwise. Carmela's rage erupts when Tony is found out by a phone call, a fingernail or perfume on his shirt. With such negative consequences it is worthwhile considering why Tony is serially unfaithful. Just as much can be learned about Tony from his *goomahs* as Carmela learns from her own romantic excursions.

Although Tony tries to be discreet, Carmela is aware of multiple indiscretions such as a weightlifter, a pre-school teacher (with the implication that it may have been a teacher of one of their own children) and Irina Peltsin. Irina is a twenty-ish Russian immigrant whom Tony sees for a couple of years. Tony ultimately breaks off the relationship when his feelings about her change. Tony grows tired when he accepted that their differing maturities and her over-dependence on him were unattractive and unhealthy. These attributes are in contrast to Carmela who, despite her faults, is a much more appropriate match for Tony. It is ironic that at the same time Tony is coming to this realization, Carmela is branching out with Victor. Though Irina is a fun time for Tony, she is not much more than that. His guilt grows when he began to feel that she is compromising her future for what he knows to be a limited term engagement. Melfi would also point out that Tony's role to Irina is paternal to a girl who only had an alcoholic father and cruel uncle. Despite Irina's threat (and attempt) of suicide, as a father figure Tony breaks up with her so she can go on to live her own life and not throw it away on vain hopes of having one with him.

The awareness of unfulfillment with Irina relates to Tony's experiences with Dr. Melfi, for whom he briefly believes he experiences feelings of love. These emotions come from the stimulating process of psychotherapy. Melfi explains that it is a common reaction for patients to misinterpret the feelings that result from therapy and misdirect them on the therapist. Melfi possesses an intelligent maturity that Irina lacks. Tony unjustly accuses Carmela of a lack of intellect based on her vice of material wealth and symptomatic nagging. This charge is misdirected frustration and a feeling of solitude with his own struggle for identity. In searching for sympathy with this struggle, Tony unconsciously seeks *goomahs* who have experience with hardship. In more ways than one, Tony finds dark women exciting. There is the physical trait of dark hair as a metaphorical antithesis to Carmela but there is also the darkness of nature and thoughts that lures him. Tony resents Carmela's material appetite and is also frustrated by her challenges to his authority. In a girlfriend, Tony seeks an unrealistic balance of independence and subservience. Tony develops a definition of the type of woman that appeals to him as an alternative to Carmela: dark and intelligent, still preferably Italian.

In the second season, Janice proposes to Carmela an explanation of the sexist behavior of men in their circle. Janice's Madonna/whore equation summarizes the expectations that mob women are forced to live with. This concept states that the men classify women as either Madonnas or whores, with zero middle ground. This concept has its origins in the primary female role model, one's mother. Mothers are experienced as nurturers. With a foundation in the value of the family, reverence and respect for motherhood is taught to each child. There is a disassociation between their mothers and sexuality, in keeping with the church's teaching of the miracle of the Virgin Mary, mother of Jesus. Tony and his fellows expect their wives to live up to this impossible role model. Women who engage in sexual pleasures beyond the necessity of conception and marital responsibility are judged unfit for motherhood and are labeled as whores. Wives are valued for their mothering potential, to give their men children. Carmela expresses frustration when Tony defines her as the mother of his children rather than his wife or a woman of whom motherhood is only part of the equation. Hypocrisy is evident when the men do not hold themselves to the same standard of fidelity. They deceive themselves that their sexual urges are irresistible and seek an outlet in their *goomahs*. Tony's extra-marital affairs, as with most of the men on the show, comes partly from a belief that sexuality contaminates motherhood.[33]

Tony's ideal alternative woman (dark, intelligent, Italian) is next found in Gloria Trillo, with whom Tony has no fatherly subtext but rather a mother connection. In contrast to Irina, Gloria is a mature yet sexy woman whom Tony feels may be the answer to his problems. As it turns out, she's the embodiment of one of his biggest problems — his mother, Livia. Once the afterglow of their *amour fou* ("crazy love") dissipates, Gloria is shown to have self-esteem issues, extreme depression and suicidal ideations. Tony finally correlates her sorrow and consuming bitterness to Livia.[34] His attraction to Gloria indicates lingering unresolved issues regarding his mother — a need to placate his mother's spirit and his own self-esteem issues. His ability to recognize these toxic behaviors in Gloria and distance himself from her indicates he's beginning to understand and move beyond these issues.

After another brief bout with fidelity, Tony falls off the wagon when he becomes involved with Valentina La Paz. This half–Italian, half–Cuban with an adolescent sense of humor defects to Tony after frustration in her relationship with Ralph. Valentina means more to Tony as a trophy of his dominance over Ralph than any feelings he has toward Valentina herself. Tony insensitively points out to Valentina that in the same way he co-opted Ralph's horse, Pie O My, he appropriated her. Like Irina, Valentina is clingy and dependent on Tony. Like Gloria, she is dark and sexy. Despite appearances of maturity and independence in Gloria and Valentina, they are revealed to be emotionally unstable. When Tony ends the relationship with Valentina she too hurls the threat of suicide at Tony in an attempt at emotional manipulation. Tony demonstrates new freedom from past demons when he coolly dismisses this.[35] He has learned about suicidal threats from his past girlfriends and also his mother, and he will no longer allow himself to be controlled by them.

Irina rears her head again when her cousin, Svetlana Kirilenko, is Tony's next conquest. Tony admires this woman for her ability to succeed in the face of intimidating obstacles. She has endured hardship in much harsher realities than most made guys or pampered mob wives. After losing a leg to a childhood disease, she fled the dysfunctional environment of Eastern Europe to seek opportunity in America and, once there, worked to start her own business. All of this she has done with quiet resignation and determination, never complaining or expressing a note of victimization. His desire for her goes beyond the satisfaction of animal urges. She appeals to his sense of strength and independence but he is stunned when she declines any furtherance of the relationship.[36] The irony of a one-legged woman not wanting to be a crutch for him bemuses Tony. He is humbled and is forced to reconsider his own faults. In Svetlana, Tony finds someone too emotionally mature and intelligent to want anything more to do with him. For once he feels pain like Carmela's — that of rejection and disappointment at prospects of happiness taken from him. It is also noteworthy that this, the relatively briefest of Tony's extra-marital relationships, is the one at the center of his separation from Carmela.

Tony has two more notable dalliances which are stopped short. The first is with Adriana, onetime *goomah* of the old-school gangster Tommy Pinto and recent fiancée to Christopher. With Christopher away, she and Tony do cocaine together and they nearly succumb to compelling sexual tension until their car accident precludes any such possibility. Tony and Ade's attraction grows out of mutual sympathy for each other's medical concerns (Ade's Irritable Bowel Syndrome and Tony's brush with skin cancer) and there are symptoms of father figure issues at work again.[37] The function of their liaison is relevant to Tony's relationship with Chris, who feels deeply betrayed. First with Carmela and then with Chris, Tony is forced to suffer the consequences of his uncontrolled libido.

As a precursor to his reunion with Carmela, Tony takes a significant evolutionary step in changing his attitude toward her and his extra-marital relationships. The change is brought about by his chance encounter with Fran Fellstein, his own father's long-time *goomah*. Tony is initially awed by Fran's apparent grace and elegance and is charmed by her connection to his father. The bloom comes off the rose, though, when Tony sees her not as the sophisticated and supportive woman he idealized her to be, but as a selfish leech. Tony is forced to consider that the women in whom he has sought solace from his friction with Carmela are no better than the ultimately tragic Fran.[38]

Tony's revolution in thinking regarding Carmela is furthered with a little help from his *Fingerspitzengefühl* in the wake of his break-up with Valentina. While staying at the Plaza Hotel, Tony has an intense dream in which he subconsciously considers his problems with Tony Blundetto in a series of stylized and symbolic scenes. What is less obvious is that the dream is equally about his feelings toward Carmela. The dream begins with a vision of a sad Carmine Lupertazzi saying he misses his wife. Tony imagines himself dialoguing with Gloria. He sees a vision of himself atop Pie O My and Carmela puts her foot down by saying he can't have his horse (phonetically *whores*) in the home. The centerpiece of the dream is a dinner table sketch including Tony, Carmela, Vin Makazian and, of all people, Annette Bening. As Makazian serenades the table with The Commodores' "Three Times a Lady," Tony admires Bening's grace and beauty and recognizes those same qualities in Carmela at his side. With this realization he appreciates what a good thing he is lucky enough to have in Carmela and carries this awareness and appreciation into his waking life.

Tony and Carmela resume their marriage and Tony renews his vow of fidelity to her. When he is later shot and comatose, Carmela stands by him, confirming her love for him and helping to nurse him back to health. On several occasions Tony gives credit for his recovery to Carmela. He gives her the status of healer and he feels new respect and appreciation for her. The second dalliance cut short occurs when Tony is at last tempted by another woman, Julianna Skiff. His old habits kick in and he plans to see her. Carmela helps dress him, unaware of the nature of his rendezvous. In the wake of his coma ordeal, the pointed camera shot of her buttoning Tony's shirt has the look and feel of mending the incision beneath the French silk. Later Julianna undoing his shirt feels unnatural and unhealthy and he stops her before they go any further. His frustration with his moral compunction exhibits itself in anger at the absence of smoked turkey in the Soprano refrigerator. He is wrestling with conflicting internal messages about marital fidelity and what it is to be a man with sexual appetites.

Although he will remain less than perfect, Tony turns another corner in his journey to being a better husband. His affairs teach him about himself and his own issues. The portraits of his *goomahs* as tragic under an idealized veneer cause Tony to appreciate the rare and precious match he has in Carmela.

The Real Carmela

In the aftermath of Wegler, Carmela mourns that she will forever be defined as Tony Soprano's wife, contaminated by him. When Carmela tells Wegler that she is going back with her husband, it is not a pre-meditated statement.[39] It is a reflex excuse to hurt Wegler and save face. Once it comes out of her mouth, though, Carmela considers its meaning. Was it just an off-hand comment or was this a reflection of subliminal intention? Does she feel entrapped by her own words to follow through or is it simply her subconscious's way of telling the conflicted Carmela which path to take? Once she finds no divorce lawyer without bias, Carmela has no options that would allow her to continue at her current standard of living. Carmela is unwilling to take a pay cut and she reluctantly resigns herself to allow her husband to return. Tony, meanwhile, truly does miss Carmela. Without her he is rudderless and engages in unhealthy behaviors such as excessive drinking, fornication, gambling and a new cocaine habit. He goes on a physical and emotional bender. Her offer to take him back is a salvation.

In the matter-of-fact, businesslike re-negotiation of their nuptials, Carmela has a price: the financing of a spec house ($600,000 for the lot plus the building costs).[40] This serves as a fine for Tony (much steeper than the five dollars for saying the f-word) and also the creation of a new outlet for Carmela's energies.[41] Carmela's decision to take Tony back has the feeling of eating crow. In her amorous explorations she sought escape from a demonized Tony. She believed in an idealized purity of Fr. Phil, Victor, Furio and Wegler. Carmela is disappointed when her idealized men show themselves to be less than perfect. This leads her to the hard realization that neither is she. In her personal evaluation of the relationship, she still blames Tony for a degree of negative influence but she begins to admit her own responsibility. In the undoing of her self-delusion she begins to recognize her true self. Relief comes when she stops blaming Tony and owns her own identity. Carmela accepts that she made a choice on her wedding day and she resolves to live with that decision to the fullest extent. Tony assumes a back-to-normal attitude, leaving Carmela's optimism for a new, better, loving relationship somewhat unrequited. Carmela embarks on a new affair — with the spec house. As a romantic substitute for Tony, she literally and figuratively gets into bed with the plans for her project.[42]

Carmela and Tony return to business as usual until Tony is shot and comatose. With the very real prospect of losing Tony, Carmela's bedside monologue confirms her love for him beyond any doubt. She seems to have come to terms with any past moral conflicts when she expresses to Dr. Melfi the sentiment that Tony is basically a good man and that there are far bigger crooks in the world.[43] In a memorable scene, Carmela tearfully opens her heart to the comatose Tony, culminating in her simple but powerful expression of "I love you." She realizes that she has been denying this sentiment to Tony and herself. The very real threat of losing her husband causes Carmela to acknowledge how much she truly does love Tony, regardless of anything else.[44]

The next hurdle for the two of them is Tony's acceptance of Carmela's new career. For the same reasons he discouraged her stock market aspirations, he does not fully support her spec house enterprise beyond minimum financing. Just as Carmela resigned herself to certain concessions, Tony eventually does as well, though motivated by the need to distract her from inquiries about Adriana's mysterious disappearance. Because the spec house is financed by him, Tony views it as his, only Carmela's in name for her edification. When the house sells, Carmela and Tony butt heads about the profits. Once Tony apologizes to Carmela and concedes all present and future interests from the spec house, it dispels the last of the clinging old-world precepts about the traditional roles of husband and wife.[45] Carmela redefined such concepts by adapting her role as a homemaker to that of a builder of homes in which other families may live.

The pivotal evolutionary moment for Carmela is her visit to Paris. Carmela is awestruck at the city's beauty and antiquity. She achieves the sensation of insignificance in contrast to the vast expanse of history and humanity. Her sense of identity is brought to the fore with renewed appreciation for the question "Who am I and where am I going?"[46] Her revelation is not about Tony or even about herself. It is about the universe and the futility of chronic worrying of which she has been guilty, perhaps for her whole life. It's as if Carmela has been wearing blinders to the bigger picture, and the circumstances of her journey finally allow them to be removed. Her epiphany allows her to shed her lingering worry, guilt and doubt and she leaves Paris with newfound perspective and appreciation of life just as Tony did after his coma.

Carmela's journey has reached a significant milestone. She once despised Tony but comes to understand that they are kindred. Their values are compatible and they operate by similar means of self-deception and manipulation. The lesson is not one of morality with respect to their *modus operandi* but the importance of wearing the same face to one's self as the multitude. Carmela's journey has been the story of her denial, anger and acceptance of her identity. She has evolved, breaking the chains of a mob wife, transcending the inherent pitfalls of that life. She has transformed what was once an existence of worry, grief and misery into relative contentedness and peace.

The arc of Tony and Carmela's relationship is an ebb and a flow. Over the first half of the series they drift away from each other by exploring other relationships and their own values. The second half of the series is the story of them returning to each other with self-knowledge and acceptance. Carmela has a career and Tony accepts it after a long, drawn-out battle. He does not lose the war, though. The key is understanding that he is not at war with Carmela. She is his greatest ally in a quest for happiness and the struggle for identity. Had she given up her ambition, it would have been a fleeting victory for Tony. If he were to subjugate her, he would lose respect for her, as she would herself, and their marriage would weaken them rather than strengthen. Rather than a tale of subjugation their story is one of hard-fought compromise. Tony and Carmela are right for each other because no one else would have been up to the task. They are worthy opponents and wonderful allies on their lifelong journey together.

6

All Tony's Children

What is it that makes Tony happy? He has creature comforts and luxuries to satisfy almost anyone. He has extra-marital affairs, takes satisfaction in a good scam, and he enjoys directing his anger at those he believes deserve it. All of these are shallow pleasures, though. If Tony has one pure joy, it is his blood family. Regardless of anything else he says or does, Tony loves Carmela, Meadow, and Anthony Jr. They bring him happiness as nothing else in his life does. For most of the series Tony has difficulty aligning his feelings for Carmela with his actions, i.e., infidelity, but that does not mean he doesn't love her. Despite the frequent *agita* they create for each other, there are truly tender and touching moments which express the depth of their relationship. Their children are an extension of their love — clean slates to teach, to give the things they didn't have, and to make happy. Tony's children are his joy, his frustration, his compass and perhaps his salvation.

Daddy's Little Girl

Meadow Soprano's journey is not unlike Carmela's. She is frustrated by both Tony and Carmela. Meadow knows of Tony's involvement in organized crime despite his cover story of waste management. She knows Tony lies, that his money comes at the expense of others, and she is angered by it. Meadow sees Carmela as an accomplice to Tony. She faults her mother for what she perceives to be the acquiescence to Tony's will, sacrificing her feminine independence and ceding moral rectitude. She sees her parents as hypocrites creating a toxic environment from which she desires to escape. Over the years, Meadow rebels by breaking curfew to be with her boyfriend, having an unauthorized party at her grandmother's empty house, dating an African-American, not applying herself at Columbia and finally pursuing a law career. When their children succeed, Tony and Carmela revel in it. Tony publicly gives credit to Carmela but he feels a deep sense of personal responsibility. Tony's sense of pride is seen regarding Meadow's prestigious college acceptances, a pride which manifests itself in bragging to Artie and Davey Scatino whose children's prospects are more restricted (respectively, due to scholastic and financial limitations).[1] There is clearly a mindset of superiority and this smug attitude has its roots in his deep need for validation. It's as if Tony sees it as a competition with his peers and their children as the players and Tony has come up the winner.

Tony has a special relationship with his daughter, being able to speak to her as an adult. While on college visits in New England they bond over the commitment to an open and honest relationship.[2] Unfortunately, as a result of Tony's work this is not always practical and Meadow senses this. Regardless of his inability to fully disclose the details of his life, Tony loves his daughter and he takes great joy from the conviction that she has loved him since she was a tiny baby.

Tony expresses the depth of his love to Meadow in the family kitchen late one night. With an open heart he professes that everything he does is for her and her brother. Meadow acknowledges Tony's dedication but demurs from his discussion of hypocrisy and demonstrates the capacity to be humble and compassionate toward Tony with the parting consolation that everyone is a hypocrite sometimes.[3] Her judgment of hypocrisy recently came to the fore as a result of his gift to her of her friend Eric Scatino's sport utility vehicle. Tony receives the vehicle as payment of a debt incurred by the friend's father and Meadow is horrified, convinced of an incompatibility between Tony's role as a father and his role as a businessman. Regardless, Meadow struggles with her own hypocrisy when she toes the party line by discrediting mafia involvement in Jackie Jr.'s death. She faithfully denies any validity to such claims while simultaneously reprimanding Jackie's sister for broaching such a discussion with an outsider present. Once she does this duty to the Family, Meadow is stricken with sorrow and guilt with the thought that Tony may have been involved in her ex-boyfriend's death.[4] Her ability to stand up for the Family with such equanimity gives an indication of Meadow's true loyalties.

Tony exhibits hypocrisy when he claims dedication to his children yet he does not give them the time or effort that might follow from that commitment. His time and energy are largely spent working. How rarely does Tony spend time with his kids and how often is he at the Bada Bing Club, Satriale's, or the Crazyhorse? Rather than time, Tony gives his children money. He sees it as his own sacrifice that he must give up time with his kids in order to provide for them. Of course he provides the obvious essentials such as a home, food, clothing, and an education but he also wants to provide them with lives independent of his criminal world. This is a Catch-22, because for every opportunity he creates for them by means of his work he also holds them back with the example he sets.

Tony's position is the common "do as I say, not as I do," but in an extreme and unique scenario. Tony tries to teach his children to be different than him. He would love for Meadow to be a doctor and the last thing he wants is for AJ to grow up a *mafioso*. However, to enable the pursuit of these goals, Tony is working from within a system that clashes with these mainstream values. With money acquired through extortion, racketeering and murder he creates opportunities for his children to escape that type of life. In a therapy session it comes out that Tony's decision to give Meadow the SUV was a subconscious effort to confront her with a thorny reality in order to compel her to evaluate moral ambiguity for herself. Dr. Melfi characterizes this as teaching her to fly.[5] Whether consciously or instinctively, Tony gives Meadow just enough pieces of the puzzle to deduce the bigger picture. From this she forms her opinions on the world and who she wants to be. She undergoes this maturation process under Tony's subtle influence, growing into the strong, shrewd, and independent woman he wants her to be.

A necessary element of Meadow and AJ's growth is an assertion of independence from Tony and his lifestyle. On one hand it is a source of aggravation for Tony that they rebel but it is an essential step in their development. With Meadow, Tony is frustrated by her challenges of his values and how he lives. Though his reflex reaction is anger, he knows this is what has to happen if Meadow is to create a life independent of his morally dubious world. It is both an indictment from Meadow and an admission of guilt on his part, though from that guilt he seeks to make amends by giving her opportunity where he felt he had none. It is irrelevant to him that the means to that end is a corrupt system. Tony is willing to lie in the bed he has made but he is determined that his children will not be required to suffer the consequences of the decisions he made for his own life.

Like her mother, Meadow explores her own value system through her romantic relationships that typically digress from her parents' expectations. The pattern that emerges is a repeating departure from and return to Family values. In her early departures she secretly dates a Dominican boy of whom Tony would not approve. Meadow's relationship with Eric Scatino begins as an entry into a world uncontaminated by crime but it ultimately forces her to decide how she will deal with others' judgment of her father reflecting on her. She dates an African-American, Noah Tannenbaum, whom she believes to be her first true love. However, to some degree she uses him to give her father a big middle finger. When she has her heart broken by Noah, Meadow returns to the Family fold by dating Jackie Aprile Jr., who fits Tony and Carmela's definition of a good boy, mostly by virtue of his Italian heritage and their close connection to his family.

Meadow learns that Jackie is not what she is looking for and embarks on a long-term relationship with Finn DeTrolio. Finn, though upright and industrious, is an outsider who is naïve to the Family dynamic. When he shares his experience of the criminality on her father's construction site, Meadow feels a subconscious urge to escape. She relentlessly badgers a marriage proposal from Finn in a tearful, three A.M. guilt trip — a technique she apparently learned from Carmela.[6] Once she's had time to consider, Meadow decides that she and Finn are incompatible and breaks off the engagement. She returns to the familiar by dating and accepting a marriage proposal from Patrick Parisi, an Italian boy whose father is one of Tony's *capos* (quite possibly this is the same boyfriend, Patrick, for whom she broke curfew in the very first episode).

In the same way that Meadow vacillates between "Family-approved" and "Family-discouraged" boyfriends, she wavers between a career in law or medicine. Carmela and Tony understand her two wonderful options but they consistently push medicine and downplay law. It's possible they might feel a greater sense of redemption and absolution for their own sins if Meadow were to be a doctor. With the contribution of a doctor to the world, a pediatrician no less, perhaps their karma would balance. If Meadow were to pursue law, it might feel like a furtherance of the unhealthy cycle to which they are party. Meadow chooses law, ironically influenced by her own experiences with the unfair treatment of Italian-Americans such as Uncle Junior, John Sacrimoni and her father — all of whom are genuine criminals.

Over time, Meadow invents herself, at the same time coming to appreciate certain aspects of Tony's point of view. Her belief in her family and the Family waxes and wanes. After exploring the world of men and careers, Meadow, by her own choice, conforms to the tradition of staying with one's own kind. She does so with her own twist, though, since Patrick and law were not her parents' first choices. She creates for herself a hybridized existence between her and her parents' initial positions and expectations. She found a comfortable compromise in the middle and in doing so Meadow found herself. Tony's pride in her maturity, perceptiveness, academic ability, and worldly acuity leads him to profess that she passed him long ago. Regardless of their differences, Meadow is Daddy's little girl, through and through.

Jackie Jr. and Tony's Surrogate Fatherhood

As previously discussed, the boss of the Family has certain obligations to the family members of deceased wiseguys. In the case of Jackie Aprile's son, Jackie Jr., Tony takes this especially to heart. Tony has a genuine interest in steering straight the surviving son of his dear friend. Though not related by blood, Tony is the closest thing Jackie Jr. has to a father. His story has significant implications for Tony and his relationship with his own son, AJ.

Jackie Jr. is introduced as a sub-par student who aspires to follow in his father's gangster footsteps under the tutelage of his Uncle Richie. Richie is not an ideal role model, so much so that Tony eventually forbids his own children from being around him. After Richie's disappearance, Jackie is left with no one to teach him the Family business and he is flunking out of Rutgers. Tony promised the dying Jackie Sr. that he would look out for his son when he (Sr.) was gone. Tony tries to steer Jackie Jr. away from the Family but Jr. is inclined toward the easy life. The only other person to take an interest in Jackie is Ralph Cifaretto, who has recently begun dating Jackie's mother. Ralph assumes the role of mentor to the idle and disrespectful Jackie, most likely out of a desire to make his own life easier by fixing this problem of Rosalie's. It is Ralph who plants the seed in Jackie's mind to court Meadow. Ralph latches onto Jackie's interest in crime and creates an opportunity to coach him in collections and beating administration.[7] When Ralph brutally beats the pregnant dancer Tracee to death, his relationship with Tony goes south.[8] Tony felt fatherly towards the Bing girl due to her age and naiveté. In Tony's mind, her death equates Ralph with a child killer. This is proven to be prophetic as Jackie's fate unwinds. Feeling unjustly disrespected by Tony, Ralph's tutelage of Jackie becomes motivated by spite. When Tony cancels Ralph's invitation to

Thanksgiving dinner, Ralph starts the process of turning Jackie against Tony, offering him an ecstasy connection and supplying him with a gun.[9] Ralph is perceptive enough to know that Tony loves Jackie and to hurt Jackie is to hurt Tony.

While Jackie is dating Meadow, Tony becomes aware of Jackie's less-than-ideal behavior such as hanging out in an illegal casino and getting lap dances at strip clubs. When he finds Jackie carrying a gun, his rage boils over and he ferociously beats Jackie in a public restroom.[10] Tony's reaction is the result of a few factors. He feels personal responsibility because he encouraged the relationship between Meadow and Jackie. When Jackie's deceptions are exposed, Tony is furious that this miscreant is wooing his daughter. Jackie betrayed Meadow even after Tony took the time to specifically warn Jackie about the high expectations of the man who would date his daughter. That which Tony professed to love more than anything else in the whole world is treated with disrespect. The paradox of the situation is that Jackie is engaging in the exact same behaviors as Tony. Tony has no compunction about applying different standards to Jackie. However, he cannot help but be aware that he is a role model to Jackie and must consider this. His words preach the straight and narrow path but his actions say something totally different. It is the actions which Jackie pays attention to, despite all of Tony's effort at guiding Jackie away from the criminal life. Jackie disrespects, distrusts and fears Tony. The fate of his uncle Richie and Ralph's guidance have clouded his faith in Tony. The ugly reality of the mafia world makes Jackie angry and creates a sense of entitlement to amend for his lost father and uncle. His entitlement is also owed to peer perception that, as Jackie Sr.'s son, he could be an heir apparent in the Family. Unfortunately, Jackie's simplicity of mind renders impossible any understanding of these circumstances which guide his behavior.

Ralph's final, fatal contribution comes when he shares with Jackie the story of Tony and Jackie Sr.'s heist of Feech LaManna's card game. This inspires Jackie to pull a heist of his own during which Sunshine, a made man and perennial card dealer, is shot to death.[11] Tony is bound by the rules of the Family to order the hit on Jackie but it greatly pains him. He recognizes Ralph's role in Jackie's fate and inconspicuously confirms it as he returns Jackie's gun to Ralph.[12] The deaths of Jackie, Tracee and Pie O My contribute to Tony's disgust and ultimate murder of Ralph Cifaretto.

Jackie's one redeeming quality is his big-brotherly quality, seen with AJ and also the little girl who beats Jackie at chess in the Boonton housing projects.[13] Although Jackie had heart, he did not have discipline. This is confirmed by Meadow's childhood memory of Jackie never being inhibited by admonitions from his parents, certain that they simply did not care. For a time, Meadow blames Tony and the Family for the death of Jackie. Tony finally convinces her that he is equally scarred by the tragedy and Meadow lets go of some of her doubt and anger regarding the Family business and her father. It's possible that Tony saw Jackie as a potential redemption in the form of escape from the gangster lifestyle but his sorrow is derived more from disappointment in his own judgment. Perhaps most of all, Tony is heartbroken by feelings that he did not keep his vow to his dear friend Jackie Sr., to protect his son. The cautionary lesson of Jackie Jr. feels frighteningly real and immediate to Tony and Carmela as they struggle to guide their own son, AJ, on his journey.

Like Father, Like Son

Whereas Tony is mostly satisfied that Meadow has learned to fly on her own, one of his greatest fears is that Anthony Jr. may never may never survive in a tough world. AJ's path takes him from his memorable ziti line in the first episode through a journey of self-discovery as he tries to find a place in the world in which to fit in. In the six seasons since that impish outburst he has developed and demonstrated an attitude that is idle, petulant and selfish.

AJ's history is littered with delinquency: chronically wasting time on video games; defiling the sacrament of holy wine from the school church[14]; smoking pot (during his own Confirmation party, no less)[15]; vandalizing his high school swimming pool[16]; being expelled from school for cheating on an exam[17]; lying to and disobeying Carmela regarding a night in Manhattan[18]; and using cocaine.[19] In most incidents AJ's actions are a result of his association with negatively influencing individuals. Virtually all of his misbehavior is in a group context with AJ being a follower rather than a leader. Jackie Jr.'s influence can be seen in relation to AJ's expulsion from high school. Jackie, who had taken on a big-brother role in coaching AJ in football, was a cheat by having Meadow do his homework.[20] AJ's expulsion is the direct result of stealing answers to a test. Unfortunately, AJ's imitation of his peers and role models is demonstrated in negative behaviors more than positive.

By this same token, AJ intuitively imitates Tony's behavior in some respects. Tony is able to misdirect attention from his crimes with outrage at anti–Italian discrimination or the defense of a soldier's code. AJ likewise misdirects from the true issues with various social or political causes.

He distracts himself and others with faux concern over the environment and the Middle East rather than put his energy into forging his own life. AJ employs excuses and looks for crutches such as a possible learning disability or his depression. He twists these phenomena, real or imagined, to his own ends. In addition to his excuses, AJ deals with legitimate emotional baggage. AJ has inherited his fair share of obstacles with Tony's depression, Livia's borderline personality, Carmela's misdirection of frustrated emotion and the DeAngelis's general unwillingness to acknowledge any feelings. The crux of AJ's journey is the challenging process of learning the way of the world and becoming an adult in the face of all his challenges, especially the demented legacy of Livia.

Both Tony and Carmela express their own apprehension that AJ was once a happy-go-lucky boy. The advent of adolescence changes that. After some minor mischief, AJ's view of the world changes thanks to existentialist thinkers such as Nietzsche and Livia Soprano.[21] These new philosophies of meaninglessness make sense to AJ in application to his relatively recent knowledge of his father's criminal work. Livia, however, perverts the existential philosophy. The resonance of her decrying of the world as meaningless is shown in his recitation of Livia's exact words seven years later.[22] It is clear that AJ's nihilistic attitude has been a dominating philosophy since the age of thirteen. He is legitimately seeking to understand the complexities of the world but is discouraged by the perplexed disapproval from his parents.

AJ's educational experience provides a context for his frustration as he tries to grasp the complexities and possible meaninglessness of existence. AJ is shown struggling to comprehend Robert Frost's poem "Stopping by Woods on a Snowy Evening." Its meaning eludes him until Meadow clarifies it for him: The snow's ominous white signifies death. This is much to AJ's consternation, having been of the belief that *black* is death. Such poetic confusion is seen in AJ's later suicide attempt when he appropriates Yeats's "The Second Coming" as a fixation for his depression.[23] His unsuccessful scholarly endeavors illustrate his difficulty in growing up. AJ's educational loss in translation is exemplified by his ignorant invocation of "Nitch" and "Yeets." Though comic relief for the audience, this is a quintessential illustration of AJ's struggle with education, confusion at the universe and how he fits in. AJ's existential crisis is an example of *The Sopranos* running commentary on education systems. Tony and Carmela are frustrated when school lessons cause AJ to question their hypocrisies. Meadow points out that such questioning is integral to education in the sense of personal growth and that simple rote memorizations of others' conclusions is pointless roboticism. David Chase and company are happy to point out hypocrisies of modern education: The dean of Columbia is depicted as a suave extortionist[24]; AJ gets a pass from his principal when the school football team is prioritized over a lesson in accountability[25]; Gloria Trillo bristles at her nephew being taught excessive political correctness in school.[26] These are all messages about the gap between what true education is and what it should be.

AJ's rare pro-active efforts wilt at the first sign of adversity. He once aspired to go to school at West Point but gave up the notion when he could not see himself fitting in with any college crowd. When he finally enters the workforce, his tenures are brief. He gets fired from Blockbuster Video when he steals promotional materials and he later gives up his construction job.[27] His best effort is seen as he works his way to night manager at Beansie's Pizzeria but he quits in grief over his broken relationship with Blanca.[28] AJ is frustrated by what he perceives to be lack of support from his parents. He wants to be treated as an adult but does little to earn that right. He feels that simple tasks are beneath him, such as helping out around the house or the prospect of being a busboy. Instead he wants to jump straight into managing a night club. Exasperated, Tony moans that AJ feels the world owes him a living and Carmela suggests Tony may have contributed to such a disposition. Tony believes AJ's educational needs can be better served by the school of hard knocks. Rosalie Aprile succinctly sums up AJ as a selfish boy with no regard.[29]

Despite his lofty and unrealistic aspirations, AJ has a fear of responsibility which is indicated by his bouts with panic attacks. His first attack takes place on the football field when his coach promotes AJ to defensive captain with the suggestion that AJ might be a leader one day. This prospect overwhelms AJ, who drops to the ground unconscious.[30] AJ experiences his second panic attack when he is faced with the real possibility of military school.[31] Both attacks arise from the immediate circumstances but they also have meaning beyond that. The attacks indicate a fear that he may be expected to follow in his father's footsteps. With such big shoes to fill, in addition to the moral and existential implications, AJ's fight-or-flight response takes over and flight wins out.

Tony is frustrated by the realization that his son's maturation process is stunted and he sees too much of himself in AJ to avoid a sense of personal fault. AJ imitates many of Tony's negative behaviors: He swears; he eats in an unhealthy way; he does poorly academically; he lies; he defies his mother; he has panic attacks. Like father like son. Tony's primary preoccupation is with his son's potential to repeat the mistakes of his father, specifically dropping out of school and getting involved in organized crime.

When AJ goes astray, Tony feels both angry and intensely guilty. This has led to acute incidents of depression. Despite initial claims that Carmela prevented him from straightening out AJ with corporal punishment, Tony admits that she is a good mother who does everything she can.[32] At the heart of the issue, Tony blames himself by way of his genes for AJ not developing to his (Tony's) expectations. An insightful disparity in Tony's logic is seen in his willingness to accept blame for his children's outcomes but the great difficulty he has in allowing any responsibility for his own circumstances to be assessed to his own parents, despite their tremendous shortcomings. Tony frequently complains to Melfi that Carmela's coddling of AJ made their son into a disappointment. Melfi points out that Carmela's protection of AJ is the same thing Tony secretly wished Livia had done for him.[33] Livia's influence on AJ is clear, exhibited by his repetition of her favorite mantra of "poor you." Tony feels it necessary to accept all the blame, to carry the world on his own shoulders.

Tony's paradoxical excuse of genetics and fate in the face of personal guilt and responsibility is shattered when he holds himself to the same standard as Carmela by asking himself if he is doing everything he can to help AJ. Tony begins to feel and see the impact of his own actions, or lack of, on AJ's path. This new perspective leads to his most pivotal fatherly moments in season six. The first of these comes after AJ's failed attempt on Junior's life to avenge Tony's shooting. AJ echoes Meadow's accusation of hypocrisy in Tony, but from a different perspective. He tearfully expresses frustration at Tony for not appreciating the parallel between his actions and those of Al Pacino in similar circumstances in *The Godfather*, revenge for an attempt on his father's life. Tony is dismayed at AJ's convoluted perception of how the real world works. In a clear instance of identity struggle, Tony tells AJ that such vengeance is not in his nature. AJ's nature is that of a nice guy, which is nothing to be ashamed of but a good thing. He confronts AJ with the most direct advice he's ever given his son — that he has to grow up.[34] Tony says this with deep love for his son and the pertinence of this painful truth is authenticated by AJ's vomiting and, later, his third panic attack. Tony correlates his advice with action when he mandates (by way of smashing the windshield of AJ's SUV) that AJ work a job in construction.[35] It's honest work, even if it is obtained by Tony's influence, and the preliminary results are favorable. AJ demonstrates new maturity at work and in a romantic relationship with Blanca Selgado. He also expresses a conscious divergence from Tony's criminal world in the rejection of Tony's offer of presumably stolen jewelry. AJ's accomplishments are leveled, though, by his poor handling of another adversity, Blanca's rejection of him.

Tony tries again to steer AJ by association with new friends. When one of them offers to get AJ started in a gambling operation, AJ demurs with the excuse that he's not good with numbers (supporting this claim with his 450 math SAT score). This draws a parallel to the way Artie has rebuffed offers from Tony to become more involved in the Family business, with the claim that he is a culinary artiste not gifted with the ability to do the math.[36] When Artie dabbled in the Family business, he failed and attempted suicide, failing in that as well. The same happens with AJ. His situation results from his repulsion when he witnesses the violence of crime, but more so because he realizes he's found another group of people with whom he does not fit in.

Feeling despondent at the lack of prospects for happiness, AJ's flight response once again kicks in. With deep, genuine pain he attempts suicide and Tony literally comes to his rescue in an emotionally wrenching scene. Debatably, AJ's suicide attempt is a cry for help rather than a genuine attempt on his own life. It seems effective as Tony, Carmela and Meadow all are confronted with the frightening severity of AJ's problems. Much like Blanca influences AJ to embrace adult responsibilities, the importance of female support to him is reinforced as his recovery is facilitated by a new girlfriend, Rhiannon. AJ shows signs of getting his act together but when he plans to enlist in the army, Tony and Carmela step in by getting him a job in low-budget movie production with Carmine Lupertazzi Jr.[37] This job as a "D-Boy" solidifies AJ's dependence on his father, just like Little Carmine never rose above being a boss's son.

Though AJ wants to be like Michael Corleone, he is more like Fredo, the naïve brother. Tony and Carmela come to terms with this, accepting AJ for who he is. They are consoled by the first-hand knowledge that there are worse fates. AJ won't be a brain surgeon but he won't end up in Boonton with his face blown off like Jackie Jr. AJ will never be his father and neither will he be entirely independent. He finds peace of mind in Tony's advice to focus on the good times. These words of wisdom predate Livia's influential and toxic lessons of meaninglessness. That AJ can apply Tony's optimistic philosophy to his own existence indicates that despite the painful trials of adolescence, AJ may survive his own demons after all, with the help of his father.

Christopher

Christopher Moltisanti is Tony's second cousin whom Tony calls his nephew. In practice Christopher is more like a son to Tony. Ever since

Christopher's birth, Tony has been a father figure to him, especially after the death of Chris's father, Dickie. Chris idolizes Tony the way Tony idolized Dickie Moltisanti. His allegiance is to Tony above all else, even Adriana whom he loves. Chris declares his identity as a soldier in Tony's army, at times proudly and at times bitterly. Tony mentors Chris in the Family business and grooms him as his successor. Chris's journey is his struggle with father issues, chemical addiction, Family values, Hollywood dreams and, above all, his Uncle Tony.

Chris's initial concerns revolve around his desire for fame. He wants to make a name for himself in the Family. He also entertains dreams of being in the movie business. Chris's arc starts with his frustrations in the pursuit of fame in these divergent paths. Hindering him are lingering issues from not having a father and his ever-worsening drug abuse. When he visits a movie set for the first time he is intoxicated, enchanted by the sights, sounds and smells — the buzz of movie magic in the air.[38] His attempts to recreate this high and alleviate frustrations to his movie dreams take the form of drug abuse. When Chris feels betrayed by Hollywood players, he renews his dedication to Tony with the understanding of a life-long commitment.

Chris's conflicting loyalties and his fate parallel Adriana's seemingly untenable pressure from federal agents. Over the two seasons which Adriana's primary storyline stretches, there is an ever-increasing dread that there can be no escape for her. The conclusion seems inevitable; the Family would not tolerate her cooperation regardless of any other affection or relationship. However, the audience watches in the hope that some form of salvation will present itself. Maybe she would convince Chris to leave the Family; maybe she would get him to flip; maybe she would break up with Chris and escape unharmed; maybe their unrealized marriage would have precluded her testimony against her husband. With all these pipe dreams, the audience desperately deludes itself when her fate is a foregone conclusion. As soon as she is nabbed by the Feds, her life is forfeit and it is only a matter of time before her number comes up.

The same sense of impending doom occurs with Christopher. Even though his centrality to the cast is unquestioned, his character flaws lead the audience to speculate on a precipitous demise. Maybe he would overdose; maybe Phil would kill him in retaliation for the murder of his brother; maybe he would rat out the Family. No matter how it would play out, it becomes evident that there is a cloud over Chris's head from which he will not escape. This cloud takes the form of his chemical dependencies. It is introduced with cocaine in the pilot episode and Chris's drug addiction is the foundation for his unreliability to Tony. For years Tony deludes himself that Chris does not have a drug problem. On their trip to Italy, Chris boasts of his determination to visit Mt. Vesuvius yet pathetically languishes in his hotel room, high on heroin.[39] Tony only peripherally notices Chris's absence but does not pursue the reason why. At Livia's wake, Chris is stoned out of his mind, rambling incoherently, yet Tony fails to take notice.[40] When Tony calls on him to exact revenge for Chris's father's death by killing Detective Barry Haydu, Chris is caught unaware, having just smoked heroin with a high-class escort.[41] Tony does not pick up on it. When Tony again surprises Chris with work, to inform him of his intention to prepare Chris for Family leadership, Chris is high on heroin.[42]

When Tony, for the first time, questions him on his suspicious behavior, Chris lies, saying he had wine with Adriana. When Tony calls on Chris for help in dealing with Ralph's corpse, Chris still has the needle in his vein. Again Tony picks up on his odd behavior and Chris lies, pleading the lesser evil of smoking a joint. This time Tony sees through the subterfuge, understanding it to be heroin use. However, the unusual circumstances of the moment require that it be put on the back burner. Chris continues to lie, minimizing the severity of his abuse to rare recreational use. Tony points out that they had actually done coke together to express that his is not a zero tolerance policy, but his concern is the bottom line. If it's negatively affecting business or the Family, then it is a problem that has to be dealt with.[43] The sum of that experience is more of a bonding moment in their collaboration in the disposal of Ralph's body, and Chris's drug use is swept under the carpet, typical of their inability to truly deal with Chris's biggest problem.

Repressed feelings about his father first erupt in an acting class when Chris punches a man, unprovoked. He later delights at the thought of fratricide in his screenplay, obscurely abstracted from a suggestion by actor-director Jon Favreau. Tony seems to know this, whether consciously or by *Fingerspitzengefühl.* When he deliberately begins the process of inseparably bonding his nephew to himself, he does so by providing Chris with his father's killer, allowing him to exact revenge and to exorcise his demons. Just as with anyone for whom Tony does a favor, Chris becomes irretrievably indebted to Tony.

There Was a Girl...

The only person who understands Chris's obstacles is the companion on his journey, Adriana. Adriana loves and supports her "Christofuh" in his Hollywood dreams but she is pivotal in his relationship with Tony and his ultimate fate. When Adriana comes to the Sopranos for help after Chris beats her, Tony's solution is an in-family intervention. Tony lives most of his life in denial about Chris's drug use. When directly confronted with it, Tony shows anger and disappointment. Though these are genuine feelings, they only come out when the drug problem is brought into his own home in the form of Adriana's blackened eye, appealing to his wife Carmela. Only when the delicate balance of his home life is at risk and Chris's drug abuse has gotten out of control, when it intrudes on his wife's happiness and his own stress level, does Tony go through the motions of acceptance, appearing to shed his denial. At this moment he consults with Uncle Junior who, despite some recent incidents of confusion, offers Tony sound business advice. Unclouded by emotional ties to Christopher, Junior sagely counsels Tony to put Chris out of his misery just as one would a horse with a broken leg. Tony knows this is the smartest move but balks, giving in to the temptation of the course of action championed by his heart — to give Chris another chance. Tony explains to Chris that for anyone else acting in such a way — drug-addicted, demonstrating their undependability, beating their fiancée — his life would have been already forfeit.[44] Chris seems to accept this second chance with gratitude and the intention of permanently cleaning up, like a man reborn (again). Once he is finished with rehabilitation, Chris is clean, sober and focused. After some shallow testing, Tony accepts this as truth, proceeding on the belief that Chris is "cured" and the chemical abuse chapter in his life is over. This only sets the stage for a new period of denial.

Chris most commonly abuses drugs to relieve his frustration with his job and Tony. Tony is the catalyst for recidivism when he and Adriana get in a car wreck, fueling rumors of a sexual encounter between them. This enrages Christopher and (although he tries to control his emotions and maintain his sobriety and a productive working relationship with Tony), the pressure is ultimately too much for him. Chris binges on alcohol and threatens Tony's life in a drunken rage. In a moment of truth, Chris's life is again in jeopardy at the hands of Tony when the threat of a gun clarifies the implications of his unwillingness to accept Tony's innocence. Tony is a big fish in his pond but he relies on the obedience and respect of the little fish. Peer perception is directly related to respect, one of the greatest values of Tony Soprano and his associates. Christopher expresses dismay at the effect of the gossip. Regardless of the merits of the allegation, Chris would be exposed for his own weakness — for not being strong enough to induce fidelity in Adriana. He recognizes that public perception of him will be defined by the belief that his fiancée cheated on him with his Uncle Tony.

Tony is considerate of Chris's position and acts to make amends for his own role in the state of affairs, though not openly accepting responsibility. He is mindful of the impact that others' opinions have on Christopher's and his own freedom to live as they wish, with respect. By making a public display of good will toward Christopher in the manner of a dinner at Nuovo Vesuvio, he welcomes his nephew back into the fold as a prodigal son. Tony's motivation, however, is not entirely selfless. He acts to maintain his own reputation, too. As well as hurting Christopher, the rumors create doubt in the minds of his associates regarding Tony's trustworthiness, a situation which would negatively impact Tony's effectiveness as a manager. In making up with Christopher, he puts those concerns to bed with plausible deniability regarding any wrongdoing with Adriana in the first place. By clever deception, Tony is able to continue to operate free from negative consequences of his actions while Chris is irreversibly scarred.[45] Chris's urge for chemicals is revitalized and his recession deeper into his addiction is shown piecemeal — starting with beer, then wine, then liquor, and ultimately heroin.

During his alcoholic binge, Chris narrowly avoids death for the third time in the series. Chris clearly does not forget nor forgive Tony nor Adriana. The mentoring role Tony has been working so hard to develop is tainted at this moment. It may never have come to this without the conjunction of several variables: Chris being out of town; Ade needing a father figure; Tony not being able to keep it in his pants; the two of them sharing a coke hobby; and a mutual desire for sympathy for their current medical tribulations. When Chris learns that Adriana has been taken in by the Feds, he feels torn. Chris weighs his love for Adriana against his sense of loyalty to the Family. His decision becomes simpler when he observes a tableau of "regular life." At a gas station he sees a man his own age with a wife and kids whose clothes, car and mullet reflect lower-class status. Chris sees in the man's eyes a look of restrained bitterness and resentment. He thinks, "There, but for the grace of Tony, go I." It is at this moment that Chris knows which course to take.[46] Chris's decision to side with Tony and sign Adriana's death warrant is essentially selfish, motivated by his unwillingness to live with daily tedium as a "Joe Jerkoff." Years later, Chris expresses his evaluation that this crossroads was where his relationship with Tony was poisoned. The roots of this poisoning, however, are in Tony and Ade's dalliance and betrayal of Chris.

It's a Disease!

Tony's frustration and disappointment with Chris are largely due to his inability to understand and accept Chris's addiction as a disease rather than an excuse. This is deftly illustrated in two separate restaurant dinner scenes in which a bonding moment between them turns sour. In the first, Tony and Tony B. have fun at Chris's expense, including passive aggressive ridicule of his abstention from alcohol.[47] Tony's frustration with Chris comes from his own incomprehension of Chris's struggle. A year later Chris and Tony heist a load of wine and drink in celebration. Tony enables Chris with his reverent comment that wine is like food for true Italians.[48] Tony holds Chris to the double standard that drugs are wrong but to abstain from wine is also wrong. In these ways and others, Tony shows his fundamental misunderstanding of Chris's condition and his disease. With constant temptation, ignorant peer expectations and judgments, Chris's Family environment is not conducive to sobriety.

Chris wants to be loyal and (in the strict Family sense) he is. His loyalty can be called into question, however, when considering his fidelity to the Family from a different perspective — his disregard for cautions against his drug use. Chris was told many times to stay away from the drugs. Adriana was the most consistent voice in this regard due to her unique familiarity with the extent of his abuse and her deep personal interest in his emotional and physical well-being. However, she was not above occasional recreational drug use. Tony made clear his feelings about drugs on more than one occasion, though his denial prevented him from taking *every* opportunity. Paulie, perhaps Chris's closest friend, also warned Chris about the dangers of letting his drug habit get beyond his control. At the intervention, Chris is confronted by a large sampling of the important people in his life expressing their great concern for him. When Chris's new girlfriend, Kelli, becomes pregnant with his child, Chris sees it as an opportunity to go straight. He marries Kelli in the vain hope that family responsibility will force him to remain sober. He later regrets this decision when the proposition does not work in practice. In various phases of his life he accepts the truth and well-meaning intentions in the advice of those who love him. At other times, they were obscured from his mind while in the grip of his disease.

In the same way Tony gives superstitious credence to the curse of "The Soprano Gene," he comes to feel that Christopher is genetically cursed. From the second season it is understood that Chris's mother is an alcoholic.[49] Joanne Moltisanti is shown to be an unhappy person and it is probable that this is partly due to the premature death of her husband, when Chris was just a baby. However, it seems unlikely, though not impossible, that she would carry that grief so conspicuously for more than thirty years. Her generally weary and cheerless aspect are a symptom of her alcoholism. She waxes and wanes in sobriety just as Chris does. Joanne experiences a certain joylessness when she is sober and she self-medicates in times of stress. When Chris is hospitalized for a gunshot and upon his death some years later, she uses alcohol to assuage her fear and grief.

It is revealed very late in the series that Chris's father was also a chemical abuser. Chris shares with Tony his understanding that Dickie Moltisanti drank, did cocaine and possibly heroin. The status of a junkie attributed to Christopher's father makes sense in that he and Joanne could have supported each other in their addictions, enabling each other. This leads to a theory that Dickie and Joanne's relationship may have been founded on co-dependency. The revelation that Dickie had a drug and alcohol problem also raises the possibility that his death may have been the lesser of two evils. Although there are indisputable challenges to being a fatherless child, as Christopher was, there is sufficient reason to believe that Dickie's problems would not make for a suitable patriarchal role model. Chris may have been worse off with a junkie father instead of Tony.

Tony believes in genetic predisposition as a result of his personal struggles with AJ and the possibility of inherited tendency toward depression. With parents like Joanne and Dickie, Chris was born with a predisposition to addiction, both by nature and nurture. The struggle set before him was to live without drugs or alcohol. Had he been able to overcome this painful and difficult impediment, he might have been a father to his daughter, a husband to his wife and a dedicated Family man to fulfill Tony's hopes and plans. Tony's fundamental inability to understand Chris's addiction as a disease prevents him from supporting Chris in his struggle to maintain his sobriety. Chris confronts his uncle with this, looking for understanding and support. Tony interprets Chris's meaning with a foundation in his own personal experience of disease in his mother, his Uncle Junior and his son, AJ. AJ's depression is something that Tony understands because he suffers from it himself. Tony does not fully grasp Livia's borderline personality or Junior's dementia. At different times and in different ways Tony has claimed Livia and Junior to be dead to him. Tony expresses his conviction that Alzheimer's is a death sentence.[50] Uncle Junior and AJ are clinically diagnosed with dementia and depression, respectively, yet they weren't going to negatively affect his business. Chris is a threat to the security of the Family and Tony is directed by the rules of business to nip this risk in the bud. Tony's belief in a genetic curse comes to be understood, in Chris, as a genetic death sentence.

A Loyal Soldier in Tony's Army

On more than one occasion Chris bemoans what he perceives to be a lack of criminal ethics and loyalty among the thieves within the Family. He expresses frustration with Tony's criticism and feels de-prioritized when Tony B. gets out of jail. At times, when frustrated with Tony's leadership, Chris contemplates breaking his oath of *omertà*. One thing which can be considered a credit to Christopher (in this morally relativistic environment) is that he never followed through on this ideation. Tony admitted being concerned about the possibility that his nephew might someday rat him out as a result of his chemical dependency. But this never happened. Chris feels rage toward Tony but represses it, stuffing it into the *Cleaver* movie project. In *Cleaver*, Chris finds a therapeutic outlet for his emotions of rage and sense of betrayal. It is not likely that Chris is aware of this dynamic since on numerous occasions he is in denial or simply oblivious to similarities between the movie and his own life. Christopher is battling feelings of not being loved. His experience with Tony is one of disappointment, frustration and anger. It is Chris's perception that Tony is unappreciative of his efforts in sobriety, family and business. It is true that after the release of *Cleaver* Tony closes the books on Christopher, having decided that Chris has turned against him with hate in his heart and dope in his veins. Chris needs a father and Tony, with all his heart and willingness to be that person for Christopher, is tragically disappointed by the premature death of that relationship. This premature death occurred not in a wrecked Cadillac EXT in a roadside ditch but over a lifetime of mutual attempts, failures and disappointments in the pursuit of happy coexistence. They are both numb to the fact as they wrestle with a new discomfort in each other in the months after Adriana and then *Cleaver*. Maybe Chris never truly loved Tony for who he was but instead was fiercely devoted to him for who he represented, Dickie Moltisanti, his own father lost before memory.

Chris's dedication to his work is a very real thing. However, it's more accurately a dedication to his father. Chris bangs his head against the wall the whole time he tries to succeed in the Family while succumbing to his vice. Despite his boiling frustration with Tony, Paulie and the Business, Chris reserves action. Even when Paulie publicly insults Chris's baby daughter, Chris shows remarkable restraint. Considering the great disrespect Paulie shows Chris, it is not inconceivable for a punch to be thrown, even if to do so would complicate Chris's work environment with potentially significant consequences. Rather he avoids conflict by immediately escaping the desire and opportunity to fight with the Family Underboss. Chris drunkenly but prudently makes an exit before his emotions get the better of him. When he arrives at JT Dolan's apartment, they discuss sobriety and the program. Chris gives great significance to JT's unintentional affront, especially less significant in comparison to what he endured from Tony and Paulie. Yes, JT unfortunately used the term mafia — an ill-advised course of action regardless of their personal relationship. However, Chris initiated the discussion with allusory talk of his criminal deeds, including names. Chris shoots JT for his disrespect and poorly chosen words but actually it is a subconscious action to release all the violent emotions at Paulie and Tony which he had been corking under immense pressure.[51]

Chris has a history of taking out his aggressions regarding the Family on lesser offenders. He may not deal with life's challenges well but he does deal with them in such a way to preserve his loyalty to, and relationship with, his Uncle Tony and the Family. In the first season Chris shoots the bakery clerk in the foot for a blatant lack of respect.[52] Chris's frustration with Paulie results in a dead waiter.[53] Part of his physical abuse of Adriana comes from his Family stresses. When Chris shoots JT, his anger is not only at Paulie for his offensive comments but the whole room of company who laugh *with* Paulie. Most damning is the sickening grin of Tony, reflective of the chasm between them. Chris once again feels deep unfulfillment of his need for a compatible father figure and a family he can trust to help him rather than drag him down. The problem is not that his Family does nothing for him, it's that they don't go *all the way* for him. Tony and company have demonstrated concern for Chris over the years: they had an intervention (though with violent outcome); Tony made a legitimately questionable business decision by not whacking Chris for his drug habit; Tony spared Chris's life when he violently threatened Tony (upon hearing rumors of oral sex between Tony and Ade). Tony has been genuinely heartbroken at Chris's failings as if they were his own. However, there is a limit. Where the two finally diverge is *Cleaver*, which Chris professes to be insignificant fiction while Tony believes it reveals Chris's subconscious revulsion of him. Tony gives up after years of pinning his hopes and support on Chris. Christopher feels this shift in loyalty and is hurt by it. Chris's loyalty knows no bounds, though. He attempts to employ his sacred oath of *omertà* as a guiding principle in sobriety. He takes the principle of a higher power from Alcoholics Anonymous and seeks sobriety by living up to the soldier's code.[54] Unfortunately, this turns out to be faulty logic. The frustration Chris feels with Tony and the Family is the result of the disparity in their commitment to give 100 percent. Chris and Tony are each looking for a fifty-fifty split but they are only willing to go as far as sixty-forty.

The Gates of Hell

David Chase's guiding hand skillfully creates suspense in the telling of Chris's story. It is very much like Adriana's situation in that the audience holds out hope for a happy ending when all the while there is the nagging sense that it is not in the cards for Christopher. There is a desire to see Chris triumph over his demons and for Tony's patience and compassion to be rewarded. The audience wants them both to be find happiness through strength and coexistence. However, there can only be a finite number of second chances and Chris has more than his share. Fate knocks on the door yet again when his car swerves off the road with Tony in the passenger seat, much like the accident with Adriana. Chris's life is on the line, in a microcosm of Chris's arc. An apprehensive audience is aware that this could be the end yet hopeful that it won't be.

In the wrecked Cadillac the severely injured Christopher admits to Tony his inability to pass a drug test. When Chris coughs up thick blood, his prognosis looks bleak and the possibility of death by car accident seems very real. Then Chase unleashes the plot twist which he's been sitting on: When Tony aborts his initial call to 9-1-1, the tragic turn in the journey is revealed. It becomes even more heart-rending when, rather than simply letting Chris die of his injuries, Tony actively facilitates his death by suffocation. Their eyes meet one last time and they part silently.[55]

There are many factors which contribute to Tony's decision to kill Christopher. Tony professes to Melfi that he held Chris's hand through the single greatest crisis of his life (Adriana's murder) because he felt pity for Chris. In return for his help and pity, Tony feels he was not appreciated.[56] Tony feels that Chris gave Tony the lip service regarding gratitude but his actions spoke otherwise — specifically, the continued drug abuse and the production of *Cleaver*. Chris did not ingratiate himself to Tony any further when, on more than one occasion, he would invoke his personal sacrifice in following the Family code of getting rid of Adriana once her cooperation with the Feds came to light. Tony considers Adriana's situation to be a problem of Chris's own making, one for which he never accepted responsibility and for which Tony felt obliged to pick up the slack. He feels that Chris never fully appreciates what he did to eliminate this problem of Christopher's. Of course, given the Family operation, any problem of Chris's is automatically a problem for Tony. His action to order the death of Adriana was just as much a selfish, necessary business precaution as it was helping his nephew whom he loved. Had Tony not done the deed, it is likely that the Feds would have been able to keep her under their thumb and in their own control to wield against Tony in any possible criminal proceedings. Tony minimizes, if not totally ignores, this aspect of his decision regarding Adriana and his subsequent relationship with Christopher.

Tony's decision to kill Chris is not spur-of-the-moment but the sum of chronic disappointment: Adriana, the drugs, ingratitude, divided loyalties with movie fame, cultural incompatibility, his role in Jackie Jr.'s crime and fate, Chris's liability to his wife, daughter and, above all else, the Family. Upon the release of *Cleaver*, Tony is broken-hearted about his relationship with Christopher. Just like Livia and Uncle Junior before, Tony realizes that Chris no longer loves him, if in fact any of them ever did love him in the first place. Their recent discussion about Dickie Moltisanti, the nature of addiction and Chris's admission of recidivism are the final bricks in the tomb Chris built for himself, with Tony's help. The directives of business and the sorrow in their hearts require action. By virtue of *Cleaver* and his *Fingerspitzengefühl*, Tony subconsciously knows what he must do long before he and Chris take their fatal drive. When the opportunity presents itself, he dutifully accepts the burden with a heavy heart and swiftly executes.

After Tony kills Christopher, he naturally experiences complicated feelings. Because of the legal and moral ramifications, Tony is not able to discuss this with Melfi. He dreams of coming clean with her about that murder and also those of Pussy and Tony B. In a session with Melfi he touches on some of his feelings and relationship with Christopher but he cannot go into particulars. This leaves an enormous bundle of powerful and complex emotions unresolved. Tony hits upon an unorthodox solution to alleviate his intense need to process these emotions: He goes to Vegas. On the surface Tony goes to Vegas to get away from the depression and mourning for Christopher. He gambles and he dines but it seems there is deeper motivation when he visits a friend of Chris's, Sonya. Tony's intentions appear to be the courtesy of delivering, in person, the news of Christopher's death. Knowing Tony, there is also a suspicion that he's interested in a romantic encounter, which does come about. Only after all this is Tony's true purpose in being in Las Vegas revealed: He seeks a psychedelic experience. Tony claims he always wanted to try it but never did because of a sense of duty and responsibility to his families. He remembers Chris telling him of taking peyote with Sonya. At this moment it is evident that such an experience was Tony's motivation to go to Vegas from the very beginning. Sonya obliges, and Tony's first psychedelic experience delivers to him the therapy he seeks.

Tony's first revelation comes at the roulette table. After winning three in a row he finds new meaning in Chris's death — his own luck has changed. As if he had shed an albatross around his neck, Tony feels freedom. The great weight of Christopher has been lifted from his shoulders. Tony falls prostrate with uncontrollable laughter. Tony and Sonya visit nature, a scenic desert valley. As Tony watches the sun rise he has a vision. The sun flashes for a split second, reminiscent of the beacon on the horizon of Tony's coma experience and the Eiffel Tower which Carmela watches from a distance. In a moment of relief and revelation he shouts to the world, "I get it!" Tears of joy come to his eyes and Tony seems to turn a corner in his grieving process for Chris but also, perhaps, in his own life.[57] In this way — psychedelic drugs and a personal connection to Chris's more innocent younger days, in the form of Sonya — Tony has a substitute for the therapeutic process he usually gets with Dr. Melfi. His mind is put in a state in which he can ask himself the same types of difficult and probing questions he is faced with in psychotherapy. On his own he is able to assemble the pieces of his puzzle. It is an unorthodox process, but Tony's process has always been eccentric. Tony gains insight and understanding of Chris's death that provides him with a sense of peace and closure.

Only Tony Soprano will ever know what he means when he screams to the desert valley that he gets it. It is impossible to encapsulate in a single sentence, paragraph or volume what such an experience could mean for any individual. The audience can learn from clues in what he says and how he acts in the following months. One of the last things Christopher said before his death was a gentle reminder to Tony about stopping to smell the roses. Chris, with all his faults, shares in common with Tony an understanding of this sentiment. Although Tony would suffocate Chris mere moments later, he grasps the importance of this counsel. Tony renews his allegiance to this philosophy and this is part of Christopher's legacy.

Despite their differences, Tony and Chris did the best they could. Chris sought to substitute for the love of a father with an incompatible Family, drugs and fame. He was unable to beat the odds. He engaged in a long, drawn-out subconscious suicide. The only question was whether his implement would be drugs or crime. Chris had a big heart but could not stop himself from polluting it. He loved his fiancée Adriana and his Uncle Tony and his loss of them broke that heart. The achievement of his dreams with the production of *Cleaver* also finalized his death sentence. Tony's decision to kill Chris was a painful one but he followed it through with the belief that it was for the greater good, for the many to whom Chris was a liability. In a bitter twist, Christopher's death created for his daughter the same fatherless challenge with which he struggled his whole life. In accordance with Uncle Junior's counsel years earlier, Tony put Chris out of his misery like a horse with a broken leg. Tony was guided by the business tenet that more is lost by indecision than by wrong decisions and he will have to live with his decision as he continues on his journey without his second son, Christopher. Chris proudly professed that he would follow his Uncle Tony to the gates of Hell and beyond. Wherever they are going, it will be Tony that follows Christopher.

Meadow, AJ, Chris and Jackie Jr. are all Tony's children. They provide the audience with insight into Tony's journey as well as theirs. They are each examples of struggles with their own natures. The tragedies of Jackie and Chris's inability to come to terms with their identities is tempered by the relative successes of Tony's own blood children to do so. The stories of the Soprano children provide structure to consider morality, parenting, education, maturation, responsibility, rebellion and, above all, the search for and acceptance of identity.

7

Internal Conflicts and Symptomatic Behavior

An organized crime Family such as Tony Soprano's is a sub-culture, with values and modes of operation that differ greatly from the greater American societal standards. However, it is impossible for the Family to live independent of the law-abiding citizenry because the Family preys on the citizens for a living. A Family like Tony's must live within the greater American system. The wiseguy angle is to bend that system to their benefit when possible and otherwise avoid it. Family associates face the ever-present threat of incarceration at the hands of law enforcement. These men enter into the criminal life believing that they can beat the system. Since odds-making is part of their work, a wiseguy knows that such a proposition is a gamble. However, one of the core values of this sub-culture is that it is better to live a short life by one's own rules than a long life by someone else's.

The practice of this wiseguy philosophy entails complications. There are unavoidable clashes with societal rules. Moral considerations enter into the equation. The attempts to manage these complications often result in negative side effects. Characters in Tony's mob Family are constantly lying. They suffer from stress and are often unhappy. They indulge in vices and are capable of brutal violence. These side effects are seen in every episode of *The Sopranos* and are grist for David Chase's mill. This chapter is an examination of the internal conflicts and common external symptoms, with consideration for how they fit into the Big Picture.

Hypocrisy by the Rules

A mob story is appealing to audiences because it allows them a glimpse into an exciting, foreign world. The gangsters populating the genre play for high stakes. These are enigmatic and contradictory non-conformists who get what they want and don't let anyone stand in their way. The gangster genre provides escapism to the typical viewers who look for adventure they don't get in a nine-to-five job. Mob life is independent of the bureaucracy of modern life with unequivocal translation to action. It hearkens back to a simpler, tribal existence where the individual is empowered. The gangster story allows an audience the vicarious thrill of temporarily having the world on their terms. Then, when the anti-hero gets his comeuppance at the end of the cautionary tale, they are reassured their nine-to-five existence is worthwhile. There is no avoiding the fact that fictional wiseguys, objects of audience envy and condemnation, are criminals in violation of societal laws. Tony Soprano and his associates do not feel an obligation to society. Their loyalties are to each other and their families.

The gangsters portrayed in *The Sopranos* have entered into the life of crime for various reasons: There is a degree of freedom in not having the humdrum office job; wiseguys are respected amongst each other and feared by outsiders; and, of course, there is the money above all else. The downside to their existence is frustration with business partners who are unscrupulous and the risk of legal repercussions. These people must also deal with life and death — the taking of others' lives and the possibility of their own premature deaths. The subsequent stress of these downsides is considerable. It's difficult to say if the benefits outweigh the drawbacks but once these people enter the Family, there is no getting out and they must live with their decision.

It seems that each wiseguy has a slightly different guiding principle in reconciling his actions with concepts of morality. Tony and Paulie present two of them in the second season. Paulie's principle lies in the Catholic Church. He believes he will pay for his sins in a harsh but acceptable sentence in purgatory. The sentence is determined by a convenient conversion equation of venial and mortal sins into the equivalent of a prison term. Paulie comes to question this perspective, though, when Chris shares his personal vision of Hell.[1]

In the same episode, Dr. Melfi asks Tony's view on Hell and he explains that he and his associates approach their line of work as if they are soldiers in war. This is echoed at other times: when Christopher professes himself to be a soldier in Tony's army; Paulie thinks of Tony as a general; Silvio draws comparisons between Tony and Winston Churchill, Tony and Napoleon; Tony's History Channel interest is military history. Tony explains that those who enter into *La Cosa Nostra* know the stakes and accept the rules. This means the potential for wealth and the potential for death. Either way, it is the individual's choice and they must live (or not!) with the consequences. Additional insight to Tony's philosophy on his work comes in an exchange with Valentina in season four. As she pursues Tony, he rebuffs her advances because she is Ralph's *goomah*. She sarcastically accuses him of having morals. He deflects the question of morals but asserts his strong belief in living by rules.[2] By simply putting aside the question of morality and following the soldier's code, Tony is able to provide for his wife and children and consider himself basically a good man.

A fascinating testament to the writers of *The Sopranos* is their power to put viewers into the same mindset as Tony, if just for an hour at a time. Tony Soprano is portrayed by James Gandolfini with thorough complexity, at times subtle and nuanced and at others brutal and fierce. Tony is charismatic, savvy, deceitful, thoughtful, emotional, violent, pitiful, reprehensible and deeply conflicted. Through all of it he comes across as sympathetic and relatable. In Tony Soprano the audience recognizes the admirable and acknowledges the despicable and on both counts they see something of themselves. They have lived with him for years and have come to know him better than many people in their own lives. The audience can find justification for his murders and entertainment in his lesser crimes. They may not agree with everything that Tony does or says but they can understand his transgressions because they have walked six seasons in his shoes. The bond has made him family to them and a *Sopranos* audience understands that blood is thicker than water.

As Tony tells Melfi that, by the rules of war, soldiers are allowed to kill other soldiers without moral condemnation, he appears to be trying to convince himself as much as her. Both Tony and Paulie exhibit signs of doubt after verbalizing their justifications. Each character, including the women who marry these wiseguys, deals with doubt about their existence. Once in the Family, though, their path is irreversible and the time for questioning morality is past.

Telling Lies So Long, They Don't Know When to Stop

On *The Sopranos* everyone lies to everyone for self-preservation and in attempts to stifle their doubts. There is not one relationship that is excluded from this phenomenon. Even the sacrament of marriage is shown to be subservient to lies when Carmela laughs off Tony's claim that she is the only person in the whole world with whom he is completely honest. The nature of This Thing of Ours is secretive. It requires the denial of its existence to outsiders. To maintain secrecy, Tony cannot disclose details about his work to his wife. This is to prevent her from legally becoming an accessory to his crime but Tony also lies to her about the business because it makes his life easier. If Carmela were privy to all the sordid details of Tony's business practices, it would complicate Tony's situation — and his situation is complicated enough. Lying is done out of convenience to conceal one's true nature. In personal relationships, lies generally serve to avoid judgment. In Family business, the lies are about maximizing profitability. It can be done overtly or subtly. In can be premeditated, accidental or simply reflexive.

As these characters lie to each other they also lie to themselves. It is crucial to always keep in mind the Nathaniel Hawthorne quotation presented in the first season: "No man can wear one face to himself and another to the multitude without finally getting bewildered as to which may be true."[3] This codifies one of the main sources of conflict for these characters. They struggle with their discontent which is a result of the bewilderment which they each deliver on themselves. With so many people lying to each other all the time, it becomes practically impossible to find any firm ground on which to stand, to sort out the causes of their unhappiness. When Tony struggles for an outlet or remedy for his powerful emotions he frequently acts on his destructive impulses. Whether seeking solace in the company of a prostitute after making the difficult decision to whack Vito, smashing a wall with his fist in an argument with Carmela or beating Ralphie to death for killing Pie O My — Tony follows through on his violent, destructive urges as an outlet for his stress.[4] What differentiates the audience from Tony is that, even though they might have internal conflicts and violent impulses, they usually stop short of the destructive action. One of the strongest appeals of Tony Soprano is his function as a conduit for the audience's animal instincts, which are sometimes selfish or violent. Part of what makes Tony so compelling to watch is the vicarious thrill that is felt in watching him do what one only wishes they could do in their own worlds. Where most people sublimate their animal instincts for the sake of societal standards of conduct, Tony puts himself and his families first. In real life it is necessary that one control those instincts in favor of the community, or at the very least so he or she doesn't get taken to jail. It is not easy, though, because there is rarely a direct one-to-one reward for exercising that control. It is a prioritization of the whole over the individual which, in the end, is the course necessary to create the best chance for greater good. What's more, it actually works to erode feelings of isolation in a constructive way. Such isolation is something that Tony feels acutely and it is an obstacle to his happiness. What Tony experiences as isolation, he tries to translate to stoicism. In Tony's first session with Dr. Melfi he expresses ennui at the standard helplessness and dependence in America by recalling the image of film star Gary Cooper. Tony admires Cooper's calm fortitude in the face of adversity. Tony will rely on this role model and call upon it several other times in the series. However, despite his frequent invocation of Gary Cooper as the idealized strong and silent man, there is a disassociation in Tony between the ideal and the actual. Even though he admires and strives to act in accordance with this personal hero, Tony falls short in trying circumstances. He is equally likely to place blame or wallow in self-pity at his fortune. Between the ideal and the actual there is a loss in translation. At times Tony is aware of this disparity and at others he is completely oblivious.

Always With the Excuses

Tony's feeling of disappointment is seen in most of the characters on *The Sopranos*. This disappointment is linked to their suppressed feelings about participating in a morally corrupt environment. In order to live with this condition, they each create their own prisms through which to interpret their worlds without being forced to confront the causes head-on. These are twisted, deranged, quirky and self-deceptive points of view which allow them to live without being crushed by the 400-pound gorilla of guilt they live with.

Tony presents biased interpretations of events for the purpose of distracting those around him from his own possible guilt. On numerous occasions Tony has assigned the blame for his predicaments to genetic predisposition. Tony fixates on the power of heredity. His depressive personality is supposedly inherited from his mother. Tony feels a sense of personal genetic responsibility for his son's academic mediocrity and panic attacks, a fault he resentfully calls "The Soprano Gene." By deferring to genetic predeterminism he seeks to excuse himself from accountability in the eyes of others. He metaphorically throws his hands in the air and professes to be powerless to change it. The genetic argument begs the Darwinian consideration of Tony's environment. Tony claims that he was born into the life of crime, a circumstance beyond his control. This is another excuse which he uses to treat feelings of guilt and shame for not living in harmony with all of his values. However, this claim is not completely without validity. When determining the relative impacts of nature vs. nurture, it is difficult to ignore the role of the parenting he received. As evidenced, first-hand and anecdotally, there was not much nurturing going on in the Soprano household of his youth. With a mother who once threatened to stick a fork in his eye and a father who Tony witnessed chop off a man's finger with a butcher's knife, it is understandable that his survival instincts would take over and do what had to be done to endure an emotionally and physically hostile environment.[5]

His pretext of genetic predisposition relates to his excuse of fate, another means of surrendering control and acquitting himself from responsibility. When circumstances don't seem to be going his way, Tony explains it as a result of a willful, supernatural force in the universe. Tony's pleas are only a smokescreen behind which he hides guilt. For a long time he is more willing to live with disappointment and accept pity from others than he is to address the guilt and make the difficult changes necessary to fix the issues.

These excuses of genetics and fate are intended for the benefit of others but as Tony wears this mask for others, he becomes bewildered himself. When he begins to believe his own lies, he becomes further removed from his Gary Cooper worship and application of those principles. This leads to the consideration of how Tony lives his work ethic. Tony claims cultural and social heredity as major determinants of his line of work. His choice to live the criminal life is occasionally examined in reference to other characters on the show that make an "honest" living. Most frequently this dichotomy is illustrated in relationship to Tony's childhood friend, Artie Bucco. In the course of their association Tony and Artie are always aware of the fact that they came from similar backgrounds yet ended up living very different lives. Tony is a crime boss with wealth, power and women while Artie is a chef who struggles financially, and feels inconsequential and imprisoned. Even though Artie may occasionally flirt with Tony's world, for the most part he lives on the straight and narrow path. The two men question their relative happiness in this context.

Just as Tony feels deeply about the disparity of actual happiness and the discouraging pursuit, Artie feels there is not justice in the return on his honest toil. He shares with Tony his father's influential words encouraging him in the belief that honest work has its rewards.[6] Artie has come to believe it to be a fairy tale. His quest for happiness is a failure even though he is the one who took up the mantle of legitimate work, rejecting the life of crime as the immoral and easy road. Tony, though, makes an argument to the contrary. Tony's life is easy in the sense that he has all the marks of success but there are hidden dynamics which contradict the presumption of ease: He received no love from his mother; she conspired with his uncle to have Tony whacked; support systems are limited to him by the nature of his job's secrecy and illegality; Tony is the one who lives with decisions of life and death — the murders of Pussy and his cousin Tony Blundetto, the jailing of Feech LaManna, and the decision to whack Vito are all necessitated by the rules of the business that he is in. These are all great stressors in Tony's life. For these and many other reasons, Tony's life is by no means easy. From his perspective it can be argued that Artie took the easy way out by not having to deal with these complicated situations with much higher stakes. Nevertheless, for the most part Tony respects Artie's choice to remain a legitimate businessman because it is congruent with who Artie is, his nature. Both Tony and Artie do what they think is right given their respective circumstances. Their relationship is not about judging each other. It's about their demonstration of the human tendency to believe that the grass is always greener on the other side of the fence no matter what choices one makes in their pursuit of happiness.

Italian pride is everpresent in *The Sopranos*. As a point of identity the characters have a tendency to pervert it to serve their own purposes. Tony's view of the Italian immigration of the early twentieth century and Paulie's dislike for a national coffee chain's capitalization on espresso and cappuccino are examples.[7] They both express a sense of victimization, that the early Italian-Americans were stolen from and taken advantage of. Tony and Paulie carry resentment for the burdens of their ancestors and use this to justify their crimes in the name of reparations. Racism is symptomatic of the intense and twisted cultural identity these characters champion. By pointing the finger of blame at other cultures, they make excuses to distract from their own misdeeds. Wiseguys use other people to their own ends, whether it's exploitation for financial gain or demonization by propagandistic ethnic slurs. No matter where a person's ancestors came from, their differences are used against them to reinforce stereotypes and further personal causes.

In Tony Soprano's New Jersey, African-Americans are the victims of lingering resentment from the racial tension in the 1960s. When Tony or someone in his family needs someone to blame, they often rely on existing prejudice to fabricate a readily accepted patsy — that of "unidentified black males." When Tony has his panic attack at the time of Tony B.'s arrest, he lies that black men mugged him.[8] When Jackie Jr. is shot and killed, the initial story is that it occurred in a drug deal with black men.[9] When Tony B. suffers a broken toe in the unsanctioned hit of Joe Peeps, he claims he sustained his injury when he was assaulted by black men.[10] On two occasions the Family employs a black male tandem as hit men — the attempt on Tony's life and that of Carmine Lupertazzi Sr.[11] Such criminal stereotypes are reinforced when Tony and AJ encounter African-American crack addicts or by the MTV images of gangster rappers that influence AJ's fashion sense.[12] Nowhere is Tony's racism plainer than his frank conversation with Meadow's African-American boyfriend. Tony makes it clear that a black man is not welcome to date his daughter. Tony prefers to restrict his contact with African-Americans to business.[13] When he is given a speeding ticket by a black police officer, Tony uses his connections to have it squashed and the officer demoted, as a matter of principle.[14] Tony has respectful, though casual, exchanges with black business partners Reverend James and Maurice Tiffen but seems to base his treatment of African-Americans on business, as he does with everyone.

The characters on *The Sopranos* displace blame on other racial groups as well. Chris's vision of Hell is an Irish bar where it's always St. Patrick's Day. In his vision the Irish are persecutors of Roman soldiers, an identification of Chris's Italian heritage.[15] This indicates an antithetical construct on the part of the Italian gangsters toward the Irish. In the first season, Junior orders the death of a man named Rusty Irish who is despised for selling drugs to a boy who then committed suicide.[16] When Vito is on the run, his fate is foreshadowed with his choice of a Notre Dame University ball cap.[17] By choosing the emblem of the Fighting Irish, Vito subliminally communicates his outsider status and betrayal of Family values. When celebrating the legacy of Christopher Columbus, Father Phil invites a speaker who is Italian by birth but married an Irish man. Her speech contains moral judgments of those involved in *La Cosa Nostra* to which the mob wives take great offense.[18] She is seen as a compromise of loyalty and betrayal of her people.

Prejudice against Asians is heard from Chris when visiting Tony B.'s new massage therapy office and again when Hesh's son-in-law is beaten.[19] Rosalie Aprile is led to believe that her son's killers were Chinese.[20] Paulie demonstrates bigotry toward Valery the Russian as an outlet for his frustrations with Tony and Silvio.[21] The Middle Easterners Ahmed and Mohammed are suspected of terrorist connections. Ralph and Tony, on separate occasions, belittle Middle East cultural identity with the ignorant reductionist use of the word "shish kebab."[22] Tony doesn't want Meadow to date a black nor does he want her dating a Dominican nor AJ a Puerto Rican.[23] Tony is suspicious of a Latino boy who wants to buy AJ's drum set.[24] Interestingly, David Chase's two on-screen cameos are in the background of Neapolitan characters.[25]

Tony and those in his Family take pride in their cultural identity. They abuse this identity by asserting its superiority. They prefer to believe stereotypes that don't complicate their lives and, in fact, make it easier for them to continue their criminal and morally questionable behavior. Excuses are a ready weapon in the hands of a Soprano, whether it's genetics, fate or the easy road less traveled. By propagating such excuses and deception, they are able to continue to distract themselves from their internal conflicts.

Fuhgeddabout Those Distractions

The Family is a culture that feels entitled to a satisfying and happy life. Its members do not experience happiness but pain at the subconscious awareness of what they don't have — fundamentals such as love, true self-esteem and sense of worth. To make up for these absent rewards of life, they exceed in the indulgence of vices and luxuries. These characters engage in crime and try to maintain a semblance of normality with chronic deception. Their internal conflict grows when they don't acknowledge it. Ignoring their guilt, fear and shame is how they are able to continue to survive without succumbing to these feelings. Not coincidentally, organized crime provides numerous distractions in the form of luxuries and vices such as drugs, pornography, prostitution and gambling.

The gangster lifestyle is marked by excesses. Tony and his associates drive expensive cars, wear fine Italian suits, adorn themselves with gold chains and have fancy homes. The luxuries serve to provide the illusion of happiness and success. Jewelry and fur coats are common gifts for mob wives. Frequently Tony gives gifts to Carmela when he feels guilty over something or he simply wants to distract her from another issue. He supplies his children with scooters and drum sets and credit cards. All of this is done under the guise of providing for his family but its true function is to distract from his crimes.

One means of self-distraction is the use of various drugs. Christopher is the touchstone for the vice of drugs because of his addiction. Chris self-medicates his job frustration with heroin and alcohol. His heroin abuse is unacceptable to the Family. Apart from his addiction, however, his practice of using alcohol is similar to that of his associates. Chris calls attention to the saturation of alcohol among their circle. These wiseguys use alcohol in social situations but abuse it to smooth over the internal conflict they may have about their lives. Even though it is under the guise of social drinking, these made men always have alcohol near at hand. They have wine with lunch; at the Bing or the Crazyhorse, Tony and the guys are always ready to drink a Scotch; they do shots of tequila in preparation for killing Pussy or Sambuca to mourn the death of Jackie Jr. Instead of its popular definition as a social lubricant, in the Family alcohol is a criminal lubricant. Tobacco use is also quite prevalent as a means of managing stress. Christopher and Silvio both smoke to relieve anxiety but no one smokes like Johnny Sack, who is practically defined by his smoking (and ultimately dies of lung cancer as a result). His decision to quit once incarcerated indicates an acknowledgment that the habit is self-destructive, as are all of the habits discussed in this chapter. All these chemicals are employed to assuage feelings of guilt and doubt about their lives and choices.

Sexual vice is another major outlet for wiseguys. To them, pornographic magazines are the equivalent of *Time* or *Newsweek*. When idly passing time, Tony and his associates are frequently shown to peruse porn. Tony has no qualms about engaging in prostitution, either. Many of the Bing dancers, in addition to stripping, are also prostitutes. In honor of Chris being made, the entertainment is prostitution.[26] When Tony stays at the Plaza Hotel, he hires an escort.[27] *Goomahs* are rarely more than prostitutes engaged for a longer term. These habits distract them from greater questions of morality with fleeting thrills but they also reflect an attitude towards women that indicates why these wiseguys might experience frustration with their wives.

Apart from prostitution, practically all Family associates indulge in illegal gambling as a source of entertainment and distraction. Gamblers are often described as degenerates and are marked as prey. Wiseguys understand that it is a weakness but that does not prevent them from employing a double standard and participating themselves. Though gambling is generally a business tool to get others' money, Tony and the guys still hold private card games and even have their own secret casino. For a while Tony becomes deeply ensnared by a losing gambling habit to the exclusion of others' welfare and consideration.[28] The single greatest commentary on gambling comes from Tony's father, Johnny Boy, who imparted the stern lesson to young Tony that he should *never* gamble.[29] The irony of this commentary is that the entire gangster lifestyle is a gamble. By joining the Family, these mobsters know the stakes — the potential for wealth or death. Tony estimates that someone like himself ends up dead or in jail eighty percent of the time.[30] This means he's doing everything he can to be part of the twenty percent but he's prepared to be a statistic. Just like gambling, there is an illusion of control in the life of a gangster. However, there is also a large element of chance when one has to play the cards they are dealt. These mobsters want to burn bright rather than fade away and the criminal life provides them with that opportunity. The question is, "How long will they be able to ride it out until their number comes up?" Every day they wake up is a roll of the dice and it's only a matter of time before they crap out. Tony knows that in life, just like in gambling, sometimes he's up and sometimes he's down. After Tony's gambling frenzy abates, he shares with Carmela the idea that surviving the coma was like winning a lottery jackpot, against impossible odds. He feels that in the Big Picture he is way up and with Christopher's death he feels that his luck returns to him, literally and metaphorically.

Gambling, prostitution, drugs, luxury — these are all symptomatic of the criminal enterprise as a means of revenue. However, they also provide escapism for Tony and company as they try to live with crimes with deep moral implications and ambiguity.

Going About in Pity for One's Self

Audience ability to find empathy for Tony is derived from his relationships and the emotions they arouse. Tony is: a husband to Carmela; a father to Meadow and AJ; a son of Johnny and Livia; a brother to Janice and Barbara; a peer to his contemporaries; and, of course, the boss of a crime family. *Sopranos* viewers live all these roles (crime bosses less so) and seeing Tony in similar relationships taps into viewers' pre-existing emotions and establishes a link between viewer and Tony. When Tony is frustrated by Anthony Jr.'s fixation on video games, many viewers can identify with that specific situation. When Tony's job is causing him stress, much of the audience knows what that feels like. When Janice manipulates people or situations, viewers feel their anger rise with Tony's because they have known similar personalities in their own lives, whether in a sibling or not. When Tony endures feelings of guilt and shame, the audience's hearts go out to him because they know how awful that feels.

All of these negative emotions suffered on the television screen connect to an audience's internal experience of the world for which it rarely has a healthy forum. Livia zealously encapsulates the feeling with the belief that happiness is a myth and each person is ultimately alone.[31] Such an expression, though extreme, touches upon experiences with despair. The simple broaching of the subject creates the forum the audience seeks, both for release and understanding of their emotions. The difference with Livia is that she has not had the benefit of release or understanding. She has held onto her pain and based her whole world-view on it. This is the unfortunate parenting model with whom Tony was forced to grow up.

Interestingly, even though one of the tenets of Livia's bleak philosophy is isolation she also implies belief that it's a condition shared by all. "Everyone is alone"— this paradoxical koan is one of the pillars of *The Sopranos*. The symptoms of self-centeredness and narcissism are consistently demonstrated in Tony and others. When it comes to assessing the world around them, most of the characters are focused solely on themselves, inconsiderate of their fellows. They are convinced of their centrality to any event or remark. Christopher, Junior, Paulie, Janice, AJ and others are all strong examples of this mentality. Tony is right there along with them, as is exemplified in a season five rebuttal of Silvio's attempt to give Tony some advice. Tony expresses a sentiment of nearly overwhelming responsibility and solitude.[32] Although there are extenuating circumstances from Tony's position as boss of the Family, his feelings are not unlike the other characters' nor those of the audience. Just as the audience is familiar with Livia's sense of despair, though on a different scale, they also understand this sense of isolation. Others can only approximate an individual's emotional state arrived at by the many contributing factors experienced throughout their lives. No one can truly and fully know how another feels and the knowledge of that solitude in the face of life's challenges is often frightening and discouraging.

Livia is a template for Tony in how he attempts to counteract his sense of isolation. In turn, Tony's charismatic personality makes him a template for those around him. The lying, excuses and passive aggression are all propagated by other *Sopranos* characters as well. These behaviors make Tony feel better about himself because they reassure him that he's not alone in his suffering. These are attempts to control suffering. In the end there are things in life which one cannot control. In the face of, this many feel helpless rather than resigned to, or even empowered by it. Tony's actions reflect his Family culture's tendencies toward seeing the glass as half-empty in the face of such circumstances.

When the guys are not sufficiently distracted by vice and luxury, the internal conflicts have a way of bubbling to the surface. This leads to one of the major symptoms of the criminal life: taking internal frustrations out on others through passive aggression. It is a running theme throughout *The Sopranos* that these characters find amusement in other people's pain. Tony and company's discontent is largely exhibited in complaining, "breakin' balls" to devalue others, and through emotional manipulation to insure that they are not alone in their suffering. They are subject to pain and misery, and reminding others of that fact makes them feel better about themselves. This is most succinctly codified by Tony's misinterpretation of Gloria Trillo's summary of a Buddhist philosophy which states that one must participate joyfully in the sorrows of the world.[33] The original intention of this teaching is to inspire individuals not to succumb to the potentially overwhelming quantity of pain, suffering, and sorrow in the world. In Gloria's case this philosophy is initially a thing which keeps her centered and sane. However, she ultimately is unable to overcome her own crushing depression. She puts herself in a position of secondary suicide, in which she goads and baits Tony into nearly strangling her to death. The Buddhist koan appeals to Tony but his is a perverted interpretation. His take is a guilt-free reasoning of others' suffering, an absence of sympathy for others' pain. His demeanor implies the acknowledgment of his own sorrow and finding solace in the fact that others suffer as well. This attitude deflects culpability for his own and others' unhappiness. It is a grim outlook on his fate and not in keeping with the true spirit of the Buddhist view. From it, Tony claims to feel a new freedom and enjoyment of life. It is empty, though, as is evidenced by the realization that Gloria is in many ways a reincarnation of Livia. He sees that such an approach is emulation of Livia by disqualifying the expectation of happiness for himself or others. Upon this realization, Tony reconsiders embracing this philosophy of joyful participation in the sorrows of the world because he sees that the messenger is kindred to the mother who he largely blames for the bad things in his life. What he thought might be the answer to being happy, he finally abandons as an empty promise.

This perverted practice of participating in the world's sorrow by adding to it is seen in most of the characters on *The Sopranos*. They subconsciously reframe this concept to fit their existing view of the world rather than change their own view. They misinterpret their role in the world's sorrow in ways which reinforce their way of living and the choices they have made. Rather than assess their own responsibility for their internal conflict, they deceive themselves that sorrow is the human condition.

Their frustration is then released on friends and associates who may or may not have a role in the creation of the conflict. These characters constantly displace their anxiety from their internal conflicts on others. In a twisted practice of the belief that a sorrow shared is a sorrow lessened, none of the characters on *The Sopranos* keep their discontent to themselves. Their emotions manifest themselves in various behaviors, sometimes subconsciously enacted and at other times willfully malicious: The ubiquitous habit of complaining is a plea for sympathy; the time-honored tradition of "breakin' balls" is the passive aggressive outlet for feelings of inadequacy; the sophisticated practice of manipulating others' emotions is employed for one's own dark glee or personal gain.

All the characters are self-centered, selfish, self-absorbed in some way. They have a penchant for complaining and it is often carried too far, to the point of self-pity demonstrated in Tony but even more excessively in the supporting cast. A fair portion of the dialogue in this show is dedicated to characterization in the form of self-pity. Uncle Junior, Paulie, Chris, Janice, Jackie Jr., Ralph, Richie — all feel that not only has life been unfair to then but insist on convincing those around them of that belief. This is one form of twisted joyful participation in the sorrow of the world. In a sense, these characters who have lemons make sour lemonade to give to their friends, family, and associates. They tell others their afflictions in search of sympathy. This is antithetical to Tony's ideal of Gary Cooper who kept quiet and dealt with his own problems. This touches on one of the reasons that Tony initially has difficulty with therapy because to whine and complain about his own problems to someone else is a demonstration of weakness. It also presumes that one's tribulations are more important than those around them. All the characters suffer from this condition and it reflects their desire to be excused from fault rather than address their problems directly.

"Breakin' balls" is another form of releasing one's frustration. This term can be applied to nagging or pestering of an individual but it is more commonly seen in the form of passive aggressive banter among associates. This is a practice of pointing out an individual's weakness under the guise of humor. It is accepted as good-natured ribbing but it truly reveals personal insecurities. For example, when Tony and Tony B. make fun of Chris's sobriety, they explain that they're just kidding around and mean no real disrespect.[34] However, it reveals a certain insecurity on their part because they don't understand Chris's disease and they feel a sense of loss at his being different. The negative effects of "breakin' balls" can be seen when Chris takes this as genuine criticism and disrespect. To a certain degree he is right. Rather than deal openly and honestly with issues, they discount them with passive aggressive derision.

A final category of misdirected frustration also takes form in passive aggression — that of emotional manipulation. However, while "breakin' balls" is somewhat of a misunderstood learned behavior, emotional manipulation is a more willful act upon peers. The quintessential emotional manipulator is, of course, Livia Soprano. She recognizes others' fears and insecurities and exploits them. By making others miserable, she lessens her own sense of unhappiness. Tony and Janice both learned this practice from their mother. It is a means of creating a sense of control and it also works as a leveler of those who may temporarily seem to be outside the grasp of despair. An example of this is seen when Tony witnesses Janice finding a new peace with the world. His envy cannot allow him to resist pushing her buttons. At the appearance that Janice is growing beyond the Sopranos family curse of emotional dysfunctionality, he puts a smile back his own face by pulling her back in by provoking her with indirect accusations of being a bad mother to her son, Harpo. In a calculated approach, Tony casually needles Janice about her estranged son to the point of an explosive re-emergence of her rage.[35] When Livia dies, Janice applies guilt to Tony to persuade him to have a wake against Livia's and his own wishes.[36] Such emotional button-pushing is seen in many characters and is a means of minimizing one's own misery by adding to the misery of others.

All of these behaviors — complaining, "breakin' balls" and emotional manipulation — are vents for stress that results from internal conflicts. At times Tony exhibits qualities of his mother wherein he spreads the suffering around to those who earn it (perceived incompetents, subordinates, inconsiderates, the Happy Wanderers, or inferiors with less worldly wisdom). This attitude is reflected in Tony's desire to control his anger and direct it at those who deserve it. Rather than accept the responsibility of dealing with their internal conflicts, the characters of *The Sopranos* distract themselves and others from the real issues.

Sometimes a character's internal conflicts become too great to be subsided by habits of passive aggression. Their anger occasionally manifests itself in physical violence unto peripheral players. Paulie forgets about his mother issues by beating Jason Barone.[37] Johnny Sack beats Donny K as an outlet for his rage at Ralph.[38] The greatest example of such a victim is the bartender Georgie, who fills the role of whipping boy. On four separate occasions, Tony takes out his frustrations from his business and personal life on Georgie. When Livia gives Tony *agita* (agitation), he takes

Georgie's telephone confusion as an excuse to beat him.[39] Georgie innocently brings a Billy Bass into the Bing and when it reminds Tony of his feelings regarding the death of Pussy, he unleashes on Georgie.[40] When Tony is preoccupied with the Family's negative financial growth, he beats Georgie for supposedly wasting ice.[41] In the fifth season, Georgie tries to sympathize with Tony about the fear of terrorism but Tony beats him again, because Tony is frustrated by Janice, Johnny Sack and Christopher.[42] Ralph even takes his internal conflict out on Georgie with a chain, a displacement of his difficulties with the dancer Tracee.[43] Physical violence from displaced anger can even go so far as murder, as it does with Tracee at the hands of Ralph. Tony's murder of Ralph is just as much about his own internal conflict as it is the death of Pie O My.[44] Conflict between Chris and Paulie results in the collateral deaths of JT Dolan and an innocent waiter.[45]

The Sopranos is unique from other entries in the long history of the gangster genre because it presents a more rounded portrait of the internal conflicts involved in the criminal enterprise. Granted many of these characters are psychopaths and sociopaths but they remain human because they are not entirely inconsiderate of doubt and questions of guilt. David Chase's presentation of life in the Family is more realistic because it examines the negative personal side effects of crime rather than simply showing these gangsters live the high life. They rationalize their actions with convoluted logic. Lying is second nature. They make excuses for their problems. They distract themselves from dealing with their unhappiness directly. They use passive aggression as an outlet for their frustrations, and when that fails they erupt in physical violence. The illustration of these symptoms illuminates a dysfunctionality endemic to the world of organized crime. The root of these gangsters' unhappiness is their fear of dealing with the cause of their condition rather than the symptoms. The greatest obstacles on Tony's journey are of his own invention. The words of the Italian mafia boss Annalisa ring true: Tony is his own worst enemy, as is every man.

8

Therapy

David Chase's original idea for *The Sopranos* was a mob boss seeing a psychotherapist about his relationship with his mother. This simple combination of elements opened up many wonderful possibilities for great television. Because of the unique tone imparted to the show by Chase, *The Sopranos* has a therapeutic nature of its own. It presents its viewers with complicated characters and it is not strictly passive entertainment. The audience is compelled to analyze these characters and consider what they think and feel about them. Equipped with those answers, it's then up to each viewer to tailor their own individual diagnosis and self-prescribe accordingly. *The Sopranos* presents characters who are relatable in their human struggle. The audience ends up loving and/or hating Tony because they understand the complicated and frustrating emotional peaks and valleys he endures in searching for his own peace of mind. Viewers are given this forum where they can share their joys and sorrows but also learn how to understand them.

The Talking Cure

The Sopranos acts much like a comedian who generates a physical response of laughter by pointing his finger at contradictions, truths and frustrations of life. This is correlated by Tony's comments in the first episode in which he describes himself as a sad clown.[1] In an alternative function of his Pagliacci identification, Tony makes the audience laugh with his blunt expressions of sorrow and joy. He acknowledges and verbalizes unspoken yet common sentiments. Like the comedian, Tony and other characters provide emotional expressions that the viewers commonly feel but don't know how to voice. These expressions pinpoint certain feelings and ideas which engender affection from an audience that either couldn't put its finger on or was afraid to acknowledge. In one session, Melfi presents to Tony the normality of people secretly wishing for the death of a terminally ill or seriously degraded loved one.[2] She normalizes his feelings, no matter how contradictory, to previously learned thinking. *The Sopranos* does the same normalization for its audience in regards to various internal conflicts and this is part of its therapeutic nature.

One of the public services provided by *The Sopranos* is education of the audience about psychotherapy, which is commonly misunderstood and its validity sometimes questioned. Therapy is subject to skepticism for several reasons. First, psychotherapy deals with mental illness, a phenomenon which is not very well understood and is consequently feared. Mental illness is not a tangible ailment like a broken arm. There are many forms of mental illness and their symptoms are equally diverse. Secondly, psychotherapy is relatively new as a science with concepts that are still debated today. Thirdly, many people don't have an accurate understanding of the practice of psychotherapy. It is something that is conducted in private and only a minority of the population has experienced it firsthand. Tony Soprano, Dr. Melfi and David Chase serve millions of viewers by taking them through the process of psychotherapy vicariously. In doing so, much of the mystery and suspicion are dispelled.

In Tony Soprano's world there are even further problems with therapy. Psychotherapy carries with it an outright stigma in this group of Italian-Americans of north Jersey. Livia Soprano sums up the Family sentiment by telling her grandson that psychiatry is a racket devised by and benefiting Jews.[3] The more practical aspect of *La Cosa Nostra* that disinclines its members from participating in psychotherapy is the imperative of silence. The code of *omertà* demands that Family business not be discussed with outsiders. The whole concept of psychotherapy is to talk out one's deep and complicated inner emotions; it is ill-advised for a made guy to participate in such talk therapy.

There are a significant number of challenges to the proposition of Tony in therapy. Tony decides to see a therapist after losing consciousness in a panic attack. Although Tony is dubious about this assessment, he follows Dr. Cusamano's advice and sees Dr. Melfi. He is able to proceed on the basis that it is treatment for his attack which is a definite, physical symptom. This gives Tony a loophole that allows him to engage in this taboo endeavor. Tony may have concerns about personal issues not directly related to his attack and he sees this as an opportunity to secretly address them. He was under no strict medical direction to consult Melfi but rather it is his own choice and one which would greatly impact the remainder of his life's journey. Coming from a background that stressed personal strength and independence, this must be a very difficult step for him. By seeing Melfi, Tony admits to himself, though not openly to anyone else, that he has problems and he needs help. These two acknowledgments are an example of the evolutionary advancement of Tony's thinking. It is a demonstration of his ability to think outside the Family box.

Dr. Melfi appeals to Tony because of her Italian heritage and because she's a woman. He professes to feel comfortable with someone from a similar background. Tony's choice of a *paisan* has its benefits. Even though Tony represents a complex conundrum with a temper, Melfi demonstrates certain tact about how to approach Tony and his Italian-American machismo. Melfi also appeals to Tony by virtue of her sex. Tony is known to be strongly guided by his libido and, given the option, he prefers a female doctor. Melfi also demonstrates diplomacy regarding Tony's work. For all these reasons, Dr. Melfi is a good match for Tony, who would have a hard time developing a relationship of similar value with anyone else.

The presentation of therapy is largely informed by Chase's personal experience (he himself was a participant in psychotherapy for years).[4] The silences in scenes between Tony and Dr. Melfi are intended to add to the realism. Melfi may act as a guide through certain discussions but she must also let their direction and subject matter be guided by her patient. As they talk, she draws out the pertinent points. It is of critical importance that she be a listener more than a lecturer. Melfi must be able to identify underlying issues and she does this by giving her patient time and space to speak about what's dominating his mind and emotions. Patients frequently do not know how to express causes for their situation. Just as a medical doctor will sift pertinent information from a patient, so does Melfi. When she sees or hears something which indicates that there is more under the surface of a statement, she must take note and encourage Tony to pursue that line of thought. The psychiatrist's greatest tool is broad, leading questions which gently encourage a patient to approach the real issue behind their symptoms. Ultimately, the patient must do the work of complicated and difficult self-examination. The psychotherapist's function is to help them do that work and also share professional insights, opinions and recommendations for understanding their issues.

Some Simple Ground Rules

The psychiatry sessions between Tony and Dr. Melfi inform the audience about this New Jersey mob boss's internal conflicts. Tony opens up to Dr. Melfi like he doesn't with anyone else, not even his wife. As a characterization device, the therapy sessions allow the audience insight into Tony's views on the world that he would not express in any other forum. It is these moments with Melfi that give Tony freedom from distraction to discuss his condition. Tony tries to come to terms with stress, depression, anger, sorrow, guilt and shame and by doing so becomes more in touch with his true identity. The audience is privileged to see discrepancies in his behavior and words in session as opposed to outside. They thus see his contradictions and come to understand his motivations without being told directly. Therapy is a vehicle for the journey of Tony Soprano and the audience's perception of him.

As Tony begins this foreign practice of talking about his feelings for an hour at a time, he must learn the nature of talk therapy. There are some initial hurdles to clear as Tony meets and acclimates himself to Dr. Melfi. Tony seats himself in the chair rather than reclining on the couch, demonstrating his desire to remain in control with the appearance of strength. Tony proceeds to question Melfi about her medical qualifications. At one point he makes a flirtatious comment and Melfi must take this opportunity to define her role to Tony. She knocks down any consideration of romance and asserts herself as a highly skilled and qualified physician who may be able to help him. This puts the two of them on equal ground. It is necessary for Tony to set his braggadocio, machismo, larger-than-life, charismatic demeanor aside if the two of them are going to make any progress.

They also must make accommodation for his unique work situation. It seems likely that Dr. Melfi has some prior knowledge of Tony's mafia affiliation, either from reputation or from Dr. Cusamano. Melfi makes clear that there are doctor-patient confidentiality privileges but in certain situations involving details of impending criminality she is legally and ethically directed to advise the authorities. She adds her own personal disclaimer, though, indicating that is "technically" her obligation. The implication is a clever nudge for Tony to understand that discussion of certain aspects of his life should be subject to a "don't ask, don't tell" policy. This does well to insulate Melfi from criminal conspiracy and Tony from self-incrimination. The drawback is that this occasionally creates a roadblock to psychiatric progress in certain cases where pertinent information is withheld by Tony and his symptoms go undiagnosed because of it.

Part of the stigma of psychotherapy comes from a belief that there is weakness in asking for help. Tony introduces his admiration for Gary Cooper in this context. Strength is equated with silence and this complements his oath of *omertà*. Tony's concept of a real man is one who can handle his problems on his own. Tony initially sees therapy as a place for those who cannot, those who would rather whine and complain. Tony must re-evaluate many of his preconceptions in order to participate successfully in therapy. He is presented with strength and silence on the one hand, accepting help by discussing emotions on the other. Once this hurdle is overcome, Tony opens up a little bit at a time, and Dr. Melfi is able to arrive at a diagnosis of depression.

The next step of acceptance on Tony's part is in regards to medication. In addition to twice-weekly therapy sessions, Melfi prescribes Prozac to Tony. This touches on his skepticism of psychiatry and the notion that it is strictly a racket to take money from the pockets of those willing to be victims and suckers. Despite his doubts, Tony is shown to take his medication, sometimes eagerly. This implies that he has been maintaining an outward condemnation of pharmacology while secretly hoping it will work. Based on his initial habits it appears that Tony hopes the Prozac will be a quick and easy cure for his depression. Melfi informs him that there is no simple solution in pill form but the Prozac is merely a part of the larger therapeutic process. The talk therapy, not the Prozac, is what has given him some success in mood and outlook. Tony is dismayed at the work involved in therapy.

The first realization which solidifies for Tony the merit of therapy revolves around the ducks who live in Tony's pool, then fly away. When Melfi prods him to examine why the ducks were so important to him, the emotions that Tony has bottled up come out. For the first time Tony cries on screen, a scene in which James Gandolfini masterfully creates a convincing and sympathetic man in emotional pain. He professes that his loss of the ducks tapped into feelings he has been harboring about his family and a fear of losing them.[5] That Melfi has led him to something meaningful convinces him of therapy's value. This is not to say that all of his doubts are put to rest. He clearly maintains skepticism about certain aspects of psychiatry. At times he ridicules and at others he expresses genuine frustration. As Tony continues his therapy, Melfi teaches him about theories of the subconscious mind. He is initially doubtful about the validity of such theories but he eventually begins to see truth in them. When there are no forthcoming breakthroughs on par with the ducks, he considers abandoning therapy. What convinces him to stay is his ability to find in session an unorthodox solution to a major business problem with his Uncle Junior.[6] Tony begins to look at therapy as a mafia strategy brainstorming session.

As Tony proceeds, his mother Livia becomes a frequent topic of discussion. Initially, Tony expresses frustration regarding Livia's stubbornness about living in a retirement community-nursing home. It soon becomes apparent to Dr. Melfi that Livia is the source of more problems than Tony lets on. Tony initially demurs at Melfi's direction to explore his feelings about his mother, dismissing her suggestion as a Freudian misadventure. The limits of Tony's higher education are expressed in his reduction of psychiatry to the concept of the Oedipal complex. He finds this proposition repulsive and ridiculous. He denies any merit to the possibility that he has complicated emotions wrapped up in Livia. Tony's emotions boil and when Melfi suggests that Livia may have conspired against his life, Tony explodes in anger. He violently smashes her glass table and looms threateningly, an inch from her face. Again, Gandolfini's performance causes the audience to recoil in fear as if Tony Soprano might next leap through their television screen and be in their own face. Next, Tony is forced to accept Livia's fault in his emotional condition when Agent Cubitoso plays for Tony tape recordings of her and Junior conspiring.[7] From that point, Tony's depression takes on a new form stemming from his confrontation with hard evidence that his mother does not love him. The depth of his emotion is a source of shame for Tony. That this one woman's love of him, or lack thereof, affects him so deeply makes Tony feel weak and this contributes to his unwillingness to speak about her.

Understanding Livia's impact on Tony is the arc of the first season's therapy. What follows is Tony trying to find a way to accept and live with this understanding. Tony wishes to put her out of his mind and into the past. He expresses this with the flippant dismissal that she is dead to him. Melfi, however, refuses to allow Tony to close off that part of his life because she (Melfi) is trained to recognize that many of Tony's internal conflicts and much of his negative behavior stem from Livia. Regardless of the fact that Tony now recognizes her toxicity and will not allow any further contact, there is a tangle of anger, resentment and guilt which have been with him from his childhood. Here is another psychiatric concept of which Tony is initially skeptical: that events from childhood shape his experience of the present. Therapy gives Tony the opportunity to discuss childhood experiences which he has repressed or the significance of which he has dismissed. Livia's threat to stick a fork in Tony's eye had been accepted by him as normal. Melfi forces him to re-evaluate. Tony likewise has repressed feelings of terror at overhearing Livia's willingness to smother her own children rather than move to Reno.[8] When Livia finally dies, Tony poses the suggestion that because of her death there would no longer be any need of therapy. Though Tony throws out this bait to see if he might get a bite, Melfi reasserts that Livia's physical absence does not erase her internal presence in Tony.[9] Therapy continues and even though Livia fades to the background of Tony's existence she remains indelibly present in his experience of the world.

Talkin' Helps

Tony's acceptance of the value of therapy is seen in his interactions with his associates. He becomes more understanding of the emotional struggles of others and at times he is able to be a skilled listener and counselor. When Artie is distraught about the loss of his restaurant, Tony is considerate of his feelings.[10] When Christopher exhibits *ennui* at life, Tony cautiously questions him to determine if he is depressed. He even goes so far as to boldly, though with the utmost concern, ask Chris if he ever considers suicide.[11] This is an excellent example of how Tony begins to imitate some of Dr. Melfi's behavior in a positive way.

Tony employs this practice to suit his own needs as well. When his Russian business associate Slava mourns the decline of his best friend, Tony sensitively sympathizes with him but does so with the ulterior motive of gaining information.[12] When Johnny Sack's rage causes business problems, Tony skillfully navigates to a peace by listening with empathy.[13] Tony learns how to be an amateur therapist to others. Likewise *The Sopranos* has the effect of slowly teaching its audience to emulate the role of therapists. In the aftermath of a new episode, fans would ask each other "What did you think about what happened to Tony?" or "Why did Tony do that?" The act of trying to understand all the nuances of the show subtly imitates the psychotherapeutic process. As the audience learns about the human subconscious and emotional dynamics of the *Sopranos* characters, they are able to apply these concepts to their own lives.

One of the themes presented in the second season is Tony as his own worst enemy; the obstacles to his growth are self-imposed. His limitations are internal, not external. This is evident in his chronic reticence to cooperate with Dr. Melfi. Despite his oft-repeated directive to focus on the bigger picture, Tony has great difficulty applying this in practice to his own personal growth. He avoids the larger issues, preferring to focus on the symptoms rather than the root causes. His slow pace of development comes from his unwillingness to tackle the real problems, his own inherent roadblocks. Tony drags his feet on his therapeutic journey.

An example of Tony's avoidance of root problems takes place in season five as he comes to terms with his relationship to his cousin Tony Blundetto. It takes months of therapy for Tony to confess to Melfi the true circumstances of his relationship with Tony B. For seventeen years Tony was alone with a load of remorse for his absence from the heist that sent Tony B to jail. He bottled up intense feelings of guilt about his own freedom and shame about his panic attacks and subsequent cover-up. Upon Tony B.'s release from prison, Tony gives him exceptionally favorable treatment. Despite the unauthorized hit on Joe Peeps of the New York family, Tony gives Tony B. a lucrative casino operation. Tony credits this delegation to business acumen. However, when he finally unloads the weight of guilt in therapy, he is dismayed by the realization that his actions were a subconscious attempt to make reparations, to buy forgiveness.[14]

Tony expresses great apprehension that his actions were subliminally directed by his emotions and feelings. This weighty realization gives him critical insight into human nature. It demonstrate the importance of doing the hard work of self-understanding in therapy. Tony's internal obstacles impede progress. He avoids such difficult work because he senses the inherent pain that accompanies such realizations. It is pain not only in exorcising his demons but pain at the realization that he is less of a man than he strives to be. Tony's anxiety begrudgingly acknowledges the reality that everyone is equally in the thrall of emotions from their personal histories. Such pivotal moments as his cousin's arrest shape Tony regardless of how much he distances himself, no matter how much time elapses. In minimizing the importance of such moments he exhibits symptoms such as stress, violence or panic attacks. In *The Sopranos* there are many portraits of individuals whose conduct is the result of their inability or unwillingness to look at themselves in the mirror: Christopher's drug addiction; Carmela's worry and denial of criminal responsibility; Junior's isolationism. These are behaviors which, if not examined, will trap them in a negative cycle from which there is no escape. The only way out is for them to deal with the behaviors and causes head-on. It is necessary for all of them to confront that which challenges them and embrace that which strengthens them.

One of the great obstacles to Tony's improved mental health is his unwillingness or inability to be entirely forthcoming with the details of his life. Because of the business he's in, he cannot give Melfi specifics regarding the deaths of Pussy, Tracee, Jackie Jr., Ralph, Adriana, Tony Blundetto or Christopher. He keeps this information from her out of moral and legal considerations. These passages in his life impact his mental and emotional state dramatically but he must keep them closed off from Melfi to avoid admission of first degree murder and making her an accessory. This presents a huge challenge in Melfi's treatment of Tony. She is never given the full picture. If she were privy to the particulars of Tony's business and the extreme emotional impact it has on him, she would be infinitely better equipped to treat him. Tony's code of conduct with Melfi is equivalent to consulting a physician regarding back pain and withholding the detail that he fell out of a window. Just like a poker player, Tony has certain "tells" when he withholds information. Tony's many tells take shape physically and verbally. Physical red flags are fidgeting, a forehead scratch, avoidance of eye contact, squinting or an out-of-place smile. Verbally, Tony tries to deflect uncomfortable topics with doubletalk, changing the subject, intentionally misinterpreting a question, jokes, laughter or silence. These are all common indications of avoidance for one reason or another. Tony's frustration with the lack of progress is directed at Melfi but it is his own doing, or more accurately it's the unique situation he's in. He expresses as much when he tells Silvio that, in the end, he's completely alone with the responsibility of being boss. There is no one to whom Tony can be 100 percent honest, rarely even himself.

Tony frequently uses therapy sessions as opportunities to re-write the facts of a situation with the purpose of establishing his fiction as reality to others. It also works to convince him to accept more palatable interpretations as the truth. This only takes on the surface of Tony's mind, though. Every time he makes a decision (whether conscious or subconscious) to put his own selfishly motivated spin on a situation, it adds to his own self-loathing and guilt. For one, he is adding to the external quotient of sorrow by propagating lies. Secondly, he does not deal with the issues internally either. Rather than hashing out his complex emotions, he ignores them, unwilling to endure the immense discomfort involved. Hawthorne's quote rears its head again as Tony consistently wears one face to Melfi and another to himself and he becomes increasingly confused as to his own identity.

Perhaps the greatest single breakthrough Tony and Melfi experience takes place in the weeks immediately following the death of Livia: the discovery of a connection between Tony's panic attacks and meat. As a result of renewed effort from Tony, the audience is given a revelation that has been buried in his memory, kept from scrutiny for years. The story of his father cutting off Mr. Satriale's finger ties so many of Tony's symptoms together — Tony's feelings toward his mother, his father, sex, work, violence, gambling, manhood, familial responsibility and meat. When Tony reveals that this episode of his youth ended with his first panic attack, so many pieces of the puzzle that is Tony snap into place. Melfi gets great insight and can approach Tony's treatment with more precision once she understands this root of his attacks, which brought him to therapy in the first place. Tony is less convinced of the value of sharing this memory and on more than one occasion downplays the importance of the incident. Melfi tries to encourage Tony with the understanding that this is what progress looks like and such self-knowledge will make him less vulnerable to further attacks. Even still, Tony does not qualify this as a practical application but more of something he got off his chest, relieving him of another secret.

Unloved or Unlovable?

One of the greatest impediments to Tony's peace of mind is his need of approval and assurances to allay insecurities he's had since childhood. In spite of Tony's success, intelligence and family, he lives with the fear that he is unlovable. This fear originates from his relationship with his parents, especially Livia, who was simply incapable of experiencing and giving love. From the beginning of the series Tony attempts to please his implacable mother. His visits, considerate gifts and provision for living in a retirement community are all met with her scorn. Such behavior from his mother causes him to doubt his worth. So strong is Livia's impact on Tony's insecurity that by season three he begins to rewrite history regarding his mother's conspiracy with his Uncle Junior to have Tony whacked, excusing her from any wrongdoing.[15] Given enough time, Tony reverses his attitude from condemnation to rationalized defense.

The love Tony didn't get from Livia he seeks elsewhere. With both his parents dead and gone, the focus of his unfulfilled need for affection and approval has been Tony's Uncle Junior. Junior is a father figure to Tony, characteristically similar to Livia, and is the last living family member of that generation — the strongest tangible connection to Tony's parents and an idealized past. This confluence of factors has led Tony to rely on that family bond in the belief that it would redeem him to the ghosts of Johnny and Livia. After Junior's attempt on Tony's life in season one, Tony rejoins an active relationship with his uncle. This is partly demanded by circumstances of business but not without personal motivation of the desire for a parental connection. Their tenuous relationship endures uneventfully until season five when Tony rankles under Junior's repeated chiding comments that Tony never had the makings of a varsity athlete. Tony's reaction is frustration and anger but he tempers this when Junior is tentatively diagnosed with Alzheimer's Disease. In a heart-wrenching scene he asks Junior why his symptomatic ramblings can't be positive rather than critical. Tony ultimately puts himself on the line by asking Junior if he loves him. With tears welling in his eyes, Junior says nothing. His ambiguous silence does nothing to dispel Tony's personal insecurities and need for validation.[16]

Regardless of Junior's diagnosis and emotional ambiguity towards his nephew, Tony pities Junior for his defeat at the hands of a genetic fate, having his autonomy and control stripped from him by dementia. It is truly sad to watch the disintegration of Junior over the course of the series. Much credit goes to Dominic Chianese's brilliant performance as well as the insightful writers and directors who helped create his story. Despite all the trials, literal and figurative, Tony does not abandon his uncle. Out of a sense of family loyalty, Tony sticks by Junior and at the beginning of season six has developed his role into that of a caregiver to his uncle. This is due partly to Bobby and Janice vacating that role to focus on their own family but is also the result of Tony's guilt, self-loathing and sense of familial obligation which stem from his relationship with his mother and father. Melfi directly confronts Tony on this point. She stresses that his self-imposed obstacle is his preference to believe that his mother and uncle were justified in their attempt on his life instead of accepting that Livia didn't value him.[17] Early in therapy Melfi assesses Livia as a borderline personality, consequently incapable of giving love or affection. Tony has been unable to accept Livia's condition as separate from himself; he blames himself for her issues. He is continually trying change that which cannot be changed, to quixotically right the un-rightable wrong. So great is his need to maintain the image of the honorable, immaculate matron that he would engage in self-abusive, self-destructive behavior to maintain the facade.

A simplified summary of Tony's internal process would show that the experience of not being loved by his mother led him to the conclusion that he's a bad person. Then, in an attempt to reconcile the need to validate himself and fulfill the expectation of honoring his mother, he acts in accordance with the premise that he is bad — thus being a gangster. With some regularity Tony explodes with rage when faced with painful truths in his sessions with Dr. Melfi. At other times he is at a loss for words when the significance of her words penetrate him with immediacy. Tony has no response to Melfi's assessment of his behavior regarding his uncle. His silent consideration indicates the truth in her diagnosis and is a sign of Tony's development of self-awareness. Tony comes to terms with Melfi's evaluation and expresses it succinctly to Carmela, saying that his efforts with Junior were an attempt to prove his worth and redeem himself. Tony did for Junior what he did for his mother — going well beyond what most people would consider a reasonable fulfillment of responsibility in an attempt to earn their love. What Tony takes a long time to understand is the dysfunctionality of *earning* his mother's love rather than receiving it unconditionally; this is precluded by her borderline personality. Tony is trying to get blood from a stone. Rather than accept that Livia was incapable of giving him love, Tony finds it less painful to believe that he is incapable of being loved.

Tony's need of validation from his mother leads to broad need for approval to counteract feelings of remorse for his own behavior and its consequences. This applies to other relationships in his life as well. Tony feels guilt for his ex-*goomah* Gloria's suicide, misplacing blame on himself. As a way to obtain commendation and praise he satisfies the material desires of the important people in his life: for Carmela he agrees to start a trust fund; he treats his sister Janice to an indulgent meal; he lends Artie $50,000 for a questionable business enterprise.[18] Flying in the face of his own better business judgment Tony is compelled to seek reassurance to dispel his insecurity that he is unlovable, at heart a toxic person. Tony's ability to grow beyond this insecurity is stunted because his attempt to buy the love of his peers actually works. Tony's stock rises in the opinions of Carmela, Janice, Artie and almost anyone else he uses in this way. This behavior merely provides temporary relief from his insecurities. Only in the sixth season, after the coma, does Tony better understand his feelings toward his parents. As he breaks from the past, Tony begins to have a sense of self-esteem independent of his mother, father and Junior.

Another way in which Tony deals with his own issues of self-worth relates more directly to his work. When doing business with a Hasid, Tony is accused of being a golem, the equivalent of Frankenstein's monster. Tony is concerned by this indictment because it connects to his feelings of insecurity, guilt and worthlessness. In session with Dr. Melfi he considers his identification with such a monster.[19] The monster is a thing, not human. It is undead, assembled from corpses and reanimated without emotion. It destroys those around it. Tony fears the possibility that he is inherently destructive. At various times he verbalizes fears that he may be a toxic person like Livia. Like Frankenstein's monster, Tony has anger for being created as something unnatural. With the excuse of being born into the Family, Tony must often deprioritize human compassion in order to live by the rules of business. This does not mean that he is unfeeling but his work demands that those feelings be put aside for the sake of the business. Nevertheless, Tony feels guilt for his actions and he correlates it to an inability to be loved. Just like a soldier in war, Tony believes himself capable of de-activating his intense emotions to do what has to be done for the Family. More accurately, he is not de-activating these emotions but suppressing them. His therapy sessions force him to deal with this condition. They are a means of changing his perception of himself as a monster to a more accurate understanding of his human nature.

In the second season, Dr. Melfi takes a more direct approach in forcing Tony to consider an alternative perspective on his nature and behavior. She describes to him a psychological condition called Alexithymia, whose sufferers crave constant action in order to avoid acknowledging their antisocial behaviors. (There are some artistic liberties taken in the characterization of the real condition of Alexithymia.) She opens the door to this concept by asking Tony if he knows why a shark has to keep moving to which he responds that they have to move to breathe.[20] The image of a shark is appropriate to Tony. He is a natural predator. He smells blood and his instincts take over. Sharks have to keep moving or they can't breathe. Sound like a symptom of the panic attacks of a certain mob boss? The shark is unique in the ocean kingdom. It is in a league of its own; cut from a different cloth; the boss of the ocean; godfather of the seas; a species more powerful than those that surround it. Both the shark and Tony are peerless in their worlds.

Apart from the latent correlations between Tony and the shark, the concepts of emptiness and self-loathing strike a chord with him. He is forced to consider the possibility that he could be such a person. What appears to hurt and scare Tony the most is the characterization of an Alexithymic's personality as antisocial — one whose acts are abhorrent, destructive, immoral. It pains him to consider that this may be his true identity. This feeds his self-bewildering crutch of predeterminism, the overriding power of genetics and the Frankenstein proposition. Tony's hopelessness is fed by the thought that his genes have been the drivers of his behaviors, fate guides him and destiny waits for him no matter what he does to direct his life.

Tony is antisocial in the sense that he disregards societal laws. His crimes compromise the happiness and even the lives of others. The codes that Tony follows are not those of common society but those of a criminal sub-culture. From childhood he would have felt that his options were few if he wanted to survive in his Family. Darwinism expresses itself in his animal will to simply survive, both physically and emotionally. This principle has guided Tony to where he is today and it is so ingrained in him that it is second nature. Artie identifies this trait very accurately in season four when he points out Tony's ability to instinctively sense opportunity and take advantage of it the way a hawk sees a mouse, then pounces.[21] Artie's characterization of Tony's nature as subconsciously predatory, even when it comes to his friends, has the same impact on Tony as the shark analogy: He doesn't like the thought. These assessments scare Tony because they further convince him of his lack of control and his poor grasp of his own identity. As Tony struggles to embrace his free will, these observations present obstacles to his progress. He is conflicted, one day preaching self-determinism to Silvio and the next quoting Popeye's "I yam what I yam" to Carmela.[22] It's not just about the choices he makes, because there are some things over which he genuinely has no control. It's not a question of choosing to be a gangster. It may be more accurate to say that's simply what he *is*. Just as a leopard cannot change its spots, this is Tony Soprano. This is at the heart of Tony's struggle — his understanding and acceptance of his true identity.

A larger theme is people's internal division, self-deceit and compartmentalization of their lives as a function of survival.[23] All this disjointedness and rationalization is unhealthy and the parts need to be integrated, united into a whole. Tony's quest for peace of mind is a struggle with that internal unification. The underlying question is whether the struggle is a therapeutic process to eliminate his antisocial behavior or an unhealthy obsession over the belief that he should be something he is not. It's possible that conforming to societal standards would cost him his identity rather than free it, and his animal instinct for survival is the only thing keeping him from self-destruction.

Hope Comes in Many Forms

Tony's progress toward defining his own identity is of his own determination. What he tends to ignore is that he can only get from therapy what he puts into it. But Tony's tendency is to avoid the difficult and painful work required to make valuable, lasting changes. Not every session can be a personal breakthrough or contribute to his business strategy and the therapy reaches a plateau. Tony grows impatient and periodically reaches a point of disaffection for the therapeutic process, wanting to call it quits because of the apparent absence of concrete results. Dr. Melfi tries to convince Tony that continuation of therapy is worthwhile. She believes that once the large burdens are lifted, he can work on addressing the smaller ones which continue to cause him unhappiness. Tony counters that unhappiness is simply part of life and that therapy is not yielding any further meaningful progress. Tony quits therapy and later returns when new complications arise in his life. However, the sessions are often used as an opportunity for him to vent stress rather than pro-actively deal with issues. There are some significant moments after the therapy plateaus but the greatest accomplishment is Tony's own education about his internal processes. By engaging in therapy for so many years he is able to independently apply its concepts to his life. This is not to say that Tony is relieved of all internal conflicts and external symptoms but he is much better equipped to handle them.

New perspective is given on psychotherapy in the depiction of other characters' therapy. Janice regularly consults a therapist named Sandy. Their relationship is quite different from that of Tony and Melfi. Janice's therapist's office is her home. This more casual environment seems to facilitate a warmth and discourse that more closely approximates a sisterly relationship.[24] Janice also briefly participates in group therapy for anger management.[25] Christopher also finds support in a form of group therapy, his participation in Alcoholics Anonymous. AA is a place where Chris can vent his frustrations but also learn about addiction and ways of coping by listening to others.

Carmela has her own experiences with therapy. For a while she seeks therapy in Fr. Phil, a function he's also seen to serve in his interaction with Artie. Carmela joins Tony for a few sessions with Melfi but this is focused on Tony, not her. When Carmela consults an associate of Melfi's, Carmela finds a distaste for the experience. Dr. Krakower is blunt in his assessment, advising Carmela to take the children and leave Tony's criminal world if she wants to escape moral culpability.[26] This therapy session causes Carmela to re-evaluate her role in Tony's crime and also her dependence on it. When she speaks with another priest, Fr. Obosi, she finds a reprieve in his recommendation to make the marriage work and avoid guilt by living only on Tony's legitimate earnings.[27] She once again consults Melfi while Tony is in a coma and her demeanor in this situation imitates her past experiences with Catholic confession.[28]

The Soprano children each encounter therapy as well. Tony and Carmela consider Meadow's therapy a total failure when Dr. Kobler supports Meadow's inclination to go to Europe.[29] After AJ's break up with Blanca, his dour mood forces Tony and Carmela to get him help. AJ's sessions provide insight into his growing depression and his own issues with violence and his sense of hopelessness about the future.[30] All of these presentations serve to round out the audience's perception of what therapy can be. Although Dr. Melfi is the most prominent practitioner, a psychotherapist, *The Sopranos* also shows that therapy comes in many forms and different people can have very different experiences of it.

The most notable alternative presentation of therapy is with Dr. Melfi as a patient seeing psychiatrist Dr. Elliot Kupferburg. Tony is surprised to learn that his own therapist seeks therapy for herself. Tony is concerned that the authority figure with the supposed power to "cure" him may not be mentally healthy herself. His reaction comes from his still relatively narrow understanding of what psychotherapy and mental health truly are. The presentation of Melfi's therapy sessions shows an experience entirely different from Tony's. There is no obstacle in fundamental understanding of the science of psychotherapy. Melfi and Kupferburg are able to participate in discourse with a foundation in mutual understanding and respect. Although Melfi's sessions are more of a device to delve into her character, her behavior indicates her expectations of patient conduct and commitment. Kupferburg provides a different approach of a therapist as well. In discussing Tony's reticence in discussing emotions he offers the interesting insight that the concept of *omertà*, with which Tony lives, comes from a pre-therapeutic culture.[31] In Melfi's discussions of her conflicted feelings about treating a patient in the mafia, the audience learns more about their own feelings of fascination and repulsion toward Tony Soprano. Kupferburg suggests the simile of her treatment of Tony to rollercoasters and scary movies.[32] They give a vicarious thrill which Melfi secretly may enjoy. Such a realization calls into question her motives in seeing Tony. Is she an enabler by treating to him? Does her don't-ask-don't-tell arrangement with Tony indicate a tacit endorsement of Tony's criminal activity? Is she trying to help him or is she trying to feed a personal desire for excitement? This correlates strongly to the audience experience. For eight years they looked forward to Sunday nights of being shocked and reviled, hoping somebody gets whacked. *The Sopranos* indirectly, though very intentionally, suggest these same questions about morality and motivation to the audience. By this power of suggestion, these questions are triggered within the viewer and not directly prompted by any character on screen. The self-examination is much more personal and powerful as a result. Melfi or Kupferburg would prefer to guide their patients to such a consideration rather than directly asking the question. If Melfi or Elliot were to ask such a pointed and bald-faced question, it would be dismissed as a judgment, an accusation and a criticism which natural human emotional defenses would discredit and disregard. Psychotherapy leads patients to ask the questions themselves and in the same way David Chase and company lead their audience to the same questions and perhaps some insight and understanding.

Melfi's sessions go on to cover her own bout with alcohol abuse, frustration with patients, concern over her son and most importantly her feelings following her traumatic rape. In the aftermath of the rape, Melfi considers the temptation of calling upon Tony to exact revenge on her assailant who slipped through the fingers of the justice system. This is elicited by dream interpretation, with Elliot's assistance, and it tantalizes the audience by appealing to their sense of justice and sympathy for Melfi as an innocent victim of a horrible crime. The result is a rising of bloodlust for Melfi to follow through on this vengeful ideation. When she remains silent at Tony's offer of help, there was much discussion about the disappointment at the inaction.[33] This point forces a thoughtful audience to consider their own feelings about justice and revenge. Although there would be satisfaction in the exaction of a painful wrath delivered upon Melfi's attacker, to do so would be making a deal with the devil and result in entanglement in the moral relativism she fears. Melfi would become indebted to Tony. Her principles would be compromised, creating a self-destructive scenario. Melfi demonstrates her moral fiber and great personal strength in abstention from soliciting Tony for a vendetta.

Kupferburg, too, shows a vicarious interest in Tony when he occasionally questions Melfi about her mob boss patient. When she is going through a difficult personal bout with alcohol and despondency, she shares with Kupferburg the suggestion that seeing Tony may be therapeutic for her. Kupferburg points out the nature of this excuse by reminding her that her sessions with Tony are intended for *Tony's* benefit.[34] It is imperative that she approach each patient for their own well-being, not hers. After her rape, Melfi also briefly considers Tony as a potential protector. When he seems open to an earlier suggestion of moving on to a behavioral therapist, she quickly discourages it with a hint of fear at losing him. Melfi considers the possibility that she has been conned by a sociopath, falling for Tony's lies and charmed by his subterfuge. Her concerns about this are not as much about Tony as they are about insuring her own integrity in her work, about which she feels passionately.

Is This All There Is?

The conclusion of the therapy between Dr. Melfi and Tony comes unexpectedly. Somewhat surprisingly, this turn of events occurs outside of Tony's control. Instead it is determined by the actions of Melfi and Kupferburg. In evaluating the termination of the seven-year relationship, the actions of the two psychotherapists must be considered independently.

Kupferburg shares with Melfi a professional study that concludes psychotherapy is ineffective for sociopaths. In addition, the study's findings indicate that sociopaths hone their criminal skills on their therapists. Melfi considers this suggestion but when she is not overtly receptive, Kupferburg chooses to push the issue. In an act of extreme unprofessionalism, Kupferburg apparently drafts two female accomplices to confront Melfi with the same ideas in the context of a dinner party. Kupferburg claims that those who engage in the therapy of sociopaths delude themselves with a fantasy that they can cure the criminal. Kupferburg then violates all ethical considerations when he reveals Tony's identity to the entire dinner party. He defends his breach of confidentiality with the argument that they are among professionals but his actions clearly exclude him from such classification.[35] Kupferburg's motivations are vague. He makes the dinner party into an intervention with the intention of convincing Melfi to give up what he judges to be a potentially self-destructive endeavor. He cites consideration for moral and legal consequences. It's possible he feels genuine concern for Melfi and acts with intentions of protecting her as a patient or a friend. Nevertheless, he exhibits overbearing condescension and disrespect by forcing her hand with this inexcusable professional and ethical transgression.

Although blindsided by Kupferburg's maneuver, Melfi is able to point out that the diagnosis of her patient as a sociopath is debatable. Once she's distanced herself from the dinner party intervention, Melfi must consider a number of variables in determining her course of action. First, the moral and legal repercussions take shape as a result of Kupferburg's disclosure. The fact that it is now public knowledge that she treats the mob boss of New Jersey creates new risk for Tony and for herself. Melfi also deals with guilt for accidentally revealing Tony's name to Kupferburg in the first place, years before. She reads the psychiatric report at the center of Kupferburg's crusade. Melfi is disturbed when it rings true with citations of sociopathic sentimentality for babies and pets. She is concerned by the proposition that her work may have been perverted into a criminal enterprise used to validate Tony's heinous acts (a parallel of which is seen in

AJ's use of excuses learned from therapy). Melfi feels more guilt at not recognizing some of Tony's symptomatic behaviors and the thought of herself as a criminal enabler.

Melfi approaches her next session with Tony knowing it will be their last. The writing and direction of the last therapy scene is overtly slanted to imply Tony seeking sympathy with crocodile tears. This can be interpreted as Melfi's newly biased perception or freedom from Tony's subterfuge. Once her intentions become clear to Tony, she informs him that she is acting upon her considered medical opinion. She tells Tony that she doesn't think she can help Tony therapeutically. On these statements alone, her decision seems reasonable. Her manner and tone, though, are less than professional. Tony accuses her of medical immorality. It is a painful, ugly break-up laced with judgment and regret. Considering AJ's recent suicide attempt, the timing is poor. However, these do not invalidate her professional assessment.

There is another layer to this turn of events, entirely separate from the ugliness of Kupferburg and the last session. Throughout the sixth season the conclusion of Tony's therapy is foreshadowed. Both Tony and Melfi make comments which indicate that each of them has gone as far as they can go and learned as much as they can in this undertaking. When discussing Christopher and *Cleaver*, Tony demonstrates that he has attained significant understanding of the human subconscious.[36] She later confronts Tony about the frequency of his absences. She is concerned that their sessions no longer serve to further his growth but are instead merely a vacation for him from his weekly stress. She puts to him the task of re-evaluating his commitment, to decide if he truly wants to continue therapy with her.[37] Tony accepts this task and after serious consideration he intends to end it once and for all. However, AJ's suicidal ideation puts this plan on hold. Tony then admits his proclivity for depression but tells Melfi that he is capable of handling it on his own. She acknowledges, with some pride in accomplishment, that Tony genuinely does understand depression. He despondently asks Melfi if there is nothing more to therapy than this pattern with which he has become so tiringly familiar.[38]

The greatest comment on Tony and Melfi's relationship comes as a consequence of Tony's peyote trip. He shares with her the idea that mothers are like buses and people's problems come from their fruitless attempt to get back on the bus rather than allowing it to continue on its journey. Melfi recognizes this as quite insightful.[39] It puts many of Tony's mother issues in a manageable perspective and provides behavioral guidelines. It is a milestone that Tony came to this realization himself, entirely independent of Melfi. What's even more compelling is that this analogy not only applies to Tony's relationship with Livia but his relationship with Melfi. By Melfi's own assessment, Tony has, in the past, made his therapist out to be all the things missing in his mother.[40] Therefore, she plays the role of Tony's bus. When Tony embarked on therapy, she took him places he hadn't been before, out from under the pall of his complicated and painful past. Once Tony's greatest obstacles are understood and overcome, the therapy plateaus. This is analogous to Tony trying to get back on the bus, to recreate the initial breakthroughs Melfi provided with therapy. Tony's peyote-induced revelation in the Nevada desert helps him understand that there comes a time when he has to get off the bus and continue on his journey. Melfi's breakthrough was that, like a mother to her patient, there comes a time to let one's child go. It's painful but it's necessary for the child to have a life of his own. Melfi and psychotherapy did wonderful things for Tony over seven years. Her greatest gift is his ability to independently understand his internal conflicts and how to pursue his happiness. Dr. Melfi teaches Tony to fly just like the ducks which brought him to her in the first place.

9

Art Imitating New Jersey

The richness of detail in Tony Soprano's world is the result of a talented and dedicated creative team of writers, directors, actors and crew members. Their attention to detail requires innumerable artistic decisions inspired by the characters and the story. The ideas of *The Sopranos* are primarily communicated through the characters' words and behavior. Their stories are punctuated and enhanced by a variety of recurring motifs. Symbolism, directorial touches, metaphor and unique storytelling compliment and reinforce the themes of the show. These details transcend simple window dressing and become an integral contribution to the fabric of the *Sopranos* universe. By identifying such details and patterns in their presentation one can better The Big Picture.

Symbolic Motifs

Symbolism is a traditional artistic device used to enrich the tapestry of the work and communicate concepts nonverbally. It has the wonderful quality of allowing for diverse interpretation. Everywhere in *The Sopranos* there are recurring motifs which add extra layers of realism and meaning. The purpose of this section is not to dictate meanings but to point out some consistently represented images and allow the reader to draw their own conclusions.

Throughout the series, animals have been presented in various contexts and with different connotations. Tony's love of pets is based on their innocence in contrast to his often ugly world. Of course the most significant animal in the series are the ducks which are central to Tony's first modern-day panic attack. Tony is sentimental about the ducks. They start out as a hobby but become his passion. He feeds them, he builds them a ramp, he talks to them and he reads books about them. He tries to share this new joy with his family but they do not have his enthusiasm. Tony's first panic attack occurs when he sees the baby ducks take flight for the first time. He later dreams of a duck flying off with his penis, a castration, and in dialoging with Melfi about this dream he comes to the realization that his anxiety about the ducks' departure is actually derived from his fear of losing his family.[1] This explanation concretely establishes the device of symbolism in the firmament of *The Sopranos*. This primary interpretation of ducks provides a foundation for numerous additional instances of duck details. In the moment after Tony kills Febby Petrullio, his attention is caught by a flock of ducks flying overhead, their calls echoing in the New England woods.[2] In season two Melfi recalls the ducks with a simile, pointing out that Tony imparting difficult lessons to his children is like teaching them to fly, allowing them to leave the nest.[3] In assessing Livia as a mother, Carmela describes her as a "peculiar duck."[4] Tony's lawyer helps him by getting their "ducks in a row."[5] Tony hides money in bushels of duck food.[6] Junior feels sorry for a neighborhood boy because his shoes are held together by duct tape, pronounced "duck" tape.[7] Adriana recalls Tony's ducks as she and Agent Sanseverino walk along a river parkway.[8] Carmela adventurously orders roast duck on a date with Wegler and Tony comments on her out-of-character choice as he eyes the leftovers in the refrigerator.[9] As Tony's opinion of Fran Fellstein drops, she serves him water chestnuts with a duck sauce.[10] Paulie destroys Chris's duck lawn ornament with his car.[11] At Bobby and Janice's lake house, little Domenica and her nanny sing a nursery rhyme about a family of ducks who, one by one, become lost in the wild and later, as Tony broods, a duck noticeably flies past him while he ignores it.[12]

    Some animal motifs plays a smaller role. Rats are a constant point of reference when discussing betrayal of loyalty. The common term for anyone who cooperates with the Federal government is "rat." When someone spills someone else's secret, they are said to be "ratting out" that person. Pussy, Eugene, Ray, Carlo, Jimmy Petrile, even Adriana are all rats. In a classic message job, Chris and Silvio leave Jimmy Altieri's body with a dead rat stuffed into his mouth.[13] Dogs often make an appearance: Tony is sentimental about his childhood dog Tippy[14]; a young Janice fed Tony a Milk Bone[15]; while stoned on heroin, Chris accidentally sits on Adriana's beloved Cosette with fatal results[16]; Angie Bonpensiero seeks money from the Sopranos to pay for her sick dog's veterinary bills[17]; Melfi has a dream in which Tony is represented by a Rottweiler.[18] Dogs are shown to bark at: Tony as he spies on the rat Febby Petrullio[19]; Mikey Palmice as he departs on his last jog[20]; Silvio as he whacks Burt Gervasi[21]; Tony as he gets intimately acquainted with Dick Barone's secretary.[22]

Pigs have a special place in the Soprano menagerie. Individuals who are greedy, crass or selfish are referred to as pigs. Of course there is the centrality of the pork store, Satriale's. Bears take on significance in the fifth season when a wild black bear stalks the Soprano estate.[23] A stuffed animal bear is present in Tony's coma experience, delivering the message that his elevator is out of order.[24]

Horses are frequently used throughout the series. Tony's love of animals shines on Pie O My. He shows genuine, childlike affection in caring for Pie and remembers her as a beautiful and innocent creature. In his world of theft, murder, vice and general ugliness, Pie O My is a rare thing of grace, untainted by the dreadfulness with which Tony lives. There are moments when Pie O My is drawn in close proximity to women in Tony's life. In a dream, Carmela tells Tony he can't have his horse/whores in the house.[25] Just as Carmela holds anger and resentment over Tony's *goomahs* she is initially outraged at him having yet another female in his life, albeit an equine. When Tony mentions Pie to Ralphie, Ralph responds with a commentary about Tony's good fortune in having Carmela in his life.[26] Ralph feels cheated by the woman with whom he was saddled (please pardon the pun). In the days before Tracee's brutal murder at Ralphie's hands, Silvio specifically refers to her as a thoroughbred and Tony stumbles on Tracee's photo after he kills Ralph for the death of Pie O My.[27] As Tony breaks up with Valentina and Svetlana he gives each the gift of a diamond brooch in the shape of a horseshoe.[28] Other horse instances are scattered about the series. Furio's defining trait is his *pony*tail. Matt Bevilaqua wears a Denver Broncos jersey.[29] Vito Spatafore Jr. wears a Broncos hat.[30] Junior's in-house nurse's name is Branca but Tony consistently mistakes it for "Bronco." Silvio uses the vernacular of "horse" to refer to heroin in the context of a deceased musician who worked with Hesh.[31] Hesh, coincidentally, keeps horses on his estate. Lastly, Tony romanticizes cowboys of the old west. Such cowboys' identities of independence are integrally linked to their horses.

No animal is more pervasive in the fabric of *The Sopranos* than fish. It begins in the first episode when Chris, in a nod to *The Godfather,* uses the expression "sleeps with the fishes" as a euphemism for death.[32] This is echoed in the most memorable use of fish: Tony's food poisoning-induced dream. In the form of a computer graphically-imaged anthropomorphic fish with Pussy's voice and features, Tony's *Fingerspitzengefühl* tells him that Pussy is a traitor and will soon sleep with the fish. Additionally, Tony considers the possibility that this prescient dream was induced by bad shellfish.[33] Pussy's fishy image is recalled with three separate instances of a novelty gift, the Big Mouth Billy Bass. Tony's sorrow for the loss of Pussy is triggered by the mechanical fish which sings, darkly recalling Pussy's watery burial. Paulie and Chris bury their differences in laughter over the singing fish. After bittersweet remembrances of Pussy as the neighborhood Santa Claus, Tony receives a Billy Bass as a Christmas present from Meadow.[34]

Bobby Baccalieri nickname is "Bacala" which means salted cod. When Uncle Junior is outed for his oral sex skills, Tony breaks his balls with mentions of bacala, tuna and sushi.[35] Tony cleans out his refrigerator by giving Uncle Junior fish.[36] Tony and Carmela frequent a new, trendy sushi restaurant at the beginning of season six.[37] Carmela reads aloud a *New York Times* article about an Italian court ruling in favor of a man's right to gift eighty-eight pounds of fish to influential business associates.[38] A bedside photograph of Tony and AJ on a fishing trip illustrates Tony's duality and later instills in Carmela fear of Tony's potential rage.[39] Carmela characterizes AJ's English teacher as a cold fish.[40] Phil Leotardo expresses strong opinions about fish on more than one occasion.[41] Fish platters are conspicuously included in various dining scenes. Tony gives his cousin Tony B. koi as a special touch for his massage therapy spa.[42] Tony uses a red snapper to conceal the gun with which he executes Chucky Signore.[43] When Christopher confronts his father's murderer, the scene is dominated by a large taxidermied blue marlin hanging on the wall, which Chris shoots.[44] As Chris relapses into heroin use, Tim Buckley's song "Dolphins" is prominently featured.[45] Adriana's ex-boyfriend anecdotally electrocuted himself trying to grill a trout with a downed power line.[46] After Adriana's murder, Carmela counsels a grieving Christopher that there are other fish in the sea.[47] Born-again Christian Bob Brewster defends his bottom-feeding proselytization, explaining that it's where the big fish are.[48] And, of course, Melfi's Alexithymia discussion paints Tony as a shark.[49] Each specific use means something different but fish generally carry a negative or foreboding connotation.

Departing from the motivic symbolism in the animal kingdom, the unusual device of stairs has earned a position of distinction in the fabric of *The Sopranos*. Stairs are a great metaphorical tool because they're multi-purpose: they go up and they go down. In an early session, Dr. Melfi asks Tony to recall warm and loving childhood memories of his family. Tony struggles to think of a specific instance but, at last, comes up with an anecdote from his youth in which his father fell down some stairs. The reaction of Tony, his sisters and their mother was derisive laughter. Melfi points out that the nature of that memory does not seem to be affectionate.[50] Rather, a man's own family was laughing at his misfortune and pain. Granted it was insignificant in life's larger scale but it is an amazing illustration of the passive aggressive family dynamic of Tony's youth. More recently, after nearly a year of not speaking to Livia, Tony finds himself face to face with his mother. She descends from the second floor on her chair-stair-lift. In his haste to escape her toxicity, Tony trips on the front steps of her house. His concealed gun falls into plain sight. Livia's reaction is laughter, not a glimmer of concern.[51]

The parallels between this incident and the story of Tony's father are clear. The image of Tony at the foot of the stairs looking up at Livia is one of a scared, helpless child as his mother takes delight in her own son's misstep. Carmela experiences a similar incident with AJ as she admonishes him for deceit and disobedience. When he makes his escape upstairs, she pursues him but falls on the stairs, banging her shin. AJ's response is a mixture of amusement, defiance and triumph but also a tinge of pity and regret.[52] AJ has adopted some of the negative lessons that Livia imparted and this is reflected in his behavior, although he does not comprehend the roots of his reaction.

The most brutal scene to take place on stairs, and arguably in the entire series, is the rape of Dr. Melfi. The rape is excruciatingly depicted with painful realism upon the cement stairs of her parking garage. She is left by her assailant to wail in anguish on those cold stone steps. Melfi has symptoms of post-traumatic stress following her attack. She experiences anxiety in association with the scene of the crime. The same steps which were the sight of this awful experience are the same steps she must traverse every day on her way into her office. Upon reaching the exact spot of the rape, she is overcome with a sense of dread.[53] For Melfi those stairs will be permanently associated with the most traumatic event of her life.

Bobby Baccalieri Sr.'s lung cancer causes him fits of coughing up blood, especially when aggravated by the exertion of climbing stairs. With a desire to be useful he agrees to carry out the execution of his godson but to do so requires him to scale an imposing flight of stairs. He surmounts the steps, nearly succumbing to a violent bout of coughing, but the pain is tolerable when he proves his worth by successfully whacking his god-son. As he escapes he is killed, crashing his car while struggling for his inhaler.[54]

Junior has a fateful encounter with stairs as well. In a media frenzy he is bumped on the head by a microphone boom which causes him to fall down several courthouse steps. The result is a hospital stay with diag-noses of dementia and Alzheimer's disease being considered. While ini-tially played by Tony and Junior as a delay tactic, in court Junior begins to exhibit genuine symptoms and his decline is irreversible.[55] While in his coma Tony has a dream experience that is quite similar. In it, he takes a spill down a flight of stairs which directly results in a medical diagnosis of early Alzheimer's.[56] The relationship between Janice and Ralphie piv-ots on a staircase. She intends to break up with him and approaches her opportunity with the intent of expressing her feelings in a mature, adult, non-judgmental manner. When the moment arrives, however, her fight/flight mechanism chooses a different approach: Janice explodes with anger, frustration and fear. She hits and scratches Ralphie, resulting in a painful tumble down the entire flight of steps. With an injured back Ralph gets the message.[57] When Adriana nearly confesses to her fellow mob wives her predicament with the Feds, she stops herself by fleeing. In doing so she takes a nasty spill on a single step from the Sopranos' entertainment room.[58] As a last throwaway detail, Tony and Carmela share one piece of exercise equipment—a Stairmaster![59] In the *Sopranos* universe, an encounter with stairs is cause for concern.

The symbolic use of teeth in *The Sopranos* comments on individual strength or weakness. Right before shooting Tony, Uncle Junior complains with frustrated anger that he has lost his upper dentures.[60] Not only has Junior lost his original teeth but he has also misplaced his false teeth. Another example of denture issues arises with Paulie's mother. Nucci Gualtieri's difficulty in adjusting to life at the Green Grove Retirement Community is marked by her inconstancy of putting in her teeth for social situations.[61] On the opposite end of the elder dental spectrum there is the Reverend James Sr., the father of one of Tony's business associates. In their brief meeting Tony notes a photograph of the reverend serving in World War II to which he responds with the boast that he still has the same teeth as he had in the picture taken fifty-seven years earlier.[62]

On two separate occasions, teeth are referred to in the context of Tony's views on parenting. In discussing parental discipline, Janice espouses the philosophy of ignoring nineteen of every twenty of a child's wrongs. Tony prefers the traditional wisdom that a single infraction should cost two teeth.[63] In a separate instance Tony explains to AJ that had it not been for Carmela he would have punched all of AJ's teeth out with one shot.[64] AJ's teeth come up again when Carmela plans a trip to Rome, meaning Tony will be responsible for taking AJ to the dentist.[65] On the dentistry tangent, Carlo undergoes a root canal not long before being unmasked as a rat.[66] In the early days of Tony's therapy his secret is nearly discovered when he learns Silvio's dentist is directly across the hall from Melfi.[67] Dentistry is more prominently included with Meadow's former fiancé, Finn, who studies to be a dentist. This connects to Tony's Test Dream in which he meets Finn's parents. With anxiety about preparation to kill his cousin, Tony imagines that his teeth are falling out. He then expresses his relief in the knowledge that Finn will be able to fix Meadow's teeth.[68] One of the last and most memorable teeth highlights comes in a vicious scene in which Tony stomps out the teeth of Coco Cogliano for insulting Meadow. Tony later finds one of Coco's bloody teeth in the cuff of his pants.[69] When Chris offers Amy, the D-Girl, the best *sanguishe* in Jersey, she declines because she just brushed her teeth.[70] Paulie regimentally brushes his teeth after taking naps.[71] Silvio lauds Tracee's ability as a dancer but bemoans her less than perfect teeth and so loans her money for braces.[72] Guilt-stricken Ralphie immediately brushes his teeth upon learning his order of Jackie Jr.'s death has been carried out.[73] This symbolic continuity of teeth is a subtle means of informing the audience about characters' internal dynamics.

Feet and shoes enjoy an interesting place in the palette of motifs in *The Sopranos*. In the first season, Chris shoots a disrespectful bakery clerk in the foot, an homage to actor Michael Imperioli's role in *Goodfellas*.[74] In the second season, Chris breaks his toe when he beats up a fellow student in his acting class.[75] At the Executive Game, Silvio expresses, with belligerent facetiousness, his affection for cheese in his socks.[76] When lost in the Pine Barrens, Paulie is afflicted by the loss of his shoe in the snow.[77] Janice's secret romantic relationship is discovered when Tony recognizes Ralph's dapper shoes.[78] Then, when Janice breaks up with Ralph, as a jumping-off point she uses the fact that Ralph disrespectfully does not remove his shoes upon entering her house.[79] Tony B.'s foot is run over by a car when he whacks Joe Peeps and his subsequent limp betrays his guilt.[80] Johnny Sack is unhappy with the patent leather shoes he's been given to wear to his daughter's wedding and at the ceremony Tony is required to remove his shoes as part of a security check.[81] Chris and Paulie each steal shoes for their girlfriends only to find out that they're the wrong size.[82] Paulie makes a similar error in purchasing skin diving socks for his aunt/mother.[83] In his coma experience, Tony slips off his Allen Edmonds as the episode closes in contemplation of his predicament.[84]

In the last nine episodes, shoes are even more prominent. With Johnny Sack on his death bed, his wife whitens his shoes and puts then at his bedside. The camera pointedly holds on the shoes for a beat.[85] When Bobby whacks the French Canadian drummer in a laundromat, a lone pair of shoes are shown tumbling in a dryer.[86] Paulie packs three identical pairs of white Vikings in preparation for going on the lam.[87] In the moment immediately before and after Burt Gervasi's death, camera shots linger on his feet. After killing Burt, Silvio polishes his own shoes.[88] AJ's brief dalliance with Family crime involves the disfigurement of a gambling debtor's foot with sulfuric acid.[89] After Christopher's death in the car crash, Paulie somberly notes that Chris always had a heavy foot.[90] As Silvio lies comatose in the hospital, his wife caringly gives him a pedicure.[91] Dr. Melfi notes, on more than one occasion, Tony's affection for the expression of disciplining AJ with his shoe up his son's back side.[92]

I encourage the reader to look for more of these and other examples of recurring devices throughout the series. The pantheon of symbolic motifs on *The Sopranos* has numerous honorable mentions: eggs; cars and car crashes; physical traits such as faces, hands, hair and eyes; translations of character names; pools; bells; hats; natural elements like water, wind, ice and snow; meat; cancer; use of mirrors; genetics, evolution and Darwinism; flowers; garbage; and, of course, guns. Finding and interpreting their countless instances is part of the fun of rewatching episodes. There are never fixed definitions. Interpretation is entirely based on contextual clues. Meaning should be derived strictly from within the body of the show, free of previous or external connotations. Identifiable patterns inform a studious audience. They don't dictate absolute meaning but if the shoe fits, wear it.

Buon Apetito!

The culture of *The Sopranos*, as northern New Jersey Italian-Americans, is often characterized by one of the greatest supporting characters on the show — the food! Sausages, ziti, pasta *fazool, cavadell', manigot'*, lasagne, *arrancin', zabaglione*, eggplant, *braciole*, chicken cacciatore and of course *gabagool*— food is inseparable from the identity of this community and their heritage. They are passionate about Italian cuisine. Each character's relationship with food reveals insight into their personality. Tony's mother despises northern Italian cuisine while Carmela's mother adores it, though partly out of spite.[93] Janice never learned to cook and is seen serving canned clam chowder, KFC and Outback Steakhouse take-out. When trying to win Bobby she passes off Carmela's signature lasagna as her own.[94] Tony begrudgingly microwaves rigatoni in contrast to Furio's loving preparation of an authentic carbonara.[95] Anyone who gets their Sunday gravy from a jar is frowned upon as un–Italian.[96] The Soprano family does not eat standing up and no one would ever catch Tony eating Chef Boyardee. Whenever Tony opens the refrigerator, it is a reflection of his internal state, often in relationship to Carmela. He seeks comfort in the fridge and is often frustrated with a particular food's absence. Not only does the food serve to realistically portray an authentic Italian-American experience but it carries much deeper meaning about Tony's work and love for his family.

The sharing of food is ritualized as a familial event. The family dinner is a sacred custom, an opportunity for the clan to share experiences and lessons, to reflect and to express their love for each other through the food around which they commune. The Soprano children are still in the process of developing their appreciation for this tradition. Anthony Jr. would like to have the TV on during dinner but Carmela refuses on principle. The most important tradition for any self-respecting *Sopranos* family is Sunday dinner. Despite their Catholic affiliation, the Soprano family is never shown to use that day for spiritual re-dedication but rather gastronormic celebration. Sunday dinner is their preferred sacrament. When audiences came together on Sunday night to watch a new *Sopranos*, they imitated this behavior by cooking elaborate Italian menus or simply ordering pizza. By gathering around food and *The Sopranos*, a bond is forged to the characters on the television and to other fans around the world, creating a family with whom to continue the Sunday tradition, a celebration of life.

Artie Bucco, along with his restaurant Nuovo Vesuvio, is the face of his community's passion for traditional Italian cuisine. The restaurant is named in honor of Mt. Vesuvius, which is closely identified with the Naples region of Italy where Tony and many other *Sopranos* characters can trace their ancestry. The name Vesuvio summons emotional connections to their identity, not just of national heritage but an allegiance to a specific region. In a dark irony, Artie's original restaurant exploded in fire and smoke much like the volatile volcano. Food is Artie's life but not simply eating or preparing. Artie is truly in love with the tradition, the cultural identification, the act of nourishment and artistry. Though Artie's focus sometimes falters when exasperated by the business side of his work, he has humbled himself to be happy in his simple life and the culinary tradition of his father. Artie, Nuovo Vesuvio, Sunday dinner and family all serve to illustrate *The Sopranos'* love affair with food.

Tony and his associates love to eat and their resultant physical weight carries symbolic meaning. The guys frequently break each others' balls about being overweight, Bobby and Vito especially. Both of these wiseguys experience significant weight loss. Vito's becomes a prominent part of his story. He uses his new trim physique to support his aspirations of becoming Tony's successor. While Vito loses weight, Tony gains — but Tony is comfortable with his 280. The last image of Vito is his "after" photo for The Thin Club. Considering his fate, it's plausible that weight, in this context, is a *positive* indicator signifying success and survival ability while loss of weight leads Vito to be another toothpick. In contrast, excessively thin individuals are referred to as "toothpicks" and looked upon as possibly ailing. Tony recognizes Jack Massarone as a rat by his unfounded flattery about Tony's nonexistent weight loss. These characters are big believers in comfort food to alleviate stress and grief. Tony takes solace in a bialy after whacking Tony B., Bobby eats the last ziti made by his deceased wife as part of the mourning process. Chris believes Tony eats to tamp down his feelings. Tony is a big guy with big appetites and he is the touchstone for any significance to be interpreted from individual weight.

How characters process the food so integrally connected to their identity indicates internal dynamics. Mind-body connections are frequently seen when stress in characters' lives manifests itself in physical symptoms. Digestive problems, specifically, are a recurring theme. They come in many forms and carry meaning about internal conflict. First there is the category of regurgitation. The sixth season opens with Agent Harris vomiting at the mention of the American public's taste — not a very subtle comment. Harris's nausea is the symptom of a virus he contracted on assignment in Pakistan but it is indicative of job stress and dissatisfaction.[97] It afflicts him to the end of the series. Harris is present for Adriana's projectile vomiting that results from her realization of the implications of being corralled by a federal sting.[98] Chris is shown to lose the contents of his stomach as a reaction to heroin injection. His willingness to continue in his habit while his body tries to persuade him otherwise demonstrates the power of his addiction. Tony vomits after killing Ralph, during his post-coma hospital stay and after proving his strength to his crew by beating the young Perry Annunziata.[99] In the first instance it reflects his great disgust for Ralph and distaste for his murder while also having roach killer sprayed in his face. Tony's hospital incident occurs when he's faced with Phil Leotardo's attempts to take advantage of Tony's weakened condition. The beating of Perry is clearly unpleasant to Tony considering the young man's innocent nature. The need to reassert his authority, however, forces Tony to take this step to prove he is still the alpha male in the Family. Tony's portentous dream about Pussy's betrayal results from food poisoning with all variety of gastro-intestinal symptoms.[100] Participation in unpleasantness yields corollary digestive symptoms in the *Sopranos* universe.

If sustenance makes it past the stomach, problems often arise in the bowels. Characters are shown to be blocked in more ways than one. Bobby has to buy Junior stool softener.[101] Rosalie Aprile claims that flying causes her bowels to jam up.[102] Vito is accused of taking an hour and a half to move his bowels.[103] What Phil Leotardo initially feels as bowel discomfort turns out to be a precursor to a serious heart attack.[104] As Tony recovers in the hospital, he complains that his bowels don't work. He is on a strict diet, including no more eggplant, but he eats a sausage sandwich against doctor's orders.[105] Most hauntingly, Gigi Cestone dies on the toilet. Some of his last words were complaints that Thanksgiving turkey felt like spackle in his bowels.[106] Once again such physical symptoms are often indicative of more than a physical ailment. These characters are all dealing with stress and restlessness.

A third category of digestive disorder is loss of bodily function. These instances often reflect one's loss of control in other area of their lives. As the dying Jackie Aprile Sr.'s cancer worsens, he bemoans the disobedience of his bowels. His is a depiction of a once strong man deteriorating, consumed by his disease.[107] Chris soils himself when Russian goons drag him out to the dock in a mock execution.[108] Word of this spreads quickly and is a source of much embarrassment for Chris. However, so strong is his addiction that he nostalgically reminisces about diarrhea that resulted from baby laxative used to cut his heroin.[109] Cat burglary seems to be conducive to evacuating one's bowels as both Pussy and Sean Gismonte develop this odd habit.[110] In Sean's case it seems that this is a side effect of anxiety about his criminal pursuits. In his coma vision, Tony laments a diagnosis of Alzheimer's Disease with the horrible thought of death while soiling his pajamas.[111] With this comment Tony is expressing fear at the potential loss of autonomy and identity. Chris insensitively relays the sad story of his cousin's colon cancer to Adriana.[112] Adriana is the saddest example of a loss of function. After vomiting on the federal agents, her symptoms turn into an inability to control the timing of her bowel movements. This and her diarrhea are diagnosed as Irritable Bowel Syndrome. Tony sympathizes with Adriana and tells her that Livia suffered from the same thing her entire life.[113] As the Feds continue to exert pressure on Adriana to cooperate, her symptoms worsen. Her condition deteriorates into ulcerative colitis and it's clear that FBI coercion in conflict with her dedication to Chris is ripping up her insides.[114]

Loss of urinary control carries different connotations as can be deciphered by several instances in *The Sopranos.* Matt Bevilaqua wets himself in fear of his imminent execution at the hands of Tony and Pussy.[115] When Chris, Furio and Patsy drag an associate to a shed, he loses control of his bladder, also out of fear.[116] Jackie Jr. can't hold it while serving as getaway driver for Chris and Benny in a heist of a Jewel benefit concert.[117] The graphic depiction of Eugene Pontecorvo's suicide by hanging includes the detail of bladder evacuation upon death.[118] It's possible Paulie may have some experience with common elder bladder control issues when he mourns the ravages of age, including weakened eyesight, loss of teeth and bladder laxity.[119] Paulie is also quite uncomfortable when he learns that paraplegic Beansie Gaeta must urinate into a bag.[120]

The mind-body connection is a powerful phenomenon. This digestive system symbolism is consistent throughout *The Sopranos,* where losing control in aspects of one's life is manifested in the loss of control of body functions. The control issues and stress with which they live are results of participation in the waste management business. This is a twisted metaphor because those who suffer actually cannot control their own bodily waste. These individuals are contaminated by criminality with subsequent doubt and guilt. The food they put in their mouths comes from crime. The physical symptoms of indigestion, diarrhea, vomiting or whatever are physical reflex rejections of that crime.

In Tony's Family the word "eat" is frequently employed as a euphemism for "earn." This illuminates a metaphorical connection between the work that Tony does and the food that he and his family eat. Tony tells Melfi that his work is simply a means of feeding his children. Though there is a degree of rationalization in this, it is not an entirely inaccurate representation of his motivations. Tony's view on work and food has roots in the pivotal incident from his childhood in which he witnessed his father, Johnny Boy, separate the local butcher from his pinky finger and then bring home meat to feed the family. Johnny Boy takes pride in the meats of his labors, which nourish and give pleasure to his family.[121] Tony exhibits that same pride in providing food for *his* family. His crimes fade into the background of his mind and to the fore comes a sense of validation facilitated by the belief that the end justifies the means. The end that Tony prioritizes above all else is the well-being of his children, creating for them a life that will be better than his own. This compartmentalization or vertical split is necessary for Johnny or Tony to continue to live without being consumed by an innate sense of guilt about the harm they do to others.[122] It's only a minor concern that their advantage comes at the cost of others. Johnny Boy is able to justify this to Tony with a lesson which becomes part of the blueprint of Tony's mind. Tony's father legitimizes his actions with the concept of honor. The most basic and measure of their "goodness" is their ability to put food on the table. No other directive is clearer in Tony's world. Everything else is subservient to this and it gives greater understanding to the importance of food in the *Sopranos* universe.

What Loose Ends?

The storytelling in *The Sopranos* has a tone and style unlike any other television program. One of its most powerful appeals is its defiance of convention. *The Sopranos'* unpredictability has been the source of both audience adulation and frustration. Fans have been thrilled by surprising twists and bewildered by their occasional absence. David Chase's style of storytelling is not always linear. He often introduces an idea and then leaves it, allowing audience anticipation to percolate. If and when the idea is resumed, it is rarely in keeping with expectations. Standard American audiences have been conditioned to a certain type of storytelling in television and movies. They are accustomed to the structure of a beginning, middle and end throughout which meanings are made explicit. Chase diverges from this formula by telling stories obliquely. With a cast of characters that constantly lie, nothing is ever what it seems to be on the surface. For example, the story of Jackie Jr.'s downward spiral is just as much, if not more, the story of Tony's fears and hopes for AJ's future.

Viewers have been known to be greatly confused, disappointed or even outraged by the unconventional path Chase takes in telling this story. Because of the popular template propagated by ninety-nine percent of entertainment, audiences sometimes have difficulty in seeing Chase's forest through Tony Soprano's trees. Just like Tony coaches AJ, viewers have to keep their eye on the ball and focus through distractions. Chase entertains by engaging his audience in active participation. He is like Tony giving his neighbor, Dr. Cusamano, a mysterious package wrapped in plain brown paper and neatly tied with twine. With reliance on implied subtext, Tony plays with Cusamano's fears and expectations by simply asking him to hold on to the ominous parcel for a while. The Cusamanos speculate and fret with paranoia about the contents of the package. In the same way the imagination of the audience runs wild with the thousands of possibilities. Cusamano's story ends there, with nothing further needing to be said. It's not what's in the package that's important, it's what's in the audience's imagination. This ending is typical of Chase's style which is commonly criticized for an apparent untidiness of loose ends. Audiences have been taught to expect closure in their entertainment. Acceptance of Chase's form of resolution requires an understanding of what he's talking about in the first place. Examination of some specific examples will facilitate greater understanding of Chase's method of storytelling.

Valery, the Russian who escaped Paulie and Chris in the Pine Barrens, may or may not have survived. This character's possible return for revenge was the focus of unending speculation on the part of zealous fans. It is an entertaining mystery that his fate is left untold; however, that is only a byproduct of what was really a story about Chris and Paulie. Their relationship is developed throughout the season and the incident in the Pine Barrens is the nadir of their conflict. The Russian is only an innocent bystander like JT Dolan or the unfortunate waiter who complained about his gratuity. The function of this adventure is threefold: to illustrate Paulie's potential to be a loose cannon and business liability; for Tony to confront Paulie with his responsibility for that, with the implication to straighten up and fly right; and, last but not least, it's really funny![123]

Furio is another character whom audiences felt might make a vengeful return to New Jersey. He and Carmela flirted all of season four, creating anticipation about how this story might unfold. In an anticlimactic turn, though, Furio accepts the immutability of his relationship with Carmela and simply disappears, never to be seen or heard from again. Once more the real story is not on the surface. Furio's function is to illustrate Carmela's ever-wandering heart. He serves to depict the chasm between her and Tony. Her loss of Furio brings Carmela to the precipice of finally throwing Tony out of the house after years of frustration. This is contribution enough to the saga of *The Sopranos.*

The unorthodox conclusion to the story of Dr. Melfi's rape was the subject of discussion and theorizing. Her rapist is set free on a procedural technicality and she is left without justice. When Tony expresses concern for her distress and asks if there is anything he can do to help, the tension is palpable. The audience is gripped by bloodlust but Melfi summons the strength of her moral convictions and declines his offer.[124] Fans debated the possibility that Melfi might change her mind or that Tony could find out about the rape by other means and exact justice of his own. What eludes some audiences is that everything that needed to be said on this subject is contained within the body of the episode. It's not about revenge on Melfi's assailant, it's about the audience examining their own sense of justice and morality. Melfi made her decision. What the writing implies is a call for the audience to make theirs.

There are numerous other examples of unique storytelling throughout the series. The wayward black bear never returned to maul the Soprano family. Ahmed and Muhammed were not shown to be terrorists. A vociferous minority of fans insisted on hypothesizing that Adriana somehow survived her fatal encounter with Silvio. Carmela hinted at investigating Ade's disappearance but this did not materialize. These are all examples of *The Sopranos'* many red herrings. Such instances of unmet audience expectations reflect a standard of entertainment aimed at the lowest common denominator. *Sopranos* fans appreciate Chase's alternative voice. It can be exhilarating and frustrating but it is infinitely more rewarding for those who are willing put themselves in his hands. Audience fervor is developed with a slowly unraveling story, abundant with details to stimulate their imaginations. To fully reap the rewards of *The Sopranos*, one must calibrate their expectations. It is fiction but not fantasy. Its strength and integrity lie in its realism. Just like in real life, people come and go. Their journeys intersect and diverge in unpredictable ways. Each relationship means something different to each individual. Real life does not always have neat and tidy endings and sometimes a cigar is just a cigar. Audiences have been conditioned to want escapism, not reality in their entertainment. The value of realism is so much greater because it allows practical application to one's life rather than distraction from it. Lessons are not spoon-fed to the audience. *The Sopranos* prefers the infinite and intriguing possibilities of questions to the vanity of mere statements. The one-hour installments are simply the planting of seeds. The actual cultivation takes much longer. Only after thought, effort and verbalization can one harvest the fruits of the enterprise. Those who misinterpret the story to have loose ends misunderstand the proposition of watching *The Sopranos*.

The consummate example is the series' infamous last scene. Chase's treatment of the finale was widely accused of being the granddaddy of loose ends. Many fans were disappointed at what they perceived to be an absence of resolution in any form. However, equipped with an understanding of his storytelling style, one can find all the closure needed. There are so many threads in the fabric of *The Sopranos* and as it inexorably slouches toward its finale, the possibility of tying together the various threads becomes increasingly obscure. However, there is meaning. Anticipation builds as Tony enters Holsten's in the final scene. Red herrings assault the senses as he eyes his fellow diners. Seeds of paranoia are planted. All of the details of eight years and eighty-six episodes swirl in the audience's mind. How do these innumerable puzzle pieces fit together? Tension mounts. Meadow agonizingly parallel-parks her car. What does it all mean? The music swells and anticipation builds, and builds, and builds until the inevitable end. Despite arguments to the contrary, there is an explanation. To put to rest all of the debate, speculation and theorizing, the meaning of the end of *The Sopranos* is

10

The End of the Line

After the success of the first season, David Chase envisioned the *Sopranos* saga to be four seasons, fifty-two episodes in which he would say everything he had to say about Tony Soprano and company.[1] However, the characters developed lives of their own. They had more things to say and there were more stories to tell. It probably didn't hurt that HBO was willing to throw around a lot of *scarole* to keep it going. As soon as the announcement was made that this unique mob drama would end its run after six seasons, anticipation and dread in its fans grew to unprecedented proportions. Many did not want it to end, at least not yet. Others thought it should have ended already, with the belief that the show had "jumped the shark" with the Vito storyline, the Test Dream or even as far back as the fourth season.[2] Most faithful fans agree, though, that Chase maintained a consistently high quality of writing with significant contributions from Terence Winter, Robin Green, Mitchell Burgess and others. All eighty-six episodes hold together independently and as a whole, each hour contributes to the larger meaning and character of *The Sopranos*.

When considering The End, it is important to remember that the last twenty-one episodes were crafted from the blueprint of a single season arc. The sixth season may have had the feel of two distinct seasons due to the intermission of nearly a year. However, the first twelve episodes of the season should not be viewed as a separate from the final nine. They are interdependent. The foundation for the last chapter of Tony's journey is laid in the first half of the season and culminates in the second half. The last season builds upon previously presented themes and introduces a couple new ones. With the entire series in perspective, the arc of the saga is Tony's and his families' search for happiness through acceptance of personal nature and identity.

Slouching Towards Bethlehem

The sixth season depicts a tipping point in the life of Tony Soprano and his two families. There is a mystical, cosmic feeling to the final twenty-one episodes as they begin with William S. Burroughs's narration of "The Seven Souls," a translation of Egyptian concepts of the nature of life, death and afterlife. Triggered by a near-death experience at the hands of his Uncle Junior, Tony comes to a crossroads in his life and re-evaluates his beliefs, behaviors and identity. With renewed determination to stop and smell the roses, Tony is reminded that there aren't many roses in waste management. As he contemplates the future of his Family, Tony tests the allegiance of his closest associates. AJ and Meadow grow beyond young adulthood and Carmela finds some peace of mind. Each character comes to terms with his/her identity and faces a turning point on his/her respective journeys.

The central event for Tony in the last season is a metaphysical experience wherein Tony is not a New Jersey mob boss but a simple salesman caught up in a case of mistaken identity when his own wallet and briefcase are inexplicably replaced by those of a man named Kevin Finnerty. The briefcase becomes symbolic of Tony's identity as he laments that his whole life was in his own lost case. What he's left with is Finnerty's case, Finnerty's identity, and how this came to be is a mystery. His interactions with a conference administrator and two separate hotel clerks all revolve around his having proper identification. Furthermore, Tony is unexpectedly identified as Mr. Finnerty by a group of Buddhist monks. Tony experiences frustration and confusion in trying to prove who he is. Tony is deeply dismayed and his confusion is so complete that he is forced to question his own true identity. Perhaps he *is* Kevin Finnerty after all. The culminating question that Tony asks himself is, "Who am I? Where am I going?"[3] This succinctly summarizes Tony's internal struggle. This experience is the result of his rarefied mind-body connection and it is the Rosetta Stone for interpreting Tony's arc in the sixth season and its context in his larger journey. It is the culmination of years of conflict, both internal and external. Tony's internal system has become cluttered to critical mass after years of living with stress, feelings of guilt about his role as a father, doubt about the path he chose and what his future holds. When

Tony is shot in the pancreas, his body and mind take some necessary down-time for spiritual, cognitive, and emotional maintenance and a reboot. The unconventional vision is the quintessential manifestation of Tony's *Fingerspitzengefühl.*

There is a certain dreamy hangover feeling from the coma experience felt through to the end of the series. This is reinforced by the artistic choice to frequently have Tony's first appearance in an episode to be waking in bed. Out of the final twenty-one episodes, this device of introducing Tony in bed is used a remarkable ten times![4] When Tony awakens from his coma he has a re-shaped view of the world and he puts it into practice with behavioral changes. The first change is that he begins to shed his dependence on excuses. Part of Tony's metaphysical vision as a legitimate working man addresses a subconscious curiosity to know what might have happened if he had chosen a different path in life. To entertain that idea requires Tony to first acknowledge that he is responsible for such choices. His habit of making an excuse of forces beyond his control must be recognized as a self-deception and abandoned. Only when he truly accepts responsibility for his choices can he implement real change in the direction of true happiness. Tony expresses newfound appreciation for each day as a gift and this new attitude is translated into practical applications in his life. After decades of shifting blame onto externals, Tony begins to show signs of fully accepting accountability for himself. In an argument with his sister Janice, Tony refuses to take the bait of blaming her for his shooting.[5] This would have been uncharacteristic previous to the coma when he would have been likely to place blame anywhere but on himself. Tony advises Bobby that he needs to define and prove himself on his own merits rather than relying on the crutch of being Tony's brother-in-law.[6] Though it is in the form of advice to Bobby, it is also an affirmation to himself. Tony seeks to stop making excuses and fully be his own man. He is freeing himself from the chains of excuses and reclaiming old convictions with new confidence.

Tony begins to phase out his passive aggressive behaviors as well. In the period immediately after his coma, Tony is confronted with an Ojibwe saying, "Sometimes I go about in pity for myself, and all the while a great wind carries me across the sky."[7] Although he sees such self-pity in those around him, he sees it in himself, too. He recognizes that the habit of making excuses establishes a pattern of complaining, in direct divergence from his hero Gary Cooper. He points out the unpleasant saturation of complaining among his colleagues.[8] Tony is filled with appreciation for life when he survives the coma without the likely brain damage and gets a second chance. He embraces every day as a gift to be treasured and appreciated, too precious to be wasted with complaining.

Tony also recognizes other possible perspectives. His approach is shaped by a proselytizing pastor, Bob Brewster. Even though Tony finds the man hypocritical and distasteful, one particular expression of Brewster's rings a bell with Tony: the idea that salvation isn't solely about being saved from Hell when one dies but also about being saved from oneself in life. This speaks to Tony and guides his actions in his post-coma existence. Perhaps the greatest leap in his interpretation of the coma's meaning and application to his life is inspired by a fellow convalescent named John Schwinn. While watching a boxing match on television, Schwinn expounds on a concept of perception and identity. He postulates that the different entities an individual sees, whether two boxers on television or anything else in their life, are only separate in the individual's mind because they choose to see it that way. In actuality, all the distinct things one perceives are just groupings and arrangements of molecules, all akin to each other.[9] This influences Tony tremendously as he re-evaluates the way he understands his life and how he will proceed. This concept has meaning for interpersonal conflict and its senselessness. Tony is evolving his own understanding of The Big Picture by realizing that he is part of the bigger body of the universe and a body divided against itself cannot stand. The majority of stresses in Tony's life are avoidable, unnecessary and self-imposed. Tony begins to apply this to his life by expressing his sentiments to Phil Leotardo that they needn't fight each other to survive and be happy. Tony is embracing this philosophy that everything is interconnected and he extrapolates to all aspects of existence in the pursuit of a happiness.

With Tony's new perspective comes acceptance of responsibility for his choices, discontinuation of excuses and complaints, and the conscious departure from defining relationships by opposition. What Tony is undertaking is an alignment of the face he wears to the multitude and the face he wears to himself with the belief that it is an illusion to believe them to be separate things. He is working to separate his inherent convictions from all the contaminated messages he has learned to accept from his parents and associates. It is a disentanglement of the past from the present, the internal from the external, the good from the bad. This does not mean that Tony will renounce his gangster lifestyle, go back to Seton Hall to get his degree and become a legitimate businessman, though. As the forty-seven-year-old boss of the New Jersey crime family, that option is no longer open to him. He has long passed the point of no return and he cannot change in that respect. However, what he *can* change is how he operates — his interpretation of the world and his actions therein.

Tony begins to shed old emotional baggage as part of this process. When Tony is shot by Junior, his subsequent comatose experience is a cathartic re-evaluation of his quest for Livia and Junior's love, his search for his own identity and how he demonstrates his love for his children. The coma vision is just as much the result of the confluence of these unresolved internal factors as the physical aspect of a gunshot to the pancreas. Tony's subconscious is forced to wrestle with these dynamics and come to some conclusions. Tony realizes that too much of his energy is tied up in the subconscious neuroses about his parents and the past. To change this negative behavior he begins cutting ties with his past. His disassociation from Junior is necessitated by the shooting. A mode of that separation is seen in Tony's decision to sell the old neighborhood poultry store to Jamba Juice.[10] This is influenced not only by the neighborhood's connotations to Junior and a bygone era, but by a decision to move forward by asserting his independence from the past. This break from the past is necessary for Tony to evolve. Tony is embracing his own identity rather than altering it to conform with the values of the "old school" of his uncle, father and mother. In the very first episode Tony's depression has roots in the feeling that he came in at the end of the golden era of the gangster.[11] What Tony comes to terms with in season six is that it *was* the end — for his father. Life is a series of beginnings and endings and Tony must embrace his own journey rather than trying, with futility, to complete his father's journey. The expectations of his father's generation and the circumstances of his own life are not compatible. Trying to bridge them is a vain pursuit. In his new perspective, Tony is less concerned with being who his father was and more focused on being Tony Soprano. No longer will he pigeonhole himself with where he came from but he will define himself by where he is going.

Tony's focus on the future is also evident from his renewed appreciation for his wife and children. He expresses gratitude for Carmela, shares with Meadow his interest in the prospect of grandchildren, and takes more of a hand in AJ's development. This new approach is capsulized in the midseason finale when Tony counsels Phil, after suffering a heart attack, to focus his energies on "good things" like grandkids.[12] His words reflect a desire to keep their business lives in proper perspective to their families, the people who they love. As Tony's stock in blood family goes up, his approach to his business Family changes. Not only is his allocation of time and energy to the business more balanced but he is also better able to let go of his ego. This has the effect of "spreading the wealth" and reducing his stress level. He is redefining his business identity and his identity as a family man.

As the second half of the season commences, Tony is considering his future and reviewing the key players in his Family. When Tony assigns Bobby his first hit, it isn't retaliation for their earlier fistfight.[13] It's strictly business. It is a test to see if Bobby is sufficiently dedicated to his career. He beat Tony in the fight and proved he could be a cold-blooded killer, thus passing Tony's test. Christopher fails his test when Tony sees *Cleaver*. Tony makes up his mind that Chris hates him and cannot be counted on. When the two of them get in the car wreck, it is an opportunity to pre-empt inevitable disaster. Chris's admission of drug use merely simplifies Tony's decision and Chris pays the ultimate price for his failure to serve Tony and the Family.[14] Again, it's business. When Tony borrows money from Hesh, he tests the boundaries of their personal and business relationship.[15] By callously demonstrating his dominance over Hesh, Tony severs further ties to his father and the "old school." Although there was not much doubt regarding Silvio's reliability, he proves himself by whacking Burt Gervasi who attempts to defect to New York.[16] When Tony takes Paulie on a boat trip, the purpose is to test Paulie's ability to keep quiet. Tony puts the screws to Paulie in an attempt to get him to admit his role in blabbing the Ginny Sack joke. Tony is convinced that Paulie is responsible but wants to see if he can get Paulie to concede it. Tony is ready to send Paulie into the ocean to join Pussy but when Paulie doesn't sing he proves he can be counted on to keep his mouth shut when it counts.[17] This is not the only instance of a boat as the setting for Tony's tests. At the beginning of the last season, Tony purchases a second boat, the *Stugots II*. On it, AJ expresses a desire to take revenge on Uncle Junior. Tony forbids AJ from taking any such action.[18] Tony proposes the possibility of new Family responsibility to Bobby while fishing in a boat on a lake.[19] Tony, Bobby and Carlo go to a boat show.[20] When Artie is on the verge of another nervous breakdown, Tony takes him out on the *Stugots II* to talk some sense into him.[21] As Tony goes through this testing phase, there are personal factors in his relationships with each of his men but they are ancillary to the dictums of good business management.

Tony is not the only character to reach some conclusions about his identity. Paulie experiences a very painful process of identity awareness when the woman he believes to be his mother turns out to be the sister of his birth mother, who he thought was his aunt. He goes through intense anger and depression, renouncing the woman who raised him.[22] He feels that this revelation actually changes who he is, that the identity he's lived his whole life is not his own. He experiences emotions common to Tony's relationship with Livia. Both feel abandoned, unloved and guilty. Paulie eventually resigns himself to the circumstances and decides to move on with his life by resuming the identity he previously inhabited — Nucci's son — if somewhat less enthusiastically.[23] He does the same in his relationship with Tony. After experiencing a period of doubt about his allegiance to the Family, he ultimately pledges himself in service to Tony.[24]

For some, their understanding of identity does not provide salvation. Silvio learns that being the boss is not for him. He contents himself with being Tony's Number Two, glad to be free of the stress of being boss. This is neatly reinforced with a shot of Silvio hanging a poster for a porn movie, pointedly framed with the title, *The Perfect Secretary*.[25] He truly is a very good *consigliere*. However, it is because of his position at Number Two that he is eventually shot and comatose, probably never to regain consciousness. In their last scene together Tony tenderly holds Silvio's hand as Silvio did for Tony in *his* coma.[26] Bobby takes Tony's advice to heart and dedicates himself to his work. He demonstrates his merits as an aspiring wiseguy, loving father and patient husband. He is shot while focused on a toy train, a vestigial link to his more innocent past. Bobby's wife (Tony's sister) Janice is left to raise their children alone. She wants to be a good mother but her identity is still closely derivative of her own formidable mother, Livia. At times this is quite effective but at others it is dysfunctional. Janice is acutely aware of the shadow she's in, and strives to escape it, but has yet to fully do so. Uncle Junior's deteriorated mental condition reflects his tragic loss of identity. The once intimidating tough guy who ran north Jersey crime with his brother Johnny Boy now does not recognize even himself. Chris's death is a direct result of his inability to accept that his identity was divided against itself. He wanted fame and he wanted the Family but more than both of these, he simply wanted to be loved. When he found no satisfaction in any of these he substituted alcohol and drugs which further disabled his ability to define his identity. When he demonstrated his inability to resolve this dilemma, Tony did it for him. Tony makes peace with all these people and says goodbye as the paths of their journeys diverge.

In contrast to Chris, Janice and Junior, those who accept their association to Tony rather than running from it come to terms with their identity. In addition to Paulie, there are Carmela and the children. Meadow vacillates about her future. Her relationship with Finn ultimately ends and she gets engaged to Patrick Parisi, son of Tony's *capo*, Patsy. Patrick is a young Italian-American man who loves Meadow and seems to have a good future ahead of him. After wavering between law and medicine as a career, she finally chooses law, with a focus on civil rights. She explains to Tony that her decision is largely a result of the numerous incidents of "persecution" Tony suffered in the name of law and order. After years of rebellion and internal debate, Meadow embraces her identity as a true Soprano woman.

Anthony Jr. takes a couple steps toward adulthood with an honest job and a serious romantic relationship in which he finds satisfaction. His relationship with Blanca, though, is just as much addressing his own father issues through her son. AJ continues to look for a group to fit into, first in the club scene of Generation Y delinquents and then in the aspiring Family soldiers of the future. AJ learns that these are two more groups in which he doesn't fit. When Blanca breaks up with him, he takes a couple steps back into depression and self-pity. His suicide attempt is a cry for help when his sense of hopelessness becomes overwhelming. Tony and Carmela finally accept their son's strengths and weaknesses and help him get back on his feet. AJ's identity is inextricably linked to Tony. He is slowly turning into his father with his undershirt, bathrobe, depression and psychotherapy. However, he is more Fredo Corleone than Michael Corleone. Like Little Carmine Lupertazzi, he is the boss's son and perhaps always will be. Rather than feel shame or failure for this, he, Tony and Carmela accept it and move on. AJ demonstrates signs of escaping Livia's formidable ghost which haunted his mind since his existential crisis of the second season. With a new acceptance of his "nice guy" nature and a resigned optimism he embraces Tony's advice to focus on the good times.

Carmela goes through a radical evolution in perception similar to Tony's. Her turning point is a visit to Paris.[27] Her own sense of self in the context of the world is shaken with an overwhelming sense of insignificance in the shadow of history and humanity. Carmela takes to heart one of Tony's oft-repeated sentiments that each person is part of something bigger. She, too, realizes the pointlessness of much of her worry and grief with the realization that it all gets washed away in the end. Carmela sees that the frustration she has felt in recent years is just as much her own doing as Tony's. She accepts her role in Tony's Family as well as his family. She accepts that she likes life's luxuries and decides not to feel guilty about it. Despite their differences, Carmela is resolved in her love for Tony. No longer embroiled in a fight against her nature, she aligns the face she wears to herself with the one she wears to the multitude. As an expression of her identity she is still a homemaker but in a new, literal and fulfilling sense with her real estate career.

All of these characters are going through the process of establishing or redefining their identities. This search for identity is the cornerstone of the series. After long and painful struggles to define themselves by differentiation from Tony, they come to embrace their true selves in direct relation to him. In some ways they end up back where they started. It's not their nature or their circumstances that have changed, it's their perspective. This is the story of *The Sopranos* and it comes to a fitting conclusion with a memorable finale.

The Finale

In the aftermath of the finale broadcast, public response was mixed, both critical and laudatory. Reactions ranged from disappointment, frustration and rage to confused and bemused to relief, appreciation, gratitude, celebration and respect. Many people felt cheated that The End did not meet their expectations. This sentiment is at odds with one of the great attractions of the show — that it constantly defies expectation. For eight years, Chase tickled an audience who laughed and squirmed but never quite wanted him to stop.

The stage is set for the last episode when the threat of a mob war is realized and the Soprano Family finally goes to the mattresses with New York. In a surprising twist, Tony rats out two peripheral associates of Middle Eastern origin as a bargaining chip. Even more surprising, Tony cashes it in for the cooperation of Agent Harris. Cooler heads prevail when "the little guy" from New York, Butchie DeConcini, supersedes Phil and makes peace with Tony. Meadow decides on civil law. AJ is truly his father's son, prone to depression but learning to cope with it. Despite the blindness of his vendetta, in the moment before Phil gets whacked he is following Tony's advice to focus on his grandkids. Fortunately for Tony, this leaves Phil unfocused on Walden Belfiore, who puts a bullet in Phil's head. *Un*fortunately for Tony, federal indictment seems imminent, especially considering the emergence of another rat in the Family. Carmela has established her real estate career. Tony still has an itch for therapy when he directs the session with AJ's therapist onto his own problems.

The infamous final scene is entirely in keeping with the storytelling of David Chase. As audiences watched it for the first time they held in their hearts hopes and fears, the culmination of eight years of anticipation. The Soprano family gathers one by one at Holsten's diner. Tony picks Journey's "Don't Stop Believin'" on the jukebox. The camera curiously pauses on various diner patrons. Meadow is delayed in joining them by her difficulty with parallel parking. The camera's eye seems to linger on a man in a Member's Only jacket as he heads for the restroom. The music swells. Meadow runs to the diner. Tony looks up. The music stops and the screen goes black. It stays that way for a full nine seconds. Then the credits silently roll.

An eight-year adventure had come to a close. The cut to black was so abrupt that many viewers leapt from their couches, screaming in the belief that their cable went out at the most critical moment in television history. Any other episode of *The Sopranos* was reliably a topic of discussion at the water cooler the following day. For the finale and its unorthodox ending this phenomenon was taken to exponential proportions. Controversy, uproar, and chaos erupted. Immediately after the credits rolled, the HBO website servers crashed under the weight of a record traffic volume. Every newspaper in the country had a story about The End and fan reaction. Every talk show had to mention the public furor. David Letterman, Conan O'Brien, Jon Stewart and every other television comedian had a *Sopranos* joke at the top of their show. The audience was generally divided into two camps, one believing The End was genius and the other deeming it atrocious. The great debate revolved around the meaning of the black screen and what happened next. Some theories include: Tony was whacked; the whole Soprano family was whacked; everyone but Meadow was whacked; just Meadow was whacked; the audience itself was metaphorically whacked; an FBI sting was sprung; Tony had a panic attack; or, this author's favorite, all four of the Sopranos sat down and had dinner. Cynics and optimists speculated that the open-endedness was simply a device to allow for a *Sopranos* movie in the future.

Fans vehemently debated interpretations ranging from sensible to downright delusional. Every detail was scoured for significance, analyzed, discussed and re-analyzed *ad nauseam*: Tony's shirt; the jukebox song selections; the sounding of the bell above the door; Meadow's car parking; the man in the Member's Only jacket; the man wearing the USA hat; the two unidentified black men; the Cub Scouts; Tony's hand movements; point-of-view camera shots; and, of course, the onion rings. Some people claimed to have seen a different ending where Meadow was the last image on the screen, rather than Tony. Rumors floated around that multiple endings had been filmed. As soon as one rumor was disproven, another would gather steam. The ending was parodied by Pittsburgh sports mascots and Hillary Clinton. It was absolute *mayham* [*sic*]!

Some fans felt that it lacked closure. Tony's fate remains a mystery. There are no depictions of consequences for Tony's life of crime, no come-uppance. Some expressed the opinion that it was simply weak, that Chase was too lazy to write a good ending. The anxiety on the part of many viewers was not as much the result of not *seeing* what became of Tony but not *knowing*. There was desire in some fans for Chase to give an explanation. It's not that loyal viewers didn't like the ending but that they actually felt like there was *no* ending. It's not that they wanted *this* to happen or *that* to happen but they expected something *definite and final* to happen.

Chase was deliciously noncommittal in his comments in his sole interview immediately following The End. "I have no interest in explaining, defending, reinterpreting, or adding to what is there ... it's all there."[28] The End demonstrates a consistency with historical "loose ends" like Melfi's rape or Furio's departure. There is realism in its uncertainty. Not every thread of real life is neatly tied up. There are not always concrete endings. One can argue the relative merits of knowing Tony was whacked, or jailed, or lived to see his great-grandkids. But that discussion is limited and infinitely less interesting than the one that ensued from Chase's artistic decision to end it the way he did. In an example of life imitating art, the last scene transports the viewer into the head of Tony Soprano. As a Family boss, Tony must live with the knowledge that his life is always on the line. He must constantly look over his shoulder, with the sense of a sword hanging over his head. As Tony sits in Holsten's, the viewer eyes each patron of the diner with suspicion. They see menace in every shadow. They not only understand the constant paranoia that Tony must live with but they actually *feel* it. This is an amazing directorial and editorial accomplishment.

Expectations for the finale were astronomically high. The potential for failure was great. So many ardent fans were basically split between wanting Tony to live or to die. The final scene — the circumstance, the details, the editing, the cut to black — walks the razor's edge by allowing both interpretations, and it refutes the very concept of the razor with the possibility of infinite interpretation. The cut to black allows each viewer to fill in the ending that suits them. If someone wants Tony to go down in a hail of bullets, there's room for that interpretation. If one prefers think of Tony living out his life, that's in there, too. If someone wants to think that it was all a dream, they are free to knock themselves out in that belief. Chase gave his audience enough rope to either hang themselves or free themselves.

The significance of the *nine-second cut to black* can begin to be grasped by going back to Tony's coma experience, eighteen episodes previous. When Tony seeks to find Finnerty at a family reunion, he is met by a man identical to his cousin, Tony B. The Tony B. *Doppelgänger* identifies Tony's briefcase as work, appearing to weigh a ton, and not allowed at the reunion in the bright, white, lighted house. Peering up to the house he sees the outline of a woman in the door, not dissimilar to a young Livia. Even though he claims it's not his own, Tony clings to the case, unwilling to relinquish it. This is his subconscious crossroads with implicit life-or-death consequences. Tony must choose but the full ramifications of the options are unclear. The choice is made when he hears the voice of Meadow calling him from the windblown trees and BOOM!—*cut to white for nine seconds*, before Tony regains consciousness.[29] This is perhaps the most significant overlooked detail of the last season. It supports the centrality of the coma experience as the Rosetta Stone in interpreting Tony's arc and search for identity.

One gets from art what they put into it and the audience must be willing to meet the artist halfway in that responsibility. Until that happens, entertainment will not evolve and innovative art will go underappreciated. The true standard of quality in evaluating the finale should not be "What happened to Tony?" but "What happened to the viewer?" Regardless of each individual's reaction to The End, it is a valuable lesson on their own journey. Chase has said that his number one priority with *The Sopranos* is to entertain. This ending allows for truly sublime entertainment long after the credits roll.

The Real Heroes

The success of *The Sopranos* is owed to great writing, acting, direction and the visionary guidance of David Chase. The real power of *The Sopranos* is a magical combination of all these elements to make endearing, realistic characters. The characters are not heroes. In many ways they are quite average. They are parents. They have jobs, even though unusual ones. They experience the occasional highs of life and its frequent uneventfulness. When faced with challenging situations, like a half-dead Russian, they don't demonstrate superhuman problem-solving. Rather they struggle through these situations the best they can. Sometimes they act wisely. Sometimes they make mistakes. Sometimes they say something perceptive. Sometimes they say things that are unintelligent. They become distracted by the little annoyances in life. In all these ways they are more accurate representations of people one might encounter in their daily life.

Popular entertainment typically trumpets the value of being a hero but does not tell its audience how to make the journey to that ideal. This creates for an audience the impression of unattainability. The goal is subsequently dismissed and abandoned with no progress made by anyone. *The Sopranos* goes about such a proposition tangentially, by entertaining its audience with a compelling depiction of life's challenges, the point of origin. Chase has taken great care to give a realistic presentation. From that realistic presentation, including human limitations, the desire to become the hero springs naturally. Because the desire is derived individually and internally, the motivation is more likely to overcome the obstacle of "How?" The journey toward each individual's hero concept can begin, a journey of self-discovery and acceptance leading toward happiness. Whether the ideal is reached is less important than the value of the journey itself. *The Sopranos* allows its audience to continue on that journey with a renewed sense of direction.

The disconnect from heroes exists in their predictability. Audiences are so familiar with the stereotypical fictional hero as an ideal that the outcome of their stories is a foregone conclusion. The audience understands that there will be trials and challenges to the hero's success but knows that the hero will emerge victorious in the end. With Tony Soprano, on the other hand, one doesn't know how it will end. Tony does not fit any previous model seen in movies or television. He is compelling because of the mystery of his fate. Yes, he comes from a rich lineage of anti-heroes, as do most of those represented on *The Sopranos*. The audience wants to forgive Tony his sins because they are more like him than the hero. In season four the audience is prepared for the end when Tony shares with Melfi his self-prognosis. In his estimation, the odds favor his ride ending in death or imprisonment.[30] The audience is aware of his crimes and common sense tells them that he will get his comeuppance, but they cannot bring themselves to wish his doom. Because Tony is more relatable, the audience wants to see him, an Average Joe, come out on top, giving them hope that the same is possible for them. Tony is not superhuman but he is ultrahuman. He does not have all the answers. He is not a role model but rather a role compatriot. He has moments of compassion and moments of vindictiveness. He is at times very perceptive and at others oblivious. He is sometimes appreciative of his life as a gift and sometimes mired in his depression. Sometimes he makes the right business decision and sometimes he makes the wrong one. At times he can be terribly insensitive to his wife and at others he can have tender words. His realistic humanity draws out of his audience their own humanity and therein lies the true beauty of James Gandolfini's portrayal of Tony Soprano.

Heroes may be fun to watch but there is less of a connection between a hero and his audience. A hero is an idealized version of what a viewer might hope to be. Tony Soprano is a much nearer representation what the viewer *is*, experiencing human challenges and emotional conflicts. Heroes are broad role models, homogenized to the point of unrelatability. One size does not fit all. What is inexpressible is how to pursue the heroic ideal. How does one go about it? In fact, this is an impossible proposition because no single generic prescription will cure all. It is rare and valuable art that has the power to speak to the many on a deep level. If the audience is a block of marble, then the art is a hammer with its questions as a chisel. The audience needs to wield the hammer and chisel upon themselves to chip away and reveal their true, beautiful selves. The stereotypical hero model's chisel is dull. Tony Soprano is a heavy hammer. The beauty of the art originates from the audience learning about itself. Good art is simply the trigger mechanism. Chase has his finger on the trigger and he truly has a beautiful audience.

The beauty in the audience is uncovered by the asking of questions proposed by *The Sopranos*. The question of the road not taken is one which most of its characters pose. The phantoms of regret and unhappiness, the second-guessing of their life choices, the blaming of others for their own grief are common. In Tony's comatose bout with regret and identity, his children clarify the internal debate and call him back to life. From them he receives the unconditional love he never had from his parents, and energy spent crying over spilled milk is wasted energy. Again the lesson is just a bit to the side of where the average audience is looking. One is better off living with one's decisions and making the most of them than worry about woulda-coulda been. Carmela's axiom of more being lost by indecision rather than wrong decision applies to life's crossroads.[31] As it serves as a spur to action, it also serves, in hindsight, to allay doubt and regret. While in Paris, Carmela is overwhelmed by the pointlessness of all the worrying to which she has subjected herself. In tears she realizes that it all just gets washed away and the choices one makes in life are water under the bridge.[32]

While Carmela puts aside her doubt and worry, Paulie sets aside his fears. His superstitions, made acute by a cat which stares at a photo of the deceased Christopher, cause him to turn down a promotion. Tony confronts him with the suggestion that his unfounded fears are preventing Paulie from living his life. Paulie considers this and recognizes that the true decision was made decades previous when he signed onto Johnny Boy's crew.[33] To depart from Tony at this juncture would be to flush his mob guy identity down the *pishadoo*. Despite his quirks, Paulie is a really good wiseguy. He's tough, he's a good earner and he knows how to handle himself. He will live up to his commitment with loyalty until the end, even though he may not escape his fears. It is his own way of participating joyfully in the sorrows of the world.

Realizations such as Paulie's or Carmela's are examples of the nontraditional closure on *The Sopranos*. In the first season, Chris laments to Paulie his desire for an arc, a path in life that would lead him someplace new.[34] The true nature of these characters' arcs is that they can more accurately be described as full circles. Their arcs take them back to where they started, like when Chris and Paulie reacted with disbelief that they inadvertently walked in a circle in the white wasteland of the New Jersey Pine Barrens. The audience's expectation of arc is defied in the same way as the two lost wiseguys. It's up to the characters and audience members to live with unmet expectations and make the most of it. The purpose is not to change who they are but to evolve the way they *think about* who they are. The journey comes full circle. It's not transformation but coming to terms with who they truly are and embracing that and living it, rather than making themselves unhappy by trying to be something they are not.

Meadow and AJ's journeys have brought them around to accept that they are each Sopranos at heart. Despite their chronic ball-breakin',' they have a truly loving brother-sister relationship. They, along with Carmela, are all united in their love for Tony. By the final scene they have all come to accept themselves and each other for who they are. The journey between the first and last episodes is a depiction of the process of denial, anger, learning and accepting. For six seasons these characters try to be who they are not. After years of divergence from each other, the Sopranos' journeys intersect once again; they are all at the same crossroads. They all choose to go in the same direction, together as a family, for better or worse. After exploring their options in life, they return to embrace their roots, demonstrating that the more things change the more they stay the same. They may or may not be moral but they are adherent to the wisdom of being true to one's self. Once they individually accept themselves and each other for who they are, the Sopranos can begin to approach being a happy family, not necessarily right or wrong, but happy. As Dr. Melfi tells Carmela, putting aside issues of legality and morality, clarity cannot be a bad thing.[35]

While Tony renounces excuses and takes responsibility for his action, he also accepts that there are limits to his ability to change. A shark can't metamorphose itself into a puppy. Each character has a nature. In a concession to his limits, Tony recognizes that his nature is not something he chooses consciously. It's what he *is* and it is one of the factors beyond his desire for total control. What Tony experiences for much of the series is his discomfort with this fact and his struggle to change his nature. He tries to change his nature in response to the messages he received from his mother, father, and uncle — that Tony is "bad." His wrestling with his deeds is either therapeutic for him to change his ways for the betterment of society or it is a self-destructive obsession over the belief that he should be something he is not, that he should conform to societal standards at the cost of his own individuality, his essence, his personality, his soul. This struggle is another fruitless adventure pursued under the false pretenses of heroes. This struggle is Tony continually trying to get back on the bus. The struggle abates when he decides to let the bus go.

Through a combination of skill, gift, luck, and unique human fiber, Tony manages to survive while battling his depression and uniquely challenging business environment. Given his circumstances, he makes it farther on his path than anyone expected, more than anyone else would have. This in itself is a personal victory which Tony now occasionally appreciates when he stops to smell the roses. It might seem like old news but it's worth mentioning that a lot of what Tony accomplished, in the face of all his obstacles and circumstances, was a subconscious effort to win his mother's love. Livia was a black hole but, as her son, Tony strove to prove himself. He sought to demonstrate his worth, to win her love (which she was incapable of giving unconditionally) by reaching heights to which most did not aspire. As he explains to Melfi in season two, everyone including himself knows the stakes going in.[36] His journey could have ended long ago but his good fortune extended his run well beyond expectations. Tony has gambled for decades. Sometimes he has been up on chips and sometimes down. When Johnny Boy told a young Tony never to gamble, he was likely unaware of his hypocrisy, considering the entire gangster lifestyle is a gamble. When a wiseguy is winning he has money, power, perks and luxuries. When a wiseguy loses, it might be a bite out of his pie or a beating but it might also be a bullet with his name on it. Tony comes to recognize the risks he lives with and appreciates that he is way up in the game of life.[37]

Tony beats odds like no one else. He survives the attempted hit in season one.[38] He avoided Federal indictment by installing his Uncle Junior as a puppet.[39] The eyewitness to Tony's involvement in the Bevilaqua murder clams up.[40] Janice kills Richie before he could be a serious threat to Tony.[41] The FBI's surveillance lamp is neutralized.[42] Furio narrowly decides not to push Tony into helicopter blades.[43] Ray and Gene both die before they can be brought to testify against Tony.[44] Biggest of all, he survives his coma and the probability of brain damage (Tony's nurse admits that the hospital staff gave him twenty-to-one odds).[45]

The sixth and last season presents several cautionary portraits of wiseguys who lose. It starts with Eugene, whose inheritance of two million dollars turns out to be a curse when the Family won't let him retire and his wife refuses to understand. The real loss comes from being caught by the FBI, who turn him into a rat. He tragically accepts his fate and commits suicide. Vito's story serves to illustrate another wiseguy who loses and pays with his life. His problem stems from his vain attempt to live two separate and incongruent lives, as a mobster and a homosexual. He denies his homosexuality, his identity, and in trying to be a wiseguy again he goes to his death. In his last days he comes to understand the trap of his lies. Like Chris's twin desires for Hollywood and the Family, Vito tries to follow two divergent paths and it results in his demise. Johnny Sack pays his price with incarceration, separation from his beloved family, and a premature death from lung cancer. They are genuine family men who truly love their wives and children, each in their own way. This applies even to Phil who is consumed by his obsession for revenge. His obsession, though, comes from his deep love for his dead brother. All of these men's downfalls come from being caught in a difficult spot, cornered like animals; they are faced with paying the debt they incurred in the gamble of mafia life. Their predicaments are tragic but of their own doing. Each accepts the consequences of their decision to give themselves to the Family. They accept their identity as Family men. Like Johnny Boy Soprano told a young Tony, a real man honors his debts. For the sake of honor, these wiseguys meet that obligation and pay the ultimate price. They make their coffins and must lie in them, leaving disillusioned widows and fatherless children.

Tony escapes this fate, for the moment. Life goes on. He is truly carried across the sky by a great wind. His luck has been remarkable, but Tony is a big believer that one makes one's own luck in life. He counts his blessings, mindful of the unlikely words of wisdom from Little Carmine in interpreting an allegorical dream. What Carmine and Tony poignantly come to realize is that the journey is not about being the boss, but about being happy.[46]

The Journey Continues...

The Sopranos is a microcosm of therapy for the viewer. Very much like the frustration that Tony feels at the obscurity of the concrete progress achieved in his sessions, a viewer might have doubts about the quality of an episode because they did not "get it." Melfi teaches Tony that therapy is hard work with rewarding results and that meanings are elicited through verbalization. Deeper meanings and values of episodes are typically earned only after contemplation and close study. The manner in which the audience is forced to do the work of "getting it" is much like the therapeutic process. Viewers must ask themselves how they feel about the characters and events. Connecting the complex dots of *The Sopranos* invites and inspires the audience to connect the dots in their own lives. I hope this book has rekindled in each reader a desire to embark anew on this entertaining and rewarding odyssey of exploration with new perspective and passion. The book is only an intermediary step on one's journey. It does not have all the answers but encourages asking the right questions. *The Sopranos* doesn't tell its audience what to be, it helps them understand who they already are. If wielded properly, it hammers away distractions to reveal their own identity and beauty.

There are certain suggestions and principles to keep in mind if one wants to engage in the endeavor of taking up the hammer. Remember that it's not about Tony, it's about the audience. Just like anything, one gets out of it what they put into it. Ask questions and discuss with others. Look for multiple meanings by considering characters' words in various applications, not just the immediate and obvious context. Don't accept statements as facts, verify against circumstances and overall patterns of behavior. Learn from the lies. Pay close attention to the characters' faces. Walk a mile in these characters' shoes. Seek to understand character motivation; trace their history to find answers. Consider the role of the human survival instinct in their actions. Watch episodes in reverse order to piece together causes and effect. Watch episodes non-consecutively to make interesting connections and find new meanings. Apply lyrics of featured songs to various characters and contexts. Look for symbolism. One must forget about distractions and keep their eye on the ball.

If any explanation presented in this book feels like mismatched puzzle pieces jammed together, play with the pieces until a comfortable fit is found. Everybody's puzzle is different. David Chase understands this and from this understanding comes a voice that asks broad, leading questions of the audience. Fulfillment of the *Sopranos* experience then requires translation to real life. This is where the art ends and the individual begins. It's up to each viewer to piece together their personal puzzle by examining their own lives. It's up to them to do the hard work of understanding the significance of the events of their lives and define their relationships with others. One must put these pieces of their puzzle together to see The Big Picture. Embracing the lessons that resonate in the individual allows them to enact positive behaviors on a daily basis. One must ask "How does this make me feel?" "Who am I and where am I going?" and "Howyoudoin'?" Verbalization of answers in any form — discussion, talking out loud, writing — elicits meaning. Seeking root causes for circumstances and emotions facilitates personal understanding. Acknowledging values clarifies direction. Recognizing negative behaviors and understanding their origins allows one to come up with a plan for change. Meditation yields answers. Every day is a gift, an opportunity to stop and smell the roses. Unmet expectations should not be a disappointment but rather embraced as a fascinating opportunity. In the practice of these principles, a once-passive audience can gain insight about their own identity and what brings true happiness. *The Sopranos* is part of something bigger and that something is you. Chase's original concept (a mob boss seeing a psychiatrist about his mother) evolved from an interesting idea into a compelling saga that entertains and carries meaning beyond viewers' expectations. *The Sopranos* turned out to be the greatest American art of the twenty-first century. The audience travels with Tony for eight years of his journey and then his path diverges from theirs. It was a thrilling ride for which millions of viewers are grateful. Tony is like the audience's bus. It's up to each viewer not to obsess about getting back on. They must continue on their own journey, as Tony Soprano continues on his. Like Melfi did for Tony, David Chase has given his audience all the tools they need to fly on their own.

Appendix:
Episode Guide

Season 1

01 — "Pilot"
02 — "46 Long"
03 — "Denial, Anger, Acceptance"
04 — "Meadowlands"
05 — "College"
06 — "Pax Soprana"
07 — "Down Neck"
08 — "The Legend of Tennessee Moltisanti"
09 — "Boca"
10 — "A Hit Is a Hit"
11 — "Nobody Knows Anything"
12 — "Isabella"
13 — "I Dream of Jeannie Cusamano"

Season 2

14 — "Guy Walks Into a Psychiatrist's Office…"
15 — "Do Not Resuscitate"
16 — "Toodle-Fucking-Oo"

17 — "Commendatori"
18 — "Big Girls Don't Cry"
19 — "The Happy Wanderer"
20 — "D-Girl"
21 — "Full Leather Jacket"
22 — "From Where to Eternity"
23 — "Bust-Out"
24 — "House Arrest"
25 — "The Knight in White Satin Armor"
26 — "Funhouse"

Season 3

27 — "Mr. Ruggerio's Neighborhood"
28 — "Proshai, Livushka"
29 — "Fortunate Son"
30 — "Employee of the Month"
31 — "Another Toothpick"
32 — "University"
33 — "Second Opinion"
34 — "He Is Risen"
35 — "The Telltale Moozadell"

36 — "To Save Us All from Satan's Power"
37 — "Pine Barrens"
38 — "Amour Fou"
39 — "The Army of One"

Season 4

40 — "For All Debts Public and Private"
41 — "No Show"
42 — "Christopher"
43 — "The Weight"
44 — "Pie O My"
45 — "Everybody Hurts"
46 — "Watching Too Much Television"
47 — "Mergers & Acquisitions"
48 — "Whoever Did This"
49 — "The Strong, Silent Type"
50 — "Calling All Cars"
51 — "Eloise"
52 — "Whitecaps"

Season 5

53 — "Two Tony's"
54 — "Rat Pack"
55 — "Where's Johnny"
56 — "All Happy Families"
57 — "Irregular Around the Margins"
58 — "Sentimental Education"
59 — "In Camelot"

60 — "Marco Polo"
61 — "Unidentified Black Males"
62 — "Cold Cuts"
63 — "The Test Dream"
64 — "Long Term Parking"
65 — "All Due Respect"

Season 6

66 — "Members Only"
67 — "Join the Club"
68 — "Mayham"
69 — "The Fleshy Part of the Thigh"
70 — "Mr. & Mrs. John Sacrimoni Request"
71 — "Live Free or Die"
72 — "Luxury Lounge"
73 — "Johnny Cakes"
74 — "The Ride"
75 — "Moe n' Joe"
76 — "Cold Stones"
77 — "Kaisha"
78 — "Soprano Home Movies"
79 — "Stage 5"
80 — "Remember When"
81 — "Chasing It"
82 — "Walk Like a Man"
83 — "Kennedy and Heidi"
84 — "The Second Coming"
85 — "The Blue Comet"
86 — "Made in America"

Chapter Notes

Chapter 1

1. Martin, 72.
2. Oxfeld.
3. *Fresh Air*, 2001.
4. "House Arrest"
5. "Live Free or Die"
6. "Rat Pack," "Cold Cuts"
7. *Fresh Air*, 2004.
8. "College"
9. *Fresh Air*, 2001.

Chapter 2

1. "Pilot"
2. "The Happy Wanderer"
3. "In Camelot"
4. "I Dream of Jeannie Cusamano," "Funhouse"
5. "Another Toothpick"
6. "Watching Too Much Television"
7. "Guy Walks Into a Psychiatrist's Office"
8. "Soprano Home Movies"
9. "Down Neck"
10. "Watching Too Much Television"
11. "Down Neck"
12. "Down Neck," "Boca"
13. "The Strong, Silent Type," "Made in America"
14. "Down Neck"
15. "Soprano Home Movies"
16. "Down Neck"
17. "The Ride"
18. "Soprano Home Movies"
19. "Down Neck"
20. "Down Neck"
21. "Down Neck"
22. "Watching Too Much Television"
23. "Down Neck"
24. "Rat Pack"
25. "Big Girls Don't Cry"
26. "Fortunate Son"
27. "To Save Us All from Satan's Power"
28. "Moe n' Joe"
29. "Stage 5"
30. "For All Debts Public and Private"
31. "Full Leather Jacket"
32. "A Hit Is a Hit"
33. "Down Neck"
34. "Fortunate Son"
35. "Soprano Home Movies"
36. "In Camelot"
37. "Boca"
38. "In Camelot"
39. "Cold Cuts"
40. "The Happy Wanderer"
41. "D-Girl," "Where's Johnny"
42. "Fortunate Son"
43. "The Test Dream"
44. "Meadowlands"
45. "D-Girl"
46. "Moe n' Joe"
47. "Soprano Home Movies"
48. "Guy Walks Into a Psychiatrist's Office," "Where's Johnny"
49. "Moe n' Joe"

50. "Proshai, Livushka," "Cold Cuts"
51. "In Camelot"
52. "Soprano Home Movies"
53. "Mayham"
54. "Denial, Anger, Acceptance"
55. "Join the Club"
56. "Pilot," "Second Opinion"
57. "Amour Fou"
58. "College"
59. "Amour Fou"
60. "Eloise"
61. "Proshai, Livushka"
62. "In Camelot"
63. "Full Leather Jacket"
64. "He Is Risen"
65. "Guy Walks Into a Psychiatrist's Office"

Chapter 3

1. "Pilot"
2. "Down Neck"
3. "Remember When," "In Camelot," "A Hit Is a Hit"
4. "To Save Us All from Satan's Power"
5. "Commendatori"
6. "The Happy Wanderer"
7. "For All Debts Public and Private"
8. "Cold Cuts"
9. "Another Toothpick"
10. "Amour Fou"
11. "From Where to Eternity"
12. "The Two Tony's"
13. "For All Debts Public and Private"
14. "College"
15. "Amour Fou"
16. "The Army of One"
17. "The Test Dream"
18. "Remember When"
19. "Full Leather Jacket"
20. "College"
21. "Big Girls Don't Cry," "Two Tony's"
22. "Unidentified Black Males"
23. "Pilot"
24. "To Save Us All from Satan's Power"
25. "46 Long"
26. "Anger, Denial, Acceptance"
27. "I Dream of Jeannie Cusamano"
28. "Guy Walks Into a Psychiatrist's Office"
29. "Funhouse"
30. "No Show"
31. "The Strong, Silent Type"
32. "The Second Coming"
33. "All Due Respect"
34. "Mayham"
35. "Remember When," "Eloise"
36. "The Ride"
37. "Amour Fou"
38. "Second Opinion," "Remember When"
39. "He Is Risen"
40. "From Where to Eternity," "Made in America"
41. "The Fleshy Part of the Thigh"
42. "Pilot," "Whoever Did This"
43. "Pilot"
44. "Watching Too Much Television"
45. "To Save Us All from Satan's Power"
46. "Bust-Out"
47. "To Save Us All from Satan's Power"
48. "A Hit Is a Hit"
49. "Fortunate Son"
50. "Cold Stones"
51. "Calling All Cars," "The Weight"
52. "Remember When"
53. "Pine Barrens"
54. "Commendatori"
55. "Luxury Lounge," "The Blue Comet"
56. "The Happy Wanderer"
57. "Remember When"
58. "All Happy Families"
59. "Rat Pack"
60. "Remember When"
61. "For All Debts Public and Private"
62. "Whitecaps"
63. "House Arrest"
64. "Pilot," "Denial, Anger, Acceptance," "Amour Fou"
65. "He Is Risen"
66. "Fortunate Son"
67. "All Happy Families"
68. "Pax Soprana"
69. "For All Debts Public and Private"
70. "Bust-Out"
71. "University"
72. "Whoever Did This," "The Strong, Silent Type"
73. "Cold Stones"
74. "Kennedy and Heidi"
75. "Pax Soprana"
76. "The Knight in White Satin Armor"
77. "The Strong, Silent Type"
78. "He Is Risen"
79. "All Due Respect"
80. "Funhouse"
81. "The Rat Pack"
82. "Guy Walks Into a Psychiatrist's Office"

Chapter 4

1. "Meadowlands"
2. "Legend of Tennessee Moltisanti"
3. "I Dream of Jeannie Cusamano"
4. "For All Debts Public and Private"
5. "Whitecaps"
6. "I Dream of Jeannie Cusamano"
7. "Mr. Ruggerio's Neighborhood"
8. "All Happy Families"
9. "Cold Cuts"
10. "Mr. Ruggerio's Neighborhood"
11. HBO Short Film
12. "Long Term Parking"
13. "Kaisha"
14. "Walk Like a Man"
15. "Made In America"
16. "Legend of Tennessee Moltisanti"
17. "For All Debts Public and Private"
18. "No Show"
19. *Fresh Air*, 2001.
20. "Nobody Knows Anything"
21. "I Dream of Jeannie Cusamano"
22. "To Save Us All from Satan's Power"
23. "Commendatori"
24. "D-Girl"
25. "Knight in White Satin Armor"
26. "Funhouse"
27. "Two Tony's"
28. "Members Only"

Chapter 5

1. "Join the Club"
2. "46 Long"
3. "Boca"
4. "Bust Out"
5. "Mayham," "The Fleshy Part of the Thigh"
6. "Soprano Home Movies"
7. "Full Leather Jacket"
8. "Pilot"
9. "Second Opinion"
10. Gabbard, 37.
11. "Full Leather Jacket"
12. "Sentimental Education"
13. "Second Opinion"
14. "D-Girl"
15. "The Second Coming"
16. "The Blue Comet"
17. "Join the Club"
18. "Marco Polo"
19. "Funhouse"
20. "Cold Stones"
21. "Mayham"

22. "Cold Stones"
23. "Commendatori"
24. "For All Debts Public and Private"
25. "Members Only"
26. "The Knight in White Satin Armor"
27. "Christopher"
28. "Bust-Out"
29. "The Knight in White Satin Armor"
30. "Eloise"
31. "Whitecaps"
32. "Sentimental Education"
33. Barreca, 63.
34. "Amour Fou"
35. "The Test Dream"
36. "The Strong, Silent Type"
37. "Irregular Around the Margins"
38. "In Camelot"
39. "Cold Cuts"
40. "Long Term Parking"
41. "Whitecaps"
42. "All Due Respect"
43. "Join the Club"
44. "Join the Club," "Cold Stones"
45. "Chasing It"
46. "Cold Stones"

Chapter 6

1. "The Happy Wanderer"
2. "College"
3. "Bust-Out"
4. "The Army of One"
5. "Full Leather Jacket"
6. "From Where to Eternity," "Unidentified Black Males"
7. "Employee of the Month"
8. "University"
9. "The Telltale Moozadell"
10. "To Save Us All from Satan's Power"
11. "Amour Fou"
12. "The Army of One"
13. "He Is Risen," "The Army of One"
14. "Down Neck"
15. "D-Girl"
16. "The Telltale Moozadell"
17. "The Army of One"
18. "All Happy Families"
19. "Johnny Cakes"
20. "The Telltale Moozadell"
21. "D-Girl"
22. "The Blue Comet"
23. "The Second Coming"
24. "Second Opinion"
25. "The Telltale Moozadell"
26. "Amour Fou"

27. "Cold Stones," "Soprano Home Movies"
28. "Walk Like a Man"
29. "Join the Club"
30. "Fortunate Son"
31. "The Army of One"
32. "Moe n' Joe"
33. "Cold Stones"
34. "Johnny Cakes"
35. "Cold Stones"
36. "Walk Like a Man," "Boca"
37. "Made in America"
38. "D-Girl"
39. "Commendatori"
40. "Proshai, Livushka"
41. "For All Debts Public and Private"
42. "No Show"
43. "Whoever Did This"
44. "The Strong, Silent Type"
45. "Irregular Around the Margins"
46. "Long Term Parking"
47. "Cold Cuts"
48. "The Ride"
49. "From Where to Eternity"
50. "Join the Club"
51. "Walk Like a Man"
52. "The Legend of Tennessee Moltisanti"
53. "Two Tony's"
54. "Kaisha"
55. "Kennedy and Heidi"
56. "Walk Like a Man"
57. "Kennedy and Heidi"

Chapter 7

1. "From Where to Eternity"
2. "Mergers and Acquisitions"
3. "College"
4. "Cold Stones," "Whitecaps," "Whoever Did This"
5. "Down Neck," "Fortunate Son"
6. "Luxury Lounge"
7. "46 Long," "From Where to Eternity"
8. "Unidentified Black Males"
9. "The Army of One"
10. "Marco Polo," "Unidentified Black Males"
11. "Isabella," "Whitecaps"
12. "Watching Too Much Television," "Kaisha"
13. "Fortunate Son"
14. "Another Toothpick"
15. "From Where to Eternity"

16. "Pax Soprana"
17. "Cold Stones"
18. "Christopher"
19. "Sentimental Education," "Members Only"
20. "Christopher"
21. "Pine Barrens"
22. "Employee of the Month," "Made in America"
23. "I Dream of Jeannie Cusamano," "Kaisha"
24. "Johnny Cakes"
25. "Commendatori," "Luxury Lounge"
26. "Fortunate Son"
27. "The Test Dream"
28. "Chasing It"
29. "Fortunate Son"
30. "Soprano Home Movies"
31. "D-Girl"
32. "All Due Respect"
33. "He Is Risen"
34. "Cold Cuts"
35. "Cold Cuts"
36. "Proshai, Livushka"
37. "The Fleshy Part of the Thigh"
38. "The Weight"
39. "46 Long"
40. "To Save Us All from Satan's Power"
41. "For All Debts Public and Private"
42. "Cold Cuts"
43. "University"
44. "Whoever Did This"
45. "Two Tony's," "Walk Like a Man"

Chapter 8

1. "Pilot"
2. "Proshai, Livushka"
3. "Down Neck"
4. *Fresh Air*, 2001.
5. "Pilot"
6. "Meadowlands"
7. "I Dream of Jeannie Cusamano"
8. "Down Neck"
9. "Proshai, Livushka"
10. "Pilot"
11. "The Legend of Tennessee Moltisanti"
12. "Pine Barrens"
13. "The Weight"
14. "Unidentified Black Males"
15. "The Strong, Silent Type"
16. "Where's Johnny"
17. "Members Only"
18. "Everybody Hurts"

19. "Denial, Anger, Acceptance"
20. "House Arrest"
21. "Everybody Hurts"
22. "For All Debts Public and Private," "Christopher"
23. Gabbard, 42.
24. "Christopher"
25. "Cold Cuts"
26. "Second Opinion"
27. "Eloise"
28. "Join the Club"
29. "No Show"
30. "Walk Like a Man"
31. "Mr. & Mrs. John Sacrimoni Request"
32. "House Arrest"
33. "Employee of the Month"
34. "House Arrest"
35. "The Blue Comet"
36. "Walk Like a Man"
37. "Chasing It"
38. "Walk Like a Man"
39. "The Second Coming"
40. "Pax Soprana"

Chapter 9

1. "Pilot"
2. "College"
3. "House Arrest"
4. "I Dream of Jeannie Cusamano"
5. "House Arrest"
6. "For All Debts Public and Private"
7. "Calling All Cars"
8. "Irregular Around the Margins"
9. "Sentimental Education"
10. "In Camelot"
11. "Walk Like a Man"
12. "Soprano Home Movies"
13. "I Dream of Jeannie Cusamano"
14. "In Camelot"
15. "Soprano Home Movies"
16. "The Strong, Silent Type"
17. "Second Opinion"
18. "Employee of the Month"
19. "College"
20. "I Dream of Jeannie Cusamano"
21. "The Blue Comet"
22. "House Arrest"
23. "Two Tony's"
24. "Join the Club"
25. "The Test Dream"
26. "Whoever Did This"
27. "University," "Whoever Did This…"
28. "The Strong, Silent Type"
29. "The Happy Wanderer"
30. "Cold Stones"
31. "A Hit Is a Hit"
32. "Pilot"
33. "Funhouse"
34. "To Save Us All from Satan's Power"
35. "Boca"
36. "The Strong, Silent Type"
37. "Members Only"
38. "For All Debts Public and Private"
39. "College," "Sentimental Education"
40. "Sentimental Education"
41. "Luxury Lounge," "Kaisha"
42. "Sentimental Education"
43. "I Dream of Jeannie Cusamano"
44. "For All Debts Public and Private"
45. "The Ride"
46. "A Hit Is a Hit"
47. "All Due Respect"
48. "The Fleshy Part of the Thigh"
49. "House Arrest"
50. "46 Long"
51. "The Knight in White Satin Armor"
52. "All Happy Families"
53. "Employee of the Month"
54. "Another Toothpick"
55. "Whoever Did This"
56. "Join the Club"
57. "Christopher"
58. "Rat Pack"
59. "Mr. Ruggerio's Neighborhood"
60. "Members Only"
61. "The Army of One"
62. "Do Not Resuscitate"
63. "Toodle-Fucking-Oo"
64. "Johnny Cakes"
65. "Funhouse"
66. "Walk Like a Man"
67. "Meadowlands"
68. "The Test Dream"
69. "The Second Coming"
70. "D-Girl"
71. "Fortunate Son"
72. "University"
73. "The Army of One"
74. "The Legend of Tennessee Moltisanti"
75. "Big Girls Don't Cry"
76. "The Happy Wanderer"
77. "Pine Barrens"
78. "No Show"
79. "Christopher"
80. "Marco Polo," "Unidentified Black Males"
81. "Mr. & Mrs. John Sacrimoni Request"

82. "Second Opinion"
83. "Mayham"
84. "Join the Club"
85. "Stage 5"
86. "Soprano Home Movies"
87. "Remember When"
88. "The Blue Comet"
89. "Walk Like a Man"
90. "Kennedy and Heidi"
91. "Made in America"
92. "The Second Coming," "The Blue Comet"
93. "I Dream of Jeannie Cusamano," "Marco Polo"
94. "Pie O My"
95. "The Strong, Silent Type"
96. "A Hit Is a Hit"
97. "Members Only"
98. "No Show"
99. "Whoever Did This," "The Fleshy Part of the Thigh," "Mr. & Mrs. John Sacrimoni Request"
100. "Funhouse"
101. "For All Debts Public and Private"
102. "Cold Stones"
103. "The Fleshy Part of the Thigh"
104. "Kaisha"
105. "The Fleshy Part of the Thigh"
106. "He Is Risen"
107. "46 Long"
108. "46 Long," "Denial, Anger, Acceptance"
109. "The Ride"
110. "Full Leather Jacket"
111. "Join the Club"
112. "Long Term Parking"
113. "Irregular Around the Margins"
114. "Long Term Parking"
115. "From Where to Eternity"
116. "Pie O My"
117. "Fortunate Son"
118. "Members Only"
119. "Mayham"
120. "Remember When"
121. "Fortunate Son"
122. Gabbard, 37.
123. "Pine Barrens"
124. "Employee of the Month"

Chapter 10

1. *Fresh Air*, 2004.

2. Jumptheshark.com
3. "Join the Club," "Mayham"
4. "Join the Club," "Mayham," "The Fleshy Part of the Thigh," "Johnny Cakes," "Kaisha," "Soprano Home Movies," "Remember When," "Walk Like a Man," "The Second Coming," "Made in America"
5. "Moe n' Joe"
6. "The Fleshy Part of the Thigh"
7. "The Fleshy Part of the Thigh"
8. "Luxury Lounge"
9. "The Fleshy Part of the Thigh"
10. "Johnny Cakes"
11. "Pilot"
12. "Kaisha"
13. "Sopranos Home Movies"
14. "Kennedy and Heidi"
15. "Chasing It"
16. "The Blue Comet"
17. "Remember When"
18. "Johnny Cakes"
19. "Soprano Home Movies"
20. "Chasing It"
21. "Luxury Lounge"
22. "Mayham"
23. "The Ride"
24. "Made in America"
25. "Moe n' Joe"
26. "Mayham," "Made in America"
27. "Cold Stones"
28. Sepinwall
29. "Mayham"
30. "For All Debts Public and Private"
31. "Whitecaps"
32. "Cold Stones"
33. "Made in America"
34. "The Legend of Tennessee Moltisanti"
35. "Join the Club"
36. "From Where to Eternity"
37. "Chasing It"
38. "Isabella"
39. "I Dream of Jeannie Cusamano"
40. "Bust-Out"
41. "The Knight in White Satin Armor"
42. "He Is Risen"
43. "Eloise"
44. "Members Only"
45. "The Fleshy Part of the Thigh"
46. "Stage 5"

Bibliography

Barreca, Regina, ed. *A Sitdown with The Sopranos*. New York: Palgrave Macmillan, 2002.

Bishop, David. *Bright Lights, Baked Ziti — The Unofficial and Unauthorised Guide to The Sopranos*. London: Virgin Books, 2001.

Fresh Air from WHYY. March 9, 2001.

Fresh Air from WHYY. March 2, 2004.

Gabbard, Glen O. *The Psychology of The Sopranos*. New York: Basic Books, 2002.

Greene, Richard, and Peter Vernezze, ed. *The Sopranos and Philosophy — I Kill Therefore I Am*. Chicago and La Salle, IL: Open Court Publishing, 2004.

Lavery, David, ed. *Reading The Sopranos*. New York: I.B. Tauris, 2006.

Lavery, David, ed. *This Thing of Ours, Investigating The Sopranos*. New York: Columbia University Press, 2002.

Martin, Brett. *The Sopranos: The Book*. New York: Time Inc. Home Entertainment, 2007.

The New York Times on The Sopranos. Collected articles. ibooks, 2001.

Oxfeld, Jesse. "Family Man." *Stanford Magazine*. September-October 2002.

Reddicliffe, Stephen, ed. *Sopranos Companion*. Radnor, PA: TV Guide Magazine Group, 2002.

Rucker, Allen. *The Sopranos, A Family History*. New York: New American Library, 2003.

Schneider, Anthony. *Tony Soprano on Management*. New York: Berkeley Publishing Group, 2004.

Seay, Chris. *The Gospel According to Tony Soprano*. New York: Tarcher/Putnam, 2002.

Sepinwall, Alan. "*Sopranos* creator's last word: End speaks for itself." *The Star Ledger*. Tuesday, June 12, 2007.

Simon, David R., with Tamar Love. *Tony Soprano's America*. Boulder, CO: Westview Press, 2002.

The Sopranos: Selected Scripts from Three Seasons. New York: Warner Brothers, 2002.

Yacowar, Maurice. *The Sopranos on the Couch: The Ultimate Guide.* New York: Continuum International Publishing Group, 2007.

Websites

http://plancksconstant.org/blog1/entertainment/sopranos
http://thechaselounge.net
http://www.ganglandnews.com
http://www.hbo.com/sopranos
http://www.imdb.com
http://www.televisionwithoutpity.com
http://www.the-sopranos.com

Index

187

CENTRAL